*To Hermana Peggy O'Neill of Suchitoto,
El Salvador, and to the women of Birth Choice, Oklahoma City,
Oklahoma, and Access Women's Health Justice, Oakland,
California. Across many divides, you are kindred spirits, seeing
with the heart, laboring always toward the good.*

———

*And to the memory of Beatriz Garcia,
who died October 8, 2017, at age twenty-six, from
complications of lupus and from the particular cruelty with
which the forces of poverty, class, education, power,
and gender collided to shape her destiny.*

HER
BODY,
OUR LAWS

ON THE FRONT LINES OF THE ABORTION WAR,
FROM EL SALVADOR TO OKLAHOMA

MICHELLE OBERMAN

BEACON PRESS, BOSTON

BEACON PRESS
Boston, Massachusetts
www.beacon.org

Beacon Press books
are published under the auspices of
the Unitarian Universalist Association of Congregations.

22 21 20 19   8 7 6 5 4 3 2 1

This book is printed on acid-free paper that meets the uncoated paper
ANSI/NISO specifications for permanence as revised in 1992.

Some names and other identifying characteristics of people mentioned
in this work have been changed to protect their identities.

Text design and composition by Kim Arney

Library of Congress Cataloging-in-Publication Data

Names: Oberman, Michelle, author.
Title: Her body, our laws : on the front lines of the abortion war, from El
    Salvador to Oklahoma / Michelle Oberman.
Description: Boston : Beacon Press, 2018. | Includes bibliographical
    references and index.
Identifiers: LCCN 2017041184 (print) | LCCN 2017043325 (ebook) |
    ISBN 9780807045534 (ebook) | ISBN 9780807089071 (paperback)
Subjects: LCSH: Abortion—Case studies. | Abortion—Law and legislation—
    Case studies. | Women drug addicts—Case studies. | Reproductive
    rights—Case studies. | BISAC: SOCIAL SCIENCE / Abortion & Birth
    Control. | LAW / Gender & the Law. | HEALTH & FITNESS /
    Pregnancy & Childbirth.
Classification: LCC RG734 (ebook) | LCC RG734 .O34 2018 (print) |
    DDC 362.1988/8—dc23
LC record available at https://lccn.loc.gov/2017041184

As a woman, I have no country. . . . As a woman my country is the whole world.

—VIRGINIA WOOLF, *Three Guineas*

CONTENTS

AUTHOR'S NOTE

I interviewed scores of people over the course of this project, taping some conversations and taking copious notes in all cases. For the sake of readability, I've related some of these encounters as dialogues, complete with quotation marks. Although the ideas and words I use are faithful to the speaker's comments, as recorded in my notes, the dialogues themselves are not direct quotes nor should they be read as such. (Original interview notes from Marina, and from all others mentioned in this book, are on file with the author.)

In this book, I refer to people by the terms they use to describe themselves. I do so out of courtesy for their integrity, and also because I do not think it is constructive to wage a battle over abortion by name-calling. For this reason, I use the terms "pro-life" and "pro-choice," rather than the terms each side often uses when referencing the other.

INTRODUCTION

I am a collector of stories about women's dark secrets. In my work as a law professor, I've studied pregnant women who abuse drugs. I've written articles about postpartum depression and the law, and authored two books about mothers who have killed their children.

I'm compelled by the despair at the heart of these stories, propelled by a belief that if we understand why things go wrong, we will find ways to stop them from happening.

To be sure, there's also a prurient aspect to my fascination. These stories are deeply entwined with sex, after all, and stories about sex are almost always interesting.

In retrospect, it's clear that my fascination with these sad stories began years ago, in my freshman year of college, when I started volunteering at Planned Parenthood. I'd gone there by myself to get fitted for a diaphragm. It felt like the first truly adult thing I'd done in my life: getting contraception. The women there were kind, and they reinforced my sense of having crossed over into not only adulthood but also womanhood.

Every Saturday morning, I crossed the picket lines for my four-hour shift with the women in the abortion clinic's recovery room. There were six recliners in a semicircle around the table where I sat, arranging crackers, juice, and pamphlets describing various forms of family planning. My job was to make sure no one left without contraception. We half-joked about never wanting to see them again.

Women choose abortion for a multitude of reasons, and yet, a sense of desperation is almost always present among them. The decision to end a pregnancy arises in response to the circumstances of one's life. The stories the women told me, as they rested before resuming their lives, were as varied as they were poignant.

I listened to their descriptions of the forces that shaped their decisions, making the abortion seem right, or even inevitable. I could see the way those same forces shaped my own life. Money, love, safety, shelter, health. . . . One experiences each of these things in an intensely personal, direct way: one has more or less, enough or nowhere near enough of them to thrive. But the way these forces come together in the crisis of an unplanned pregnancy lets you see them in stark relief.

The women's stories made visible the things that were going right in my life—the things I relied upon in order to make my way. Their tales were cautionary ones: their lives often seemed ordinary, too. Their stories could easily have been my own. Through their stories, then, I came to understand the way women experience vulnerability around sex.

Perhaps I intended to make a political statement by choosing to volunteer at Planned Parenthood. Yet, what I remember most about the work, which I did off and on in my twenties and thirties, has little to do with an explicit feminist agenda. It wasn't my politics that kept me going back to the clinic, week after week. I kept coming back because the women's stories populated my imagination, shaping my understanding of how it is to be a woman. I mean that their stories showed me the "most obvious, important realities," which, as David Foster Wallace notes in his parable about fish in water, are often the ones that are hardest to see.

There are two young fish swimming along and they happen to meet an older fish swimming the other way, who nods at them and says, "Morning, boys. How's the water?" And the two young fish swim on for a bit, and then eventually one of them looks over at the other and goes, "What the hell is water?"[1]

After I finished law school, I went to work at Loyola, a Catholic university in Chicago. It was there that I first came to know, at more than a superficial level, people who spoke openly of their deep moral opposition to abortion. I began teaching medical ethics, thriving on the difficult conversations, fascinated by the variety of opinions sparked by the stories around which I structured discussion.

It was the 1990s, and the media were consumed with pregnant women who used illegal drugs. Fear of a generation of crack babies animated the public imagination. The news stories evoked images of mostly black women who were portrayed as slutty and irresponsible, busy chasing their high rather than getting clean, if only for the sake of their unborn child. The solution, to some, was to prosecute them for child abuse.

The stories I knew from the abortion clinic were filled with the messy reasons why women have sex without contraception, even though they do not want to get pregnant. My hunch was that the truth about pregnant addicts was more complicated. I began collecting stories from drug rehabilitation centers, from doctors, from child abuse experts, and from the women themselves.[2]

It turned out that sex and drugs went hand in hand. Female addicts get pregnant because sex plays a central role in how they get the drugs they need. They have sex for money, they have sex in exchange for drugs, they have sex with their dealers. For many addicted women, sex has been part of the way they navigate their risky world since they were children. Female addicts are survivors of immense violence and trauma. Studies estimate that somewhere around 70 percent of them have been victims of childhood sexual abuse.[3]

Most drug-addicted women don't use drugs because they like to party, but rather because they want to be numb. Their responses to pregnancy are complicated. Unlike the callous depiction in the media, these women often want to be mothers. Actually, they want to be good mothers. Many see in a baby the prospect of unconditional love, of a new beginning, of a positive identity for themselves as mothers. Many already have lost children to the foster care system. They know the risks of losing yet another child if they continue using drugs, yet still they hold out hope that their unborn child might provide the change they so desperately want.

True, some of these women lack access to abortion, either because any money they have goes to feed their addiction or because they don't recognize their pregnancy until it's too far advanced for an abortion. But the bigger problem underlying the 1990s crisis of perinatal addiction was not that these addicts didn't have access to abortion, but rather that they didn't have access to drug rehabilitation programs. Their cases were too complex for programs developed for single men, too fraught with risk of harm to the fetus and potential liability. The overwhelming majority of drug treatment programs didn't accept pregnant women.

Once I understood their stories, it seemed obvious to me that prosecuting them wouldn't solve the problem. What we needed was an approach built upon our knowledge of addiction, one that paved a path to recovery.

It was 1992. The abortion war was raging in the United States. There were battles over parental notification laws, over clinic protesters, over the timing of viability. The US Supreme Court replaced *Roe v. Wade*'s trimester approach with the *Planned Parenthood v. Casey* decision, which created the "undue burden test." So long as they didn't create too much hardship for women seeking to exercise their constitutional right to terminate an unwanted pregnancy, states could use their power to encourage women to carry to term.

The battle intensified. Both sides argued with righteous indignation, appalled at the immorality or hypocrisy of their opponents.

As a law professor, I followed the legal debates closely, reading every decision. The struggle over abortion—the war—is deadly serious. Yet, the noisy debate over abortion law didn't seem all that connected to my research. That is to say, abortion's legal status didn't make much of a difference in the lives of pregnant addicts.

Abortion law was even less relevant to the new set of stories I'd started collecting: those of women who killed their children. It seems only logical to infer that a mother who kills her child must have been someone who wanted an abortion but, for some reason, couldn't get one. But it turns out that's totally wrong. These cases are complicated in ways that have almost nothing to do with abortion.

I began noticing news reports of mothers who kill following a call I received from a small-town defense lawyer seeking medical-legal experts to help defend a teenager accused of killing her baby by delivering it into a toilet. The girl claimed she didn't know she was pregnant. Over the next several years, I noticed so many similar stories that I began collecting them.

The Internet, even in its infancy, made it possible to track news items from around the country. I began searching for articles. I wanted to understand how a girl might conceal her pregnancy and what would make her deliver her baby at home, in the toilet. I felt that understanding why these cases happened would help me formulate my ideas about how the legal system ought to respond. I found hundreds of news stories. I met with doctors, spoke to experts, and ultimately interviewed women in prison for this crime.

I've spent decades studying these stories. They are messy and varied, but one thing is certain: these cases don't involve women who wanted to terminate their pregnancies but lacked access to legalized abortion. Instead, they involve stories like that of a sixteen-year-old whose case came my way. Eva was living with her uncle and his fiancée after her mother told her there wasn't room in her apartment.[4] Starving for love, yet certain she'd have nowhere to live if she had a baby, she spent the months waiting for someone to notice she was pregnant. No one said anything—not her father or stepmother, who later said they'd suspected she was pregnant, nor her mother, nor her friends, to whom she'd confided her predicament. In the end, she had her baby alone, on a toilet. The baby drowned.

When we spoke, I asked Eva why she didn't have an abortion. It was legal, and she could have consented without her parents' permission. It wasn't that she lacked the money, she said. Her ex-boyfriend had even offered to pay for it, before he stopped talking to her. But she didn't want an abortion. She didn't want to kill her best chance at feeling connected and loved.

The same desire to be a mother—to be a good mother—surfaced when I was researching mothers imprisoned for killing their children. Working with Dr. Cheryl Meyer, a psychologist and lawyer, I interviewed forty women in an Ohio prison for having killed their children. These women were incarcerated for crimes like beating their children and then failing to take them to the hospital in time, or standing by while their boyfriend beat their child to death.

Yet they bristled when asked whether they'd considered having an abortion. They wanted to be mothers. Most of their babies were simply victims of the chaos in their mothers' lives. The mothers didn't wish them dead. Most began our conversations about the child they'd been convicted of killing by saying, "Being a mother is the single most important thing in my life."

I was coming to believe that, for the most vulnerable and marginalized women, abortion's legal status hardly mattered. There are women who live with a chaos so profound that despair predates the unplanned pregnancy. Women for whom the notion of a planned pregnancy is itself almost meaningless.

The abortion battle has always raged in the background of my research. In the early twenty-first century, it grew louder, as lawmakers showed their opposition to abortion by enacting a broad swath of abortion-related laws.[5] As a law professor, it seemed to me that I should have been more engaged by the battle over abortion laws. But the sad stories I'd spent a lifetime gathering made me a skeptic about the hyperbolic promises of "choice" and "life."

I thought of a woman I met in prison for killing her two-year-old child. She'd begun raising her four younger siblings at age nine, because her parents were addicts. My hunch is that by the time she became pregnant, at fourteen, no amount of access to safe, affordable abortion would have tugged her to safety.[6]

The abortion debate doesn't concern itself with stories like hers; it ignores the lives of pregnant addicts. Yet, the lives of these women are circumscribed by norms and laws governing sex and motherhood. How much, I wondered, did it matter if abortion was illegal?

In 2008, I went to Chile to try answering this question. At the time, Chile had the world's strictest law against abortion—making it a crime in all cases, without exception. I wanted to learn whether banning abortion shaped the circumstances or frequency of cases involving mothers who kill.

I had clear expectations about what I would find in a country that outlawed abortion. I imagined that, in addition to tragic stories surrounding US mothers who kill, I would find cases of women who were driven to their crimes because they couldn't get a legal abortion.

I knew the studies of what happened in the United States, before legalized abortion. There would be hospital wards overflowing with women who had septic shock or had perforated their uteruses by trying to induce abortions with hangers.

Once I got to Chile, though, I became distracted. Nothing looked as I'd expected. There were no hospitals filled with women injured from illegal abortions, no epidemic of cases involving women who abandoned their newborns to die.

I shifted from worrying about mothers who kill their children to trying to understand what was going on with abortion in Chile. I found law professor Lidia Casas, a prominent Chilean lawyer who has devoted her career to challenging Chile's abortion ban. She explained that the ban was one of the final acts of the brutal dictator Augusto Pinochet when leaving office in 1988.

"Perhaps he wanted to leave a legacy other than having ordered the killing of tens of thousands of his political opponents," she suggested with a grim smile.

His legacy seemed to be intact. Other than Casas, no one seemed terribly interested in changing the law. Every day on my way to the subway, I passed the Castrense Cathedral, adorned with a plaque from 1994 that read "To the Memory of Children Assassinated Before Birth."

With Casas's help, I began making sense of how the abortion ban worked in practice. I met Dr. Ramiro Molina, director of the country's only adolescent health clinic, located within a public hospital that serves Santiago's poorest residents. When I asked him to tell me about unplanned pregnancy and abortions in Chile, he said, "Abortion is a non-issue in Chile. You can buy abortion drugs on the street anytime you like."

The abortion drug most widely available in Chile is misoprostol. It's only part of the formulation of the more effective abortion drug used in the United States. Even so, taken alone and within the first twelve weeks of a pregnancy, misoprostol will bring on a miscarriage in 90 percent of cases. Unless the bleeding is severe, there's no need to see a doctor.

I asked him where women found the drug. He opened his computer and plugged "misoprostol" into a search engine. Thousands of vendors appeared at the click of a mouse.

In spite of its being completely against the law, abortion in Chile is commonplace. Because it is illegal, estimates of how many abortions take place every year in Chile vary widely. But all agree that tens of thousands of women have abortions there every year.[7]

In contrast to the stories from US history, or from places where medical abortion is largely unavailable, in Chile the high rates of illegal abortions don't appear to have led to high rates of maternal mortality.[8] In fact, experts agree that fewer women die from illegal abortions now than they did fifty years ago, before the ban.[9]

If abortion remained commonplace in spite of being illegal, I wondered how the abortion law was enforced. Who gets prosecuted for the crime of illegal abortion when tens of thousands of women have them every year?

As both a defense lawyer and a law professor, Casas knew the answer. She'd studied prosecution patterns since the ban took effect and found evidence suggesting that prosecution rates declined, rather than increased, in the years since the abortion ban took effect.[10] Furthermore, when the state prosecuted women or doctors for illegal abortion,

Casas's research showed that conviction rates were low and punishment was light.

What was the purpose of the law, I wondered, if it wasn't going to be enforced? As an answer, she introduced me to her former client, Marina.

Casas had defended Marina in the summer of 2007, when Marina was prosecuted for the crime of abortion. Marina was one of only a handful of women prosecuted for abortion in Chile that year. She was caught when a sensational news channel ran a sting operation, filming women as they entered an abortion doctor's office, and as they exited. Afterward, the reporters approached each of the women individually, showed them the film, and offered them a deal: confess to us on film and we will tell the district attorney to make a plea agreement with you. Most of them confessed, but they all were prosecuted anyway.

"My story was the most interesting to the press because I was the oldest," Marina told me. "I was almost forty, and I had a teenage daughter. I'd been living overseas for twenty years, and had only recently returned to Chile."

"When I became pregnant, I was so ashamed," Marina continued. "My daughter could have such a thing happen to her, but not a grown woman like me. My period had been irregular for the past few years. I didn't even notice it wasn't coming."

"I made phone calls to old girlfriends," Marina continued. "I had been gone so long. I knew I couldn't keep it, though, so I called until a friend of a friend gave me a name."

"How much did it cost you?"

"$5,000. The rich women fly to Miami, you know. Women like me stay here. It costs between $5,000 and $8,000. Really, it's cheaper to fly to Miami. But then it's so obvious. And besides, there was my work and my daughter, so I never really considered it."

Marina was convicted. She had been caught on film. Yet, even though the crime carries a sentence of up to five years, like other women convicted of abortion in recent years in Chile, Marina did not have to go to prison. She didn't even have to be on probation, nor was she required to comply with any particular court orders. Marina's sentence was suspended. After the trial, Marina went free.

I returned to the United States baffled by the Chilean abortion law. If abortion was tantamount to murder under the law, how could the country be at peace with the high rates of illegal abortion and the low rates of law enforcement?

The following year, in 2009, I attended the first binational meeting of El Salvadoran and Nicaraguan abortion-rights' activists. Like Chile, both of these countries ban abortion without exception. The bans were relatively new; when El Salvador banned abortion in 1998, it became the world's third country, along with Chile and Malta, to do so. Nicaragua joined that number in 2004. In both countries, as in Chile, the bans intensified already restrictive abortion laws, which for decades had outlawed abortion except in cases of threat to maternal life or health, rape or incest, or fetal anomaly.

Lawyers, doctors, and activists from the two countries met to share information about the law's impact—largely on the poorest women in both countries—and to discuss strategies for law reform. At the gathering, it became clear that the situation in El Salvador was different from that in Nicaragua and Chile. In El Salvador, the government actively attempted to enforce the law. I heard stories of women who were shackled to hospital beds, still hemorrhaging, after seeking care in emergency rooms. In the ten years since the ban took effect, scores of women had been imprisoned for crimes related to illegal abortion.

I wanted to know more. I returned to the United States and secured funding for a new research project, looking at the impact of criminalizing abortion in the twenty-first century. Over the next five years, I returned nine times to El Salvador.

At some point during the weeks and months I spent in El Salvador, I realized I was not simply researching the impact of El Salvador's abortion ban. Instead, I was trying to solve the same puzzle in El Salvador that I'd encountered in Chile: there was widespread political support for the ban, yet illegal abortion was commonplace and prosecutions were so sporadic that it was hard to imagine they deterred women from terminating their pregnancies.

Over the six years during which I researched and wrote this book—2010–2016—the battle over abortion law in El Salvador intensified. Advocates for and against El Salvador's abortion ban garnered attention within the country and around the world as they fought over the law. The more pitched the battle, the more familiar it felt to me, until finally I realized that the war over abortion, whether in El Salvador or in the United States, takes on the same form: it becomes a struggle over abortion law.

Watching the abortion war play out in El Salvador, I slowly realized that, for all the fighting over abortion laws, once you get past the slogans, neither side seems to spend much time considering what they're fighting for.

I found I was writing a book about how and why and how much and to whom abortion laws matter. And to answer those questions, it would help to have a deeper understanding of the values and hopes that animated the people in the country I knew best.

Even as I was finishing my research in El Salvador, I set about investigating abortion politics in the United States. I started by visiting Oklahoma, one of the most pro-life US states. There, I came to know lawyers and advocates who have devoted much of their lives to fighting to make abortion once again a crime. Closer to home, I met with Californian abortion-rights scholars and activists. From them, I learned not only what they think is at stake in the fight over abortion laws, but also what issues the abortion war has left behind.

It was here in the United States, in the overwhelmingly pro-choice state of California, that I became convinced of the truth in my hunch, formed years ago when studying pregnant addicts and mothers who killed their children. For the most vulnerable girls and women, abortion's legal status doesn't make all that much difference.

———

This book is the result of my long journey through the abortion war. I hesitate to call it one war, rather than many. After all, my journey has taken me to different countries, where I've met people with vastly different life experiences and wide-ranging conceptions about abortion's morality. I've studied the laws of jurisdictions all over the world.

Yet, I've come away certain of at least one thing: the battle lines over abortion are being drawn with laws. There is one war over abortion, and laws are the weapons with which it is fought.

This book calls our collective attention to the fundamental, yet unasked question underlying our abortion war: what is it about abortion that we think will be changed by way of abortion laws?

This question is unasked because our discourse about abortion is largely limited to announcing one's position on abortion's legality. All that the abortion war requires of us is that we pick our side on the question of legality. As if the question of how and why abortion laws matter was beside the point.

I consider myself pro-choice. That is to say, I support a woman's unfettered right to choose to terminate a pregnancy. But this book is not written to persuade you to keep or change your opinion about whether abortion should be legal. Rather, it's to invite you to consider the ways in which abortion law matters—to encourage you to reconsider the utility of the terms of our debate, if not the debate itself.

I am issuing not so much an invitation, in the spirit of intellectual inquiry, but more of an exhortation, offered in the names of the countless women whose stories I carry with me. Because year after year, the war over abortion law consumes vast resources, not only in the United States but in countries worldwide. And year after year, that war does little to alter the concrete factors that shape whether a woman will consider having an abortion.

ONE

BEATRIZ AND HER CASE

I want to start our search into how abortion law matters by taking you to El Salvador. It has the strictest laws against abortion in the world: abortion is never legal there, not even if a woman needs one to save her life.

In spring 2013, a case arose that put the abortion ban to the test. A woman known only as Beatriz was just over three months pregnant when doctors learned that her fetus didn't have a brain. It had a rare condition called "anencephaly," which is always fatal. Humans cannot live without a brain; if her baby did not die in utero, it would die shortly after birth. To make matters worse, Beatriz's health status was extremely fragile because she had lupus—an incurable disease that causes the body's immune system to attack its own organs. Two years earlier, she had almost died and her kidneys became permanently impaired as a result of her pregnancy with her first child. Her doctors warned that she could easily die if she became pregnant again.

With no hope for her fetus's survival and her life in danger, anywhere else in the world, Beatriz would have been advised to have an abortion. Yet because the law in El Salvador completely prohibits abortion, that option was foreclosed.

Beatriz petitioned the Salvadoran government for permission to terminate her pregnancy. Her case triggered an international firestorm. Within El Salvador, branches of government took aim at one another. Around the world, advocates on both sides of the abortion war circulated news stories, petitions, and videos, pleading for support.

I followed Beatriz's case from the United States as it made its way through the Salvadoran legal system, stretching on for weeks and then months. Beatriz was seven-months pregnant by the time the Salvadoran Supreme Court denied her petition, concluding that an abortion was unnecessary because her life was not at imminent risk. Then, two weeks later, her doctors performed an emergency cesarean section. Beatriz's daughter died shortly after birth.

Neither side was surprised by the baby's death. The fact that the fetus was doomed was understood from the start. It was one of the only facts on which both sides agreed.

At the most basic level, the outcome in Beatriz's case seems perverse. For the sake of a fetus that would never live, Salvadoran law forced Beatriz to endure months of physical and psychological pain, gravely risking her own health and life.

But Beatriz's case cannot be understood simply at this basic level. As we will see in this chapter, Beatriz's case played out not only in the legal sphere, but also in the court of public opinion. For those who opposed the abortion law, her case was the utmost example of the law's absurdity, and a perfect case with which to challenge the ban. For those who supported the ban, Beatriz's case tested the moral and legal integrity of their position that life begins at conception. Allowing Beatriz an abortion would have made that belief seem negotiable.

I went to El Salvador to try to understand Beatriz's case, with its puzzling outcome. I came home with many stories that help to explain why things unfolded as they did. Read together, these stories permit us to understand, through fresh eyes, the purpose and the significance of abortion laws. Just as importantly, they shed light on the limited extent to which the law makes a difference in the lives of women like Beatriz.

BEATRIZ'S PREDICAMENT

Dr. Guillermo Ortiz first met Beatriz in 2011, when she was pregnant with her son, Claudio, who was two years old when the story with which we are concerned began. Ortiz is one of El Salvador's leading perinatologists, specializing in managing high-risk pregnancies, and working at La Maternidad, the country's main public hospital for obstetrics and gynecology.

"That first pregnancy was terrible," he told me. "She almost died. She got to seven-and-a-half months, but then her lungs filled with fluid and we couldn't control her blood pressure."[1]

Beatriz had been hospitalized for several months, beginning at twenty weeks of pregnancy. Her doctors worked around the clock to keep her stable so that her fetus could develop long enough that it would be able to survive outside of the womb. Beatriz was on six different medications to control her blood pressure, but finally she developed preeclampsia—a condition in which blood pressure becomes life-threateningly high, damaging other organs. Beatriz's kidneys were failing.

"We gave her an emergency cesarean section," Dr. Ortiz told me. "The newborn spent more than a month in the ICU, but he was in good condition. And we saved Beatriz's life. But as a result of that pregnancy, she now has chronic hypertension and a kidney dysfunction called lupus nephritis."

Her second pregnancy was more complicated from the start. In February 2013, suspecting she might be pregnant, Beatriz stopped taking her lupus medicine, which put her into a medical crisis. Her skin was covered with painful eruptions; she had hypertension, and her damaged kidneys were spilling protein into her urine, leaving her blood and body severely weakened.

By the time her lupus doctors verified her pregnancy and referred her to La Maternidad, she was eleven weeks pregnant and very ill.

So Beatriz found herself back at La Maternidad, pregnant and panicked because she knew too well how close she'd come to dying during her first pregnancy.

"We reassured her that we would do everything we could to keep her safe and healthy," Ortiz told me. "The surprise came a few weeks later, when we did the ultrasound and realized the fetus was anencephalic. So the probability of its survival, here and in any other hospital in the world, is zero. I tell you this because there are those who are confused by the terminology. Anencephaly is related to conditions such as microcephaly or hydrocephaly. And with those conditions, there is a possibility of survival. So there were those who said, 'I know of a case in which the baby survived.' But that's not anencephaly."

"What were your options, once you realized the fetus didn't have a brain and couldn't survive?" I asked.

"When we realized it had no chance of survival, and that the only thing we'd accomplish by continuing the pregnancy is to risk Beatriz's life, we talked to her."

The doctors told Beatriz and her mother about the risks she would face if she carried this pregnancy to term. There were all the life-threatening complications she knew firsthand from her first pregnancy: kidney failure, preeclampsia, stroke, blood clots, and more. In addition, there were risks due to the fact that the fetus was anencephalic. She would have to be hospitalized until she had the baby.

Otiz said, "She was around fourteen weeks pregnant at that point. Her situation was even more serious because her first delivery had required a cesarean section. We knew it was less risky to interrupt an early pregnancy; it was much safer than waiting to do another cesarean section, with its own risks, in addition to the risks from the lupus. We convened a meeting of the medical committee, which is what we do when there is a challenging case. We call together all the relevant experts: intensive care, obstetricians, and neonatologists, to discuss options and set a plan. In this case, we all agreed that interruption was the ideal plan."

Beatriz agreed and asked the doctors to perform the "interruption," as abortion is called there.

Ortiz continued, "But when we talked with the hospital attorney, he told us that our proposed 'interruption' put us at risk of violating the law. We sent him to consult with legal experts, including the Fiscalia de la Republica [the governmental office overseeing all prosecutions], a human rights lawyer, a family law judge, but none supported an interpretation of the law that permitted us to interrupt pregnancy. None of them said, 'Do it. We'll support you.'"

BEATRIZ'S DOCTORS' PREDICAMENT

Beatriz's request that her doctors terminate her pregnancy posed a legal dilemma. In 1998, El Salvador changed its penal code from a law permitting legal abortions in cases of rape, incest, or threat to maternal health or life to a law banning abortions in all cases.[2] There is no way to legally end a pregnancy in El Salvador, even one like Beatriz's, in which the fetus will not survive outside the womb.

At the same time, El Salvador's constitution guarantees a pregnant woman the same right to life promised to all citizens, such that the doctors who fail to provide a dying patient with life-saving treatment violate the patient's fundamental rights. Because Beatriz's doctors believed her illness threatened her life, Beatriz's case forced the state to grapple with two competing rights to life. Under Salvadoran law, both Beatriz and the fetus she carried had a right to life.

It turns out that doctors have been navigating this ambiguity at a practical level since 1998, when abortion was banned. One of the most vivid examples of the impact of the ban on abortion is seen in the way it shapes how doctors treat high-risk pregnancies.

Ortiz described the approach he and his colleagues use when treating very ill pregnant women. He calls it "conservative treatment":

> When we look to international health literature to guide us about how best to treat certain illnesses—for example, metastatic breast cancer and an early pregnancy—the experts suggest terminating pregnancy. We can't follow that suggestion, though. And, when we seek guidance on how to proceed without terminating the pregnancy, there's none to be had. And so we forge our own experience. . . . For example, in

the case of cancer, we give the lowest doses of chemo, rather than give her the best, most effective treatment, because we have to worry about the fetus.[3]

Ortiz's discomfort with conservative treatment is that it isn't really treatment at all. In the absence of established medical guidelines, let alone systematic research into how or whether breast cancer chemotherapy works when given at low doses to pregnant women, El Salvador is conducting an ongoing, unregulated medical experiment on this segment of its population—women and fetuses alike.

The impact of conservative treatment is perhaps most readily observed in the way Salvadoran doctors treat ectopic pregnancy. An ectopic pregnancy occurs when a fertilized egg gets stuck in the fallopian tube, rather than moving down into the woman's uterus. Instead of being able to grow, as it would in the uterus, the egg starts to develop inside of the tube, which is small and incapable of supporting a pregnancy. There is no chance it will develop into a fetus, let alone become a live baby. Left to grow, within twelve to sixteen weeks, the embryo explodes, destroying the tube, leading the woman to bleed profusely, and triggering health complications ranging from the risk of stroke to kidney damage and even death.[4] In addition, losing a fallopian tube may limit her ability to conceive in the future. Ectopic pregnancies are not rare. Between 2005 and 2009, the most recent years for which statistics are available, the Salvadoran Ministry of Health estimates that there were 1,567 ectopic pregnancies and another 46 abdominal pregnancies.[5]

Another of Beatriz's doctors described, with evident frustration, the way he treats ectopic pregnancies. You hospitalize the woman and then

you watch her night and day with scans, and the minute it bursts, you operate and take the tube. . . . She's in imminent risk of dying and I've got the responsibility of saving her life. Waiting is totally contrary to medical principles. It's no different from having an aneurism in the brain; one can see from scans that it's growing and growing. Why would you wait until it explodes? There's no single medical principle that would justify waiting.[6]

I pushed the doctor to clarify the connection between the ban on abortion and this approach to treating ectopic pregnancies—embryos that would never survive. His reason reflected the central puzzle of Beatriz's case: if it's a person from the moment of conception, then deliberately killing the embryo, let alone the fetus, could be considered homicide.

If the hospital lawyers interpret the law to require waiting for a tube to explode, rather than removing an ectopic pregnancy, it's easy to see why they similarly would have advised the doctors against terminating Beatriz's pregnancy. She was already fourteen weeks along; she was carrying a fetus, not merely an embryo. And in spite of its inevitable demise, her fetus was growing larger every day.

EL SALVADOR'S RESPONSE TO BEATRIZ'S REQUEST FOR AN ABORTION

When it became clear that the doctors would not terminate her pregnancy, one of her nurses reached out to a local women's group that found Beatriz a lawyer. In April, when Beatriz was seventeen weeks pregnant, the lawyer filed a petition asking the court for permission to terminate her pregnancy. The government took fifty-five days to reach a decision in her case, by which point she was nearly seven-months pregnant.

By examining the legal proceedings in the context of the climate in which they played out, it is easy to see the extent to which Beatriz's predicament came to stand for far more than the simple legal question of whether the law ought to permit her a life-saving abortion. From the start, we see how her case became a national and then international referendum on the abortion ban. From observing this clash, we understand abortion laws to have a symbolic importance that distinguishes them from ordinary crimes, such as robbery.

Beatriz Files Her Petition

Once Beatriz's doctors refused to terminate her pregnancy, Beatriz's lawyers took two actions. First, they filed a petition with the Salvadoran Supreme Court, seeking a court-ordered abortion for Beatriz. At the time, she was just over four months pregnant. The court took twelve days to respond to her petition.

In the meantime, her lawyers launched a full-scale media campaign. They began by contacting the country's Ministry of Health, the government agency charged with overseeing health care and setting policies for the country's public hospitals, which treat the vast majority of the population. After reviewing Beatriz's medical record, the ministry posted a summary of Beatriz's case on its website, and the minister of health herself gave a statement to the press publicly urging the Supreme Court to permit Beatriz's doctors to interrupt the pregnancy on the grounds that it was the only way to safeguard Beatriz's life.[7]

When the Ministry of Health released its summary of Beatriz's case, along with its recommendation that she be allowed to terminate her pregnancy, her case became a public affair, and Beatriz found herself at the center of an international uproar over abortion. Within a day of filing her petition with the Supreme Court, international organizations from the United Nations to Amnesty International issued statements supporting Beatriz's right to end her pregnancy.

In El Salvador, advocates weighed in on both sides of the debate. Local newspapers issued editorials decrying the ministry's position and urging the court to deny Beatriz's petition. Official organizations such as the Office on Human Rights, with leaders appointed by the left-leaning government, joined the Ministry of Health in calling for the state to permit Beatriz to terminate her pregnancy. They were countered by a coalition of more than fifty groups that joined forces to form the Organization for the Family, whose leaders warned that the case was being used to legalize abortion.[8]

In spite of efforts to conceal Beatriz's identity, journalists found both her mother's house and the two-room home she shared with her

husband and his parents. Television cameras camped outside both loca-
tions, and newscasters harassed her mother in order to get her opinion
on the case.[9] Beatriz, her son, and her husband went into hiding, taking
shelter in a village on the other side of the country, at the home of one
of her lawyer's friends.

Beatriz's Petition Is Referred to the IML

Twelve days after she filed her petition, the Supreme Court agreed to
hear Beatriz's case. The first step in the Supreme Court's evaluation was
to refer her case to the Instituto de Medicina Legal (IML). There's no
US equivalent to the IML, but such institutes are relatively common in
Latin America, where they operate as independent bureaus that combine data collection (e.g., tracking vital statistics and issuing birth and
death certificates) and conduct research or investigations at the behest
of the government.[10]

Rather than simply permitting each side to present medical experts,
the Salvadoran Supreme Court asked the IML to render an independent
expert opinion as to whether Beatriz needed an abortion to save her
life. As a government agency, the IML employs a handful of doctors to
advise it on simple cases. It also has the capacity to call witnesses, such
as Beatriz, and to seek input from additional experts as needed.

"The job of the IML," its director, Dr. Jose Miguel Fortin Magana,
later explained to me, "was not to advise the Supreme Court on whether
to permit the abortion. Instead, our job was simply to answer two questions: one, is Beatriz in imminent danger of dying, and two, is it the
case that terminating the pregnancy is the only treatment that will save
her life?"[11]

A bit of background will help explain how Fortin Magana conducted the inquiry into Beatriz's petition. Unlike the Ministry of Health,
in which all top administrative posts are appointed by the president and
the controlling political party, the IML is considered an independent
government agency, offering support on issues of fact and science. Because these issues are framed as apolitical, rather than conceived of as

policy driven, the director and staff serve indefinite terms of office. They may be appointed by a given president when a vacancy arises, but the expectation is that the director will serve an indefinite term.

At the time of Beatriz's petition, IML director Fortin Magana was a longtime member of the conservative political party, ARENA. By contrast, the president and the head of the Ministry of Health were members of the opposing liberal political party, Farabundo Martí National Liberation Front (FMLN). These parties are not simply political opponents, at least not by US standards. From 1980 to 1992, El Salvador was torn by a civil war in which members of ARENA and FMLN were on opposing sides. Tens of thousands were killed.[12]

Against that political backdrop, consider Fortin Magana's description of the experts appointed to evaluate Beatriz's request. In order to answer the questions of whether Beatriz was dying and whether she could be saved only by having an abortion, Fortin Magana assembled a panel of experts. He said:

> We went to the president of the country's leading medical school and he helped us identify experts. Then we brought in the presidents of the national associations of nephrology, rheumatology, and medical ethics. We didn't know them before.
>
> The Instituto de Medicina Legal brought with it the head of forensic medicine, who is an evangelical, the head of strategic development, who is a Mason, and like myself, a psychiatrist and a Catholic. We didn't need to include experts in obstetrics and gynecology, because the Instituto de Medicina Legal already has these experts on our staff. We only called for the experts we didn't already have.

Two puzzling things stand out in the assemblage of experts who made up the IML's panel. First, there was no one who specialized in high-risk pregnancy. One would expect to find an obstetrician with such expertise on the panel, as this is the branch of the medical profession best qualified to assess the very questions the Supreme Court put to the IML: was Beatriz's condition life-threatening, and was abortion the only way to save her life? The second puzzle was Fortin Magana's emphasis on religious diversity among his experts. Why did he think it important that the experts included Catholics, Masons, and evangelicals? Both of these puzzles indicate how the politics of abortion shaped the legal proceedings in Beatriz's case.

Let me discuss the second puzzle first. Although El Salvador is a democracy, it is also a country in which the vast majority of citizens are religious. Regional studies show that over 90 percent of people in Central America identify as Christians.[13] In El Salvador, the Catholic Church remains the predominant religious organization, with approximately 50 percent of Salvadorans calling themselves Catholic. But the past several decades have witnessed a surge in the popularity of evangelical Christianity, and today, as many as 40 percent of Salvadorans call themselves evangelicals.[14]

By recruiting experts from a variety of religious backgrounds, Fortin Magana was assuring the public of the legitimacy of his process. He listed the participants' religious affiliations to show he had taken steps to safeguard the process against the bias that might come if the experts all reflected a single religious perspective.

Given his attention to concerns about religious diversity, how could it have seemed fair to exclude the country's best experts on managing high-risk pregnancy? In terms of medical expertise, Fortin Magana's panel was limited, at best. As one of Beatriz's doctors later decried: "His experts were a forensic specialist in rape, an ordinary gynecologist, and himself—a psychiatrist—plus some generalists from the medical school. What sort of opinion can a nephrologist [a doctor who treats kidney disease] have on managing pregnancy in a patient with lupus?"[15]

From Fortin Magana's perspective, though, the country's leading high-risk obstetricians were not neutral experts. After the Ministry of Health published Beatriz's case on its website, El Salvador's Association of Obstetricians and Gynecologists sought permission to review Beatriz's full medical record. Shortly after its review, the association, which represents the country's small cadre of experts in treating high-risk pregnancy, went on record by publishing an opinion supporting Beatriz's petition to terminate her pregnancy.[16]

Thus, as Fortin Magana saw things, by the time the IML began to assemble its panel, the country's high-risk obstetricians were no longer neutral. They had already announced their decision about whether Beatriz's life was at risk, about whether she truly needed an abortion.

It is easy for me to slip into cynicism at this point, and to conclude that Fortin Magana, who favored the ban, excluded these medical experts because he knew they'd vote to support an abortion. And perhaps I'd be right in that Fortin Magana's support for the law may well have motivated him to find experts whose views aligned with his own.

But it's also possible to see his actions as an effort to ensure an unbiased audience for Beatriz's evaluation. In announcing their support for Beatriz's right to an abortion, these experts essentially declared they had already made up their minds. Before they met with the other experts, collectively reviewed her medical record, and evaluated her in person, they had already answered the two questions the IML was tasked with reviewing for the Supreme Court: "One, is Beatriz in imminent danger of dying and, two, is it the case that terminating the pregnancy is the only treatment that will save her life?" It was as if they'd decided the case before it was even tried.

When that happens here in the US legal system—as when a judge gives an opinion on a case that is currently or soon to be tried before her—we demand that the judge recuse herself. We worry that a judge who's already made up her mind will not give both sides a fair hearing.

In Beatriz's case, if the doctors already supported her right to abort on the grounds that this pregnancy was life threatening, then it was obvious how they would answer the court's narrower questions about imminent danger of dying and treatment alternatives.

So it is that, before we even lift the curtain on the first of Beatriz's legal hearings, we can see how the politics of abortion permeated not only the realm of law, but also that of science.

The Instituto de Medicina Legal Evaluates Beatriz's Petition

The IML panel took almost six weeks to review Beatriz's medical record. It pored over hundreds of pages describing her first pregnancy, the health crisis it precipitated, and the successful outcome after an emergency cesarean section delivery. The panel reviewed the tests and examinations pertaining to Beatriz's current pregnancy, and then, on May 3, it summoned Beatriz from the hospital to the IML offices for a physical examination. By that time, she was twenty-three-weeks pregnant.

Fortin Magana was one of three evaluating physicians. Because the hearing happened behind closed doors, all I know comes from what Beatriz told me, a year later, when I asked her to describe it:

> There were three doctors. I didn't know their names. They didn't make me undress. They just checked my face and my hands, looked at the marks on my skin. And listened to my breath. They asked about my childhood and made me do some drawings. I guess they wanted to see if I was OK in my head. Maybe they thought I was crazy because of what I wanted to do.

On May 8, Fortin Magana announced the decision on behalf of the IML. It found that Beatriz was stable and, as such, there was no need to terminate the pregnancy.[17]

"Terminating the pregnancy was not necessary," Fortin Magana told me, "nor would it remedy her chronic illness":

> Our conclusion was unanimous; we advocated conservative treatment. We never said, as was reported throughout the world, that her life wasn't important or shouldn't be saved. On the contrary, we specifically said she could terminate the pregnancy if her symptoms worsened

and her life was in danger. The doctors could put the infant in an incubator and if God wants, it will live, and if God doesn't want, it will die. But we weren't leaving Beatriz in danger of dying.[18]

After the IML's May 8 ruling, the Salvadoran Supreme Court agreed to hear arguments from both sides of Beatriz's case a week later, on May 15. During that week, her supporters mounted a publicity campaign, using political connections, social media, and the international press to plead her case. The political firestorm that ensued reminds us of the extent to which Beatriz's case became a referendum on abortion. It shows how both sides understood the stakes and gives us a sense of the pressures the case placed on the Supreme Court.

Shortly after the IML released its report finding that Beatriz was stable, Salvadoran minister of health Dr. Maria Isabel Rodriguez gave a public interview condemning the report. In it, she described Beatriz's medical condition in vivid detail and made the case for abortion, telling the press that therapeutic abortion was the only "viable and just solution," and that Fortin Magana's declarations were "crude and rude."[19]

President Mauricio Funes, who had not addressed the subject of abortion in the first four years of his five-year presidency, announced his belief that Beatriz had the right to make decisions about her own life.[20]

Beatriz's supporters filmed her, the image cropped to show only her puffy hands, blotchy and red from the lupus, folded over her obviously pregnant belly.

"I want to live," she said quietly. "I beg from my heart that you let me."

The video went viral, circulated by Amnesty International and other social media outlets throughout the world.[21]

At the same time, international pro-life groups such as Human Life International called on El Salvador to hold fast to its opposition to abortion under all circumstances.[22]

Julia Regina de Cardenal, the head of El Salvador's pro-life movement Sí a la Vida and also a columnist for *El Diario de Hoy*, one of the country's two leading newspapers, cast the debate over Beatriz as an assault on Salvadoran sovereignty:

> In our country the Constitution defends all human life against the powerful interests of those who manipulate situations like this in order to open the door to the multinational multimillion-dollar abortion industry. The IML uncovered the truth: showing that Beatriz is stable, that she can continue her pregnancy, that medical intervention will be possible as soon as any complication arises, in spite of the false declarations of pro-abortion groups, the Ministry of Health and international organizations, among others. We await the apologies of the United Nations, the International Court of Human Rights, the Organization of American States and Amnesty International for having pressured our leaders to commit a crime with grave consequences for Beatriz and her baby.[23]

The Supreme Court Proceedings

On May 15, 2013, the Supreme Court held a closed-door hearing. Beatriz arrived in an ambulance, accompanied by a caravan of trucks and cars bearing her doctors, representatives of the Ministry of Health, expert witnesses, and lawyers. The morning session was devoted to establishing the credentials of experts offered by both sides. The technicalities were strictly enforced. So strictly, in fact, that the court barred the testimony of the defense's key expert on the grounds that he had brought only a copy, rather than an original, medical diploma. That expert was world-renowned Brazilian obstetrician Dr. Anibal Faundes, who was to have testified about international standard of care in cases involving lupus during pregnancy. Without his testimony, Beatriz's lawyers lost their strongest testimony regarding the international standard of care that they had hoped to invoke in support of Beatriz's need for an abortion.[24]

After the court heard arguments from both sides, it announced that it would render its decision within fifteen working days.[25] To be sure, the case was a difficult one, forcing the justices to resolve what seemed to be an impasse between the competing rights to life of Beatriz and her fetus. On the one hand, abortion was banned. On the other hand, the Salvadoran constitution guaranteed the same fundamental rights to every person, including those not yet born. Still, fifteen days was a long time, and Beatriz's health status was growing increasingly precarious.

On May 29, 2013, the Supreme Court announced its opinion. In it, the court rejected Beatriz's petition for an abortion, citing the IML's conclusion that Beatriz's right to life was not imperiled: she was receiving treatment according to "medical science," consisting of hospitalization and constant monitoring to ensure that her health remained stable. Therefore, it concluded the state was adequately protecting Beatriz's fundamental rights to health and life.[26]

Key to the opinion is the court's refusal to choose between Beatriz's right to life and that of her fetus. Although the court acknowledged the possibility that, at some point in the future, these rights might come into conflict, it took pains to avoid privileging one life over the other.[27] Instead, it instructed the doctors to follow medical guidelines in determining the opportune moment for any intervention, noting that their decision should be based upon their clinical analysis of the best treatment to secure the lives of both the mother and the fetus.

The Aftermath of the Legal Proceedings

The court's decision placed Beatriz's doctors in what one of them called the "ridiculous" situation of "knowing that her life was going to be imperiled, yet having to wait until it actually was in order to save her."[28] Further complicating Beatriz's medical status was the fact that Beatriz had delivered her first child via a cesarean section delivery. Although vaginal births are possible after cesarean section deliveries, in El Salvador, the risks of uterine rupture and other complications are considered too high. Thus, her doctors knew Beatriz would need a cesarean section, and yet they understood the law as barring them from scheduling one until Beatriz became medically unstable. Of course, once she was medically unstable, the cesarean section would be a complex and risky operation.

Finally, when she was twenty-seven weeks pregnant, Beatriz began having pre-term contractions. Her doctors knew they couldn't let her risk going into labor. They performed a cesarean section, and Beatriz's baby girl was delivered. Beatriz bled more than normal after the surgery, but she was readily stabilized. Her newborn daughter was placed on life support in an incubator, where she died, five hours after she was born.

UNDERSTANDING THE MEANING AND PURPOSE OF ABORTION BANS: WHAT WE LEARN FROM BEATRIZ'S CASE

Try as I might to see another viewpoint, the outcome in Beatriz's case seemed to me perverse. El Salvador forced Beatriz to wait until her life was in immediate danger before allowing her to terminate her pregnancy. The law increased the chances that she would suffer permanent damage to her vital organs; it forced her to endure months of physical pain and psychological distress. And all for the sake of a fetus that everyone agreed would never survive.

A year after the decision, when it had faded from public view, I went to El Salvador to try to make sense of it all. I found doctors and lawyers on both sides of the conflict who were generous with their time and helped me to understand not only the reasons Beatriz's case unfolded as it did, but also the purpose and significance of the abortion law itself.

The Distinction Between a Life-Threatening Pregnancy and Imminent Risk of Death

One of the most outspoken medical experts in support of the government's position in Beatriz's case petition was Dr. Carlos Mayora. Both during and afterward, he appeared on media outlets throughout El Salvador. An obstetrician in his eighties who'd worked for decades in private practice, Mayora's white-jacket commentary conveyed grandfatherly authority. He gave so many interviews making the case for denying Beatriz's petition to terminate her pregnancy that he became the de facto spokesperson for the opposition.

I was determined to reach out and see whether he would be willing to talk to me about Beatriz's case. After my attempts to reach him by e-mail failed, I screwed up my courage and called his office.

"Dr. Mayora," his gravelly voice announced, when his secretary put through my call.

"Good afternoon," I said, launching into my carefully rehearsed Spanish introduction. "I'm a law professor from California. I'm researching the well-known case of Beatriz and I'm coming to El Salvador in a few weeks and was wondering whether you might be willing to let me interview you."

"*Bueno*," he answered. "Why don't you send me a description of your study?"

He had understood me. I was amazed and thrilled.

"Certainly, and I have explained it all in Spanish. I speak well in person, but I get nervous on the telephone, so I would love to send you the details. What is your e-mail address?"

"Well, that's not necessary. You can send it to my office."

"Send it by mail to El Salvador? Are you sure? Is there someone else I could e-mail it to?"

"That's not necessary. Just send it to me."

When I got to his office, I saw my papers had arrived, in spite of my doubts about the reliability of the Salvadoran postal system. Mayora had also printed out a tall stack of my articles. As I offered my thanks for agreeing to meet with me, he motioned to them, saying, "See, we know who you are," his face crinkling into a wide smile.

He'd invited his friend Delmer Rodriguez, a constitutional law professor from the Superior School of Economics and Business, to join us. In addition to a brightly painted, wooden business-card holder, Rodriguez gave me a pocket-sized copy of the Salvadoran constitution.

"Look at *Article I*," Rodriguez pointed out, opening the small book. "It's written here: life begins at conception. It's a human being. We put it there in 1998 because it's the most important part of our law—protecting human life."

"But it's not simply a legal concept; it's a scientific fact," added Mayora, lifting a heavy volume from the books on his shelf. "It's here in *Williams Obstetrics*. It's an American book. Are you familiar with it? This one is in Spanish, of course, from 2008. But it says here, 'There's a unique DNA.' The fetus is totally distinct from the moment of conception. It's an individual and the law signifies this fact."

I had encountered the "separate DNA" argument before, when talking with pro-life advocates in the United States. As they see it, the fact that a fetus has its own chromosomal makeup proves that it is a separate individual. If it is a separate individual, it deserves the same rights as does any other member of the human community. Its location inside of its mother in no way diminishes its humanity.

I understand their argument. I even agree with them that the fetus is in a sense "alive." But I reject their conclusion that, because a fetus has a unique genetic makeup, abortion is always wrong.

In my religious tradition, until a baby is born alive, it is not considered a separate human being. We don't treat fetuses like other human beings. For example, although there is grief when a woman loses a pregnancy, we don't have funerals or engage in traditional mourning practices for miscarried fetuses. My sense is that the same holds true for most other religions. So to my way of thinking, location matters: the fetus is alive and has a unique DNA, but until it is born, it is not a separate human being.

In Beatriz's case, her fetus never would survive outside her body. In the meantime, its location inside her body posed a serious threat to her life.

"What I want to know," I asked Mayora, "is why, if the mother's life is in danger, it should be illegal to terminate the pregnancy? Not with the intention of killing the fetus, but in the double-effect sense. You know, where the goal is to save her life, but the only way to do so is to end the pregnancy."

I had learned about the Catholic doctrine of double-effect years ago, when teaching medical ethics at a Catholic hospital in Chicago. In the context of abortion, this doctrine permits an exception to the general religious prohibition against abortion when the act is intended to save the mother's life. In this case, because the goal is to save the mother's life, the abortion has the double-effect of saving her life—a moral good—and the negative, but unwanted, effect of ending the fetus's life.[29] The doctrine seemed to me tailor-made for a case like this.

But Mayora did not want to discuss Catholic ethics. Instead, he was interested in the way Beatriz's case was being used to advocate for an exception to the abortion ban.

"Her doctors found that the fetus lacked a brain, which is totally incompatible with life. It looked like a worm. In my judgment, the doctors thought in good faith that this girl was carrying a fetus that couldn't survive," he said.

But he believed her supporters were exaggerating Beatriz's condition in order to get the state to make an exception to its abortion ban:

Her lawyers presented Beatriz's case very dramatically. But she already had had a child who survived. And then she got pregnant again, in spite of the fact that the doctors had warned her to take precautions against pregnancy. She got pregnant again, and had been going to and from her doctors' appointments by herself. She was living at home, seventy-five miles from San Salvador, but coming every week by public bus to her prenatal appointments. So she was healthy, you see?

Then, the advocates, a group of radical feminists, took her away to a shelter of American women. Even though we, as an organization, offered her a private lodging. The feminist group said "no." They had her isolated there, basically deprived her of her liberty, and made her an emblematic case. To make a law in favor of abortion.

How can I describe Mayora so that you'll understand why I failed to interrupt to press him for clearer answers? Surely a trained journalist or anthropologist would have managed to get to the heart of the matter. His crinkled eyes were blue, his hands enormous. The smile lines so deep they seemed sculpted. When he spoke of God, his deep voice grew quiet.

I knew the advocates. They were not Americans, but Salvadorans. They had taken Beatriz into hiding in order to escape the media frenzy.

I still couldn't understand why, if he agreed both that Beatriz's fetus was doomed and that it was only a matter of time until the pregnancy placed her life in danger, he nonetheless supported making her wait before terminating it.

When I asked him why she needed to wait, Mayora responded that, at the time of her petition to the Supreme Court for an abortion, Beatriz's medical condition was stable. And at the same time, her fetus was alive, its heart was beating, and it was growing day by day. Unless and until the pregnancy posed an "imminent threat" to Beatriz's life, it was wrong to kill the fetus.

Later, when I described this part of my conversation to Dr. Jorge Ramirez, the chief assistant to the minister of health, he bristled: "Ask them if those who survived the 9/11 attack on the Twin Towers were never in danger. Because they survived? They say things that are indefensible."[30]

I did ask Mayora at least one direct question, though: "If she'd really been dying, would you have supported her desire to terminate her pregnancy?"

And he answered, "Yes."

I managed a lawyerly follow-up: "Have you ever treated a woman whose life was in danger as a result of her pregnancy?"

"I worked for thirty-five years at Social Security—the country's second-largest public hospital system, and also in the largest one, La Maternidad," he answered. "I've been a doctor for fifty-five years. I believe medicine has grown in its capacity to respond to pregnancy-related

problems. And in this case, when the Instituto de Medicina Legal evaluated Beatriz, it saw she wasn't dying; that it had been a complete
exaggeration. "

The Law of Self-Defense and Beatriz's Life-Threatening Pregnancy

Long after the conversation with Mayora and Rodriguez, after meeting
Fortin Magana and after parsing the Supreme Court's opinion, I came
to see how El Salvador interpreted the law of self-defense in Beatriz's
case. I was so distracted by the politics of the case—by the assertions of
bad faith on both sides—that I forgot to pay attention to the law that
ultimately permitted Beatriz's doctors to interrupt her pregnancy.

The legal principle of self-defense was evident in Mayora's focus on
whether Beatriz was dying. Because the fetus was considered as much a
human being as was Beatriz, a justification for taking its life would arise
only if and when the fetus posed an imminent threat to Beatriz's life.

By relying on the law of self-defense, El Salvador's decision permitted doctors to save Beatriz's life without in any way diminishing the
moral status or the legal rights of her fetus. In El Salvador, after Beatriz's case, life still begins at conception and abortion is still completely
banned.

Self-defense is an ancient legal principle, as much a part of US law as
it is a part of El Salvador's. The conventional definition provides:

> One who is not the aggressor in an encounter is justified in using a
> reasonable amount of force against his adversary where he reasonably
> believes (a) that he is in immediate danger of unlawful bodily harm
> from his adversary and (b) that the use of such force is necessary to
> avoid this danger.[31]

It doesn't take a law degree to spot the slippery terms in this definition. Who's an *adversary*? What's *immediate danger*? And what's *unlawful bodily harm*?

El Salvador answered these questions in Beatriz's case by acknowl-
edging that the fetus would become an adversary at the point where

Beatriz's doctors could no longer stabilize her condition. At that point, when the risk of death was imminent, Beatriz's fundamental rights to health and life would be deemed imperiled.[32] As such, her doctors would be justified in interrupting the pregnancy, even if they killed the fetus in the process. Critically, the intention in intervening would be to save Beatriz's life, rather than to kill the fetus. Indeed, the opinion directed them to employ all means of saving the baby's life.[33]

Had Beatriz's case arisen here in the United States, the requirement of imminence might not have been interpreted so strictly. "The proper inquiry," says one leading commentator, "is not the immediacy of the threat but the immediacy of the response necessary in defense. If a threatened harm is such that it cannot be avoided if the intended victim waits until the last moment, the principle of self-defense must permit him to act earlier—as early as is required to defend himself effectively."[34]

The Salvadoran Supreme Court's opinion arguably allowed this option of early intervention to Beatriz's doctors. The court said that it was up to her doctors to determine the precise moment when medical protocols demanded intervention.[35] But because the opinion added that those protocols ought to be based upon evidence of "real and immediate risk to the life of the pregnant mother," and because the risk of a miscalculation on their part meant possible criminal sanctions, Beatriz's doctors elected to wait until her life hung in the balance.

My hunch is that the Supreme Court struggled when applying the law of self-defense to a fetus. How odd to cast the fetus as an assailant against whom deadly force is justified. Unlike conventional adversaries, the fetus doesn't do or intend anything toward its mother.

Perhaps, too, the court was moved, in narrowing the scope of self-defense, by a sense that Beatriz was partly to blame for her predicament. After all, Beatriz became pregnant again, against medical advice, even though her first pregnancy almost killed her.[36] My conversations with Mayora, Rodriguez, and Fortin Magana did not go deep enough to explore the possibility that they blamed Beatriz for her situation, but all mentioned the fact that she'd gotten pregnant a second time, in spite of knowing its risk to her health.

The way they invoked her choice to get pregnant a second time reminded me of a familiar undercurrent in our debate over legalized abortion here in the United States: the idea that some women are more deserving of an abortion than others. It's surprisingly common for those who would ban abortion to support exceptions in cases of rape and incest. The reasoning seems to be that these women had pregnancy forced on them when they were raped. Because they did not choose to have sex, they should not be forced to carry a pregnancy, regardless of the humanity of the developing fetus. I could spend pages exploring what's wrong with the assumption that, by having sex, a woman waives her fundamental rights to protect her own health and safety, should she become pregnant.

But in Beatriz's case, such debates are unnecessary. Because, as you'll see momentarily, Beatriz did not choose to become pregnant. Nor did she describe the sex leading to her pregnancy as voluntary.

In the media and in the courtroom, Beatriz's case was understood as a challenge to El Salvador's abortion ban. But in order to take the true measure of the ban, so that we understand how much and how little laws governing abortion matter, we need to understand Beatriz as a human being, rather than merely an abstraction.

BEATRIZ'S STORY

Arranging to meet Beatriz was easy. Having spent four years researching abortion in El Salvador, I already knew many key players in Beatriz's case. At 6 a.m., one June morning in 2014, I set out from San Salvador with Sara Garcia, one of the activists who'd advocated on her behalf.

It took two and a half hours to get from the capital to the dirt road turnoff to La Gloria (pseudonym). It took another forty-five minutes to find the home of Beatriz's mother, less than a mile away. The dirt road was muddy with the previous night's rains. We traveled slowly, trying to stay in the ruts. A herd of bony cows moved slowly in front of us. A man on horseback rode behind them, randomly whipping the stragglers so that they lumbered to one side or the other, without ever clearing the street.

The village of La Gloria has only one road. There were no signs or numbers, but Garcia didn't want to ask directions of the occasional neighbors for fear of calling attention to Beatriz's family. Beatriz and her son had moved from the house of her husband's parents and were staying with her mother, Delmy, for a while.

Delmy's high voice came over Garcia's cell phone, guiding us to a bumpy lane that angled off the main road, then opened onto a clearing with two brightly painted churches and, farther down, five or six cinder-block houses. Finally, we saw her waving to us from across a muddy yard scattered with brick stepping-stones. Chickens patrolled the yard, clucking as we passed under a wire clothesline strung from an electricity pole.

Beatriz waited in the doorway's shadow, her eyes as enormous as a baby's. Two impossibly small kittens played by her feet.

"Come in, come in," Delmy said, with hugs and a kiss on the cheek.

My eyes adjusted to the dim room. Beatriz sat on one of the two red plastic lawn chairs, inviting Garcia and me to sit in the two hammocks that crisscrossed the room. Her mother unpacked the bag of groceries—rice, beans, corn flour, cookies, and tampons—that we'd brought from the "super" market in Zacatecoluca, the nearest town. I tried to engage Claudio, Beatriz's two-and-a-half-year-old son, who was playing ball with a rectangular blow-up pillow. He kicked it around the room, until it went under the bed. He cried until Beatriz got up and coaxed it out with a broken umbrella. He'd hit his head some time ago on the bed's metal underside and wouldn't go under himself. After the fourth or fifth time, Beatriz ignored his crying and left the pillow ball under the bed.

Claudio brought out his other toy, a plastic bowl in which he carried three ketchup packets. While Garcia tried getting him to say "one, two, three," Beatriz, Delmy, and I chatted about children, theirs and mine. Delmy couldn't believe that, at fifty-three, I wasn't yet a grandmother. She's forty-one and already has several grandchildren.

As the sun angled slowly into their home, Beatriz's sixteen-year-old sister arrived, carrying her eight-month-old son. Delmy gave her three dollars and sent her to the neighbor's stand to buy Coca-Cola and some *pupusas*. She stayed and chatted for a while when she returned, then kissed her mother good-bye and left. Later, Beatriz's fourteen-year-old sister emerged from behind the curtain that separated the small bedroom in the back from the house's main room where we sat. She poured water over herself from a bucket in the outdoor basin, pulled on white knee socks, and then left for her three-hour school day. Still later, Beatriz's eighteen-year-old brother arrived, carrying a clear plastic bag filled with scores of baby tilapia. He was hoping to raise them in the gray tub next to the latrine and maybe sell them one day.

Beatriz leaned forward as I spoke, smiling as she got used to my accent. I tried sitting up in the hammock to create a lap for one of the kittens, and suddenly flipped over and fell onto the floor. Even Claudio stopped whining, and after a stunned moment, we all laughed. I dusted myself off—the cement floor was covered with a persistent layer of crisp gold sand, although we were miles from the beach—and took a seat in one of the chairs.

Beatriz was ready to tell me her story.

I already knew most of it. Her doctors had described the painful lupus sores, red and itchy, that began spreading all over her body. The way pregnancy escalated her disease, the trip to the experts in San Salvador, the ultrasound with its terrible news about the fetus. And everyone knew about the ensuing legal battle.

What caught me by surprise was not the story she told, but Beatriz herself. She'd seemed entirely passive in the public story told about her case—a person to whom things had happened. Lupus. A fetus with no brain. A girl who got pregnant a second time, in spite of her doctors' warnings. In person, though, she was not so much passive as she was trapped.

The truth is that Beatriz *chose* not to get sterilized after her first child, Claudio, was born. At first it wasn't clear whether Claudio would survive; he'd been delivered so early. She didn't get sterilized then because she wanted the chance to have a child, in case Claudio died. Later, when Claudio came home, and it became clear that he wasn't developing normally, her reasons for not getting sterilized grew more complicated.

The truth is that her life was almost impossibly difficult before she became pregnant a second time.

At her mother's home, she and Claudio slept in the front room on a thin foam mattress over a sagging metal frame. There was no money for diapers, so she awakened night after night in a puddle of urine. Claudio didn't speak and seemed unable to understand even basic commands. There were four other people sharing the two-room living space.

Beatriz had left school at age fourteen. She'd never held a job, and no one she knew earned a regular income. And she was sick. Her lupus was so advanced that medications barely controlled her blood pressure. She was weak, easily tired, and at constant risk of stroke.

There was no marked path, no clear way in which Beatriz could have stepped out of the life she was living and into one in which she had good options. Instead, she moved back and forth between her mother's home and her in-laws' home every few weeks.

She moved because her husband beat her. Inside of the cinder-block house he shared with his parents, he hit her. Then she would leave him, taking Claudio with her. They would make up. She would move back. He would beat her again.

She told me about his violence in passing, when I asked how she felt, now that her case was over and done with.

"I feel guilty," she said. "I know it wasn't my fault that the baby died. But we were guilty for not having taken precautions."

"You feel guilty for having gotten pregnant?" I asked.

"He didn't take care," she said, speaking softly. "We always have problems between us, so . . ."

Beatriz's voice trailed off, and I thought perhaps I needed to move on. But then she continued, "One day we fought. He knew that I couldn't have children, but he told me that he wanted me to get pregnant anyhow, even though he knew what could happen. So he wouldn't use a condom."

We had been talking for hours by this point. I didn't know what to say. Telling her that she'd been raped, that getting pregnant wasn't her fault, wouldn't change how she felt. And my hunch was that, in her mind, she felt guilty because she didn't get sterilized, even though she knew a second pregnancy might kill her. She knew what was at stake: she did not get sterilized because she feared that, if she did, she would lose her husband.

Claudio stood in the doorway crying. Pee ran down his leg. Beatriz got up from the chair, reached for some newspaper from a stack near the door, and laid it on the wet spot.

"Does it feel like it was a long time ago, when we talk about what happened?" I asked, hoping the present was so distracting that it might help her to forget the past.

"No, it feels like it's only a few days ago. It's not the past."

Beatriz was crying in earnest now, but she had raised her eyes and was looking straight at me.

"It's made me want to be somewhere else. Like, I always want to be with my mother when I'm with my husband. And then I want to be with my husband when I'm with my mother. Sometimes, I feel desperate in all of my body, and I don't want to be alive. But my mom tells me that I have to fight for the child that I have. God still wants me to be here, and my son needs me."

CONCLUSION

At some point on the journey home, it occurred to me how little difference it would have made had Beatriz been granted an abortion at fourteen weeks. Of course, it would have been better for her not to have lain in the hospital for months, worrying about her son, her mother, her husband, and the possibility that she would die.

But an early abortion, like the later induced delivery, would have offered no permanent relief from the things that made her life hard. Beatriz's case meant more to the war over abortion than the abortion meant to Beatriz.

To those who oppose the abortion ban, Beatriz's case offered the perfect challenge to the ban's legitimacy. Making an exception to permit Beatriz an abortion—whether because the fetus lacked a brain, or because her life was at risk, or both—would amount to an admission that the ban went too far. If Beatriz was allowed to end her pregnancy, there would be precedent for favoring a mother's rights over those of her fetus. Her case would be the first of many.

Those who supported the abortion ban understood this threat. This case was not about their conviction that Beatriz's fetus was viable or could, by some miracle, survive. Mayora, the leading spokesperson in support of denying Beatriz an abortion, had said, "It looked like a worm," and made no pretense about its chances for life.

But they understood the risk of making an exception in Beatriz's case.

In the end, Beatriz's case became a high-stakes game, played to a draw. Beatriz survived. But so did the abortion ban.

I understand both sides. If a fetus or, for that matter, a zygote is a full member of the human community, the battle over abortion must be fought in an all-or-nothing manner.[37] The law banning abortion is simply the legal embodiment of a moral truth. It is a declaration of membership in the human species.

Using the law to make moral declarations is not unusual. It's what legal theorists call the "expressive function" of the law.[38] We use the law to tell us something about ourselves—who we are and what we value.

Think of laws against prostitution, flag-burning, or organ-selling. To the extent one supports these laws, it's often for reasons beyond or even aside from a belief that the law will prevent the crime from happening. Instead, we look to the law as a way of proclaiming moral boundaries. Supporters use the law to testify to a shared moral vision.

But valuing a law because of the statement it makes does not mean that one doesn't care about its impact. Consequences matter. So, for example, if evidence showed that a law against selling human organs had the effect of intensifying the exploitation and misery of the relevant vulnerable populations, one might reconsider his or her support for that law.

Professor Cass Sunstein, in his leading work on the expressive function of law, suggests that the biggest challenge to symbolic laws arises when "the effects of such laws seem bad or ambiguous, even by reference to the values held by their supporters."[39] Only a fanatic, he reasons, would completely ignore the law's impact on the norms and values it aims to promote.[40]

Until I began my travels in El Salvador, I did not fully appreciate the moral position that life begins at conception, and the ways in which that moral conviction might lead inexorably to supporting a complete ban on abortion. But as Sunstein notes, the ultimate test of a law's legitimacy, even of a law intended primarily to make a symbolic statement, lies in its consequences.

It is not enough to assert that a law's consequence is good simply because it makes a good statement. That circularity is a fanatic's position.

Beatriz's case was, by all accounts, extraordinary. In the next chapter, we turn to the subject of ordinary abortions and of the measurable consequences of El Salvador's endeavor to outlaw them.

TWO

ASSESSING THE IMPACT OF EL SALVADOR'S ABORTION BAN

In 1998, El Salvador passed a law banning abortion under all circumstances.[1] Until that point, abortion was illegal except in cases involving risks to maternal life, severe fetal anomaly, and rape or incest. Since then, El Salvador has worked to enforce its ban, mounting an intensive effort to identify and prosecute those who violate the law. If we're hoping to understand what happens when abortion is banned, El Salvador is the perfect place to study.

Regardless of whether one favors or opposes the abortion ban, it is vital that we assess the law's impact. Recall Cass Sunstein's observation at the end of the last chapter that a law cannot be justified merely because one likes its message. Even if we like the message of the law, it is valid only to the extent that it produces results that are consistent with its message.

So what happened when abortion was outlawed in El Salvador? The evidence shows us that three things occurred: (1) abortion remained commonplace and rates did not drop even though it was illegal; (2) doctors become involved in law enforcement; and (3) innocent women were accused and convicted of abortion-related crimes. These three systems—the black market, health care, and criminal justice—all yield measurable consequences of the ban on abortion. And, as I explain below, in spite of the vast differences between El Salvador and the United States, there is good reason to expect that the United States would experience each of these three consequences were it to outlaw abortion.

ABORTIONS STILL HAPPEN

Perhaps the most surprising thing about banning abortion is what doesn't happen when abortion becomes a crime. Abortion does not go away. Indeed, the rates of abortion in countries with the most restrictive abortion laws are higher.[2]

This is true in El Salvador: by the Salvadoran government's own measure, there are tens of thousands of illegal abortions every year.[3] Indeed, the rate of abortion in countries with restrictive abortion laws far exceeds that of countries with far more liberal laws, such as the United States.[4]

The correlation of high abortion rates and restrictive abortion laws does not mean that abortion bans *cause* more women to have abortions. Any number of factors might cause these two things—abortion bans and high abortion rates—to go together. Perhaps these countries share a religious or cultural discomfort with contraception, as well as abortion. Perhaps it is hard to get contraception. Perhaps there is little sex education.

There is one thing we know for certain: abortion doesn't simply go away when it is made illegal. Because abortions are illegal, it is hard to get a complete picture of how women obtain them in El Salvador. What is clear beyond a doubt is that the advent of abortion drugs has completely altered illegal abortion.

Until recently, abortions were exclusively surgical procedures.[5] Doctors would terminate pregnancies by opening the cervix and suctioning or scraping out the contents of the uterus. Women unable to find or afford a doctor to perform an illegal abortion might try bringing on a miscarriage themselves, for example, by inserting a sharp object into their uterus. Opening the cervix typically is enough to induce a miscarriage, although it carries with it high risks of excessive bleeding and infection.

Historically, these so-called "botched" abortions provided the only proof of the crime of illegal abortion. Coat-hanger abortions, for example, were notorious in pre-*Roe* America, in part because they carried a high risk of perforating a woman's uterus, leaving behind the telltale sign that the woman had deliberately ended her pregnancy.

Beginning in the 1990s, with the advent of abortion drugs, illegal abortion became safer and harder to detect. Taken in the appropriate dose, at the right point in pregnancy, the drug known as Mifeprex or RU-486 (mifepristone is the generic name) will safely end 98 percent of pregnancies.[6] Side effects include excessive bleeding or incomplete abortion, both readily resolved by a visit to a doctor.[7]

Although they are not always safe or effective, especially when taken too late in pregnancy or at the wrong dose, compared with the risks of an illegal surgical abortion, drugs such as RU-486 or Mifeprex have completely altered women's access to illegal abortion.[8] In many countries, women find it easy to buy misoprostol, a drug conventionally used in treating gastric ulcers. It happens to be one of two of the drugs that, together, make up Mifeprex. Taken alone, misoprostol is slightly less safe and less effective than Mifeprex, ending between 75 and 90 percent of first-trimester pregnancies, as opposed to Mifeprex, which ends 98 percent of pregnancies. Still, the side effects of misoprostol, such as heavy bleeding or incomplete abortion, are minimal and easily treated, unlike those associated with incompetently performed surgical abortions.[9]

In El Salvador, and throughout Latin America, women find it easy to access misoprostol via the Internet.[10] In Brazil, for example, where abortion is illegal except in cases of rape, threat to maternal life, or anencephaly (where the fetus lacks a brain), abortion drugs play a vital role in the thriving black market. An estimated one in five Brazilian women under age forty has had an abortion.[11] Even in a poor country like El Salvador, almost everyone has a smartphone and, provided they have money and time, can go online to purchase the drugs that will end an unwanted pregnancy.

To be sure, illegal abortion remains risky.[12] Whether they use drugs or other means to terminate their pregnancies, many women experience complications from illegal abortion that necessitate medical attention. In Latin America, complications from illegal abortion constitute the leading cause of mortality in young women.[13]

The inevitability of such complications has led to the second concrete change set in motion by banning abortions: doctors become entangled in the law enforcement process.

DOCTORS AND THE PROBLEM OF DETECTING ABORTION

If the first thing that happened when El Salvador banned abortion was the proliferation of illegal, black-market abortions, the second thing that happened was that doctors were enlisted in the law enforcement effort. The overwhelming majority of abortion cases in El Salvador begin in the hospital, with a doctor's hunch that his or her patient has broken the law.

In 1998, Salvadoran government officials charged with implementing the newly passed abortion ban reached out to doctors to encourage them to report patients they suspected of terminating their pregnancies. Dr. Alejandro Guidos, former president of the El Salvadoran Association of Obstetricians and Gynecologists, described the state's approach. He told me, "Officials from the Fiscalia [the state prosecutors] went to the hospitals, advising doctors that they had a legal obligation to report women suspected of terminating their pregnancies. And the hospital directors supported the obligation to report. They collaborated."[14]

The push to enlist doctors in enforcing the abortion law succeeded. A 2006 survey of practicing obstetricians found that more than half (56 percent) of respondents reported having been involved in notifying legal authorities about a suspected unlawful abortion.[15]

Inevitably, a country seeking to enforce laws against abortion will seek doctors' collaboration. Women must turn to doctors when an illegal abortion goes wrong. Doctors are therefore in the best position to spot the crime.

But there are serious problems with using doctors to enforce abortion laws. In reporting their patients, doctors break the law and violate the oldest of ethical principles—patient confidentiality. Furthermore, in the vast majority of cases, doctors cannot tell whether a woman has had an abortion or simply a miscarriage. Thus, their reports are based on hunches, rather than on medical evidence.

Law, Ethics, and Doctors' Reports to Police

The obligation of safeguarding a patient's secrets is ancient. For over twenty-four hundred years, medical doctors have embraced the precepts articulated in the Hippocratic oath.[16] Recited at medical school gradua-tions worldwide, one of the oath's central tenets is the following pledge: "Whatever I see or hear in the lives of my patients, whether in connection with my professional practice or not, which ought not to be spoken of outside, I will keep secret, as considering all such things to be private."[17]

This principle is based in part on policy considerations. Confiden-tiality is essential to creating a solid doctor-patient relationship, dedi-cated to promoting the health and life of the patient. Doctors routinely treat patients whom they suspect or even know to have broken the law. The medical profession long has been clear that its job is to heal, rather than to work as agents of the police.

In El Salvador, as in other countries, including the United States, the ethical obligation of confidentiality has been enacted into law; it is illegal to share patient information.[18] A doctor who reveals her patients' medical information commits both a civil wrong, for which a patient might sue, and a crime, punishable by imprisonment and the suspension of the doctor's medical license.[19]

Regardless of these ethical and legal precepts, it's easy to understand why a doctor might struggle when encountering evidence of an illegal abortion. If you view abortion as the taking of a life, you might be willing to call the police, even if it means violating the norms and laws governing confidentiality.

Salvadoran law supports such breaches of confidentiality by requir-ing doctors to report suspected crimes to the state.[20] Because abortion is a "criminal act," this requirement could be construed to mean that providers must report cases of unlawful abortion to police. Plainly, this was the interpretation the Salvadoran officials meant to convey when they toured hospitals in 1998.

Legally, though, they were wrong. The law explicitly excuses doctors from this duty when the information is acquired in the course of a confidential doctor-patient relationship. The law states that "[d]octors, pharmacists, nurses and other health professionals must report unlawful criminal acts that they become aware of in the context of their professional relationship, *unless the information they acquire is protected under the terms of professional secrecy.*"[21]

There is no conflict under the law, then. Doctors are required to maintain patient confidentiality.

Still, when the state sends prosecutors to inform hospital personnel of the need to report patients they suspect of having abortions, one can understand why doctors might comply. What happened next was both inevitable and deeply troubling.

The Diagnostic Challenge: Distinguishing Abortion from Miscarriage

It's almost always impossible, even for doctors, to tell whether a woman has had an abortion or instead simply suffered a common spontaneous miscarriage. Indeed, miscarriage is so common an occurrence that, in Spanish, there is no difference between the word for miscarriage and the word for abortion. Any interruption of pregnancy is termed an *aborto*. Although women in El Salvador, like women in the United States, tend not to speak openly about losing a pregnancy to miscarriage, when they do so, they say they've had an *aborto*. There is no other way to describe their loss.

Throughout the world, as many as one in four pregnancies ends in spontaneous miscarriage.[22] Miscarriage most often happens early in pregnancy—within the first twelve weeks. A woman having a miscarriage typically experiences what feels like a heavier period than normal, perhaps passing more blood and some blood clots, along with whatever fetal tissue remained in her uterus after the fetus stopped developing.[23] A woman might seek medical care following an early miscarriage, in response to heavy bleeding or cramping, or because of the risk that her body hasn't expelled all the fetal tissue.

Herein lies the inevitable challenge for abortion law enforcement: in the absence of physical evidence such as trauma to the uterus, there is no reliable way to distinguish a woman experiencing complications from an illegal abortion from a woman who has suffered a miscarriage.

Because doctors cannot distinguish a spontaneous miscarriage from an abortion, the government will lack the evidence necessary to support a conviction against women who have early abortions.

Salvadoran lawyer Dennis Munoz, who has defended more women convicted of abortion-related offenses than any other lawyer in the country, explained it this way:

> Yes, there are many illegal abortions in El Salvador for sure. But how do you prosecute them without evidence? There's a rule here called *corpus delecti*, which requires the state to prove a crime has taken place.[24] It's much easier to prove the crime if you have a body. To catch an early abortion, you need evidence that it's provoked. Undissolved pills in the vagina or a perforated uterus. There has to be some evidence.

Munoz's observation helps explain why the law has generated a line of prosecutions against women who lost their pregnancies at or close to full term, rather than prosecute cases against women who took drugs or hired someone to terminate an unwanted pregnancy. What Munoz's observation does not explain is why reports to police are generated almost exclusively from public hospitals. When El Salvador sought to enlist doctors in enforcing its abortion ban, only those working in public hospitals complied.

The Cases: Public Hospitals, Poor Women, and Police Reports

My hunch was that a doctor's willingness to report a woman for suspected abortion would reflect his or her personal beliefs about abortion. It turns out that I was wrong.

The first comprehensive investigation in El Salvador traced the origins of abortion prosecutions over the ten-year time frame from 2001 to 2011. By traveling across the country and visiting every criminal court,

researchers identified 129 abortion prosecutions.[25] A doctor's report triggered the great majority of these prosecutions. Yet not a single one of these
reports was made by a doctor in private practice, seeing a paying patient.[26]

I wondered what might make a doctor at a public hospital more
willing to act on suspicions, so I decided to try talking to a doctor who
had made a report. This task was complicated because the doctors' police reports are anonymous. In the end, I settled for interviews with two
doctors: one whom I knew believed doctors should not report their
patients, and the other whom I suspected of having reported a patient.

Interview with Dr. Rosario

Dr. Bernadette Rosario (pseudonym) was born into a medical family and
raised in San Salvador. In her mid-forties, Rosario is a powerful woman
who has served in the country's Ministry of Health, as well as on the
faculty of the country's foremost medical school. Her office is in Colonia Médica, home to the country's leading private medical practices. The
neighborhood is only a mile or two from the public hospital where Beatriz waited out her ordeal. But whereas the entry to the public hospital was
crowded with street vendors, ragged children, and dilapidated cars, Colonia Médica is tranquil. It consists of several tall buildings arrayed around
a circular patch of grass. In the middle of the grass, a bronze statue of an
enormous golden hand cradles a tiny baby in its palm.

"Can you tell me about doctor-patient confidentiality rights in El
Salvador?" I asked at the start of our conversation.[27]

I needn't have worried about putting her on the defensive. Rosario
looked me straight in the eye and answered, "Here, the right to confidentiality comes with a price tag. Patients at the private hospitals buy
their privacy—no one ever reveals their secrets. You could lose your
medical license and spend three to six years in prison for breaching
patient confidentiality. And besides, they're your patients—you know
them, or their families, or their friends. Your reputation and your live-
lihood depend on them."

"What percentage of Salvadorans go to private doctors and hospitals?" I asked.

"Three percent. Maybe five percent." She smiled and shook her head when she saw the look on my face.

I found it hard to believe that all the elevator buildings in the Colonia Médica, the medical offices, and the small specialty hospitals served only three hundred thousand of the country's six million residents.[28]

Rosario continued, "Eighty percent of Salvadorans get their care from public hospitals located throughout the country. The rest, mostly those who are retired or on pensions, get something in between."

I'm not naive about the difference between the quality of health care received by rich and poor Americans. Generally speaking, we too live in a tiered health-care system.[29] Still, I wondered how poor women lost their right to confidentiality simply because they couldn't afford to see a private doctor.

"Why aren't doctors in public hospitals worried about breaching patient confidentiality when they report women for abortion?" I asked.

Rosario answered, "Well, a lot of doctors think they're obligated to report women they suspect of having done something to terminate their pregnancies; they do it because they think the law says they must. And then there are those who report because they really believe it's a terrible crime to terminate a pregnancy and they want to see the law enforced. And, of course, doctors in public hospitals typically are young, hoping to build a reputation and then to start a private practice. They'll do what they need to do to avoid conflict with their nurses or their superiors."

"Do women know the public hospital doctors might report them?" I asked.

"It depends," said Rosario. "Some of them are savvy enough to know exactly what sort of things separate the public from the private hospitals. But my guess is that most women don't know. No one talks much about abortion or the law, and even if they knew, poor women seek care at public hospitals simply because they're bleeding to death and they have no other option."

Rosario had done little to conceal her opinion that patient confidentiality should preclude abortion reports to police. But then, she was allied with the opponents of the abortion law. I'd gotten her name from the activists working to overturn the ban. I wondered if health-care providers who supported the ban, who believed abortion was murder, nonetheless felt bound by patient confidentiality.

Dr. Diaz's Interview

There is a stigma to breaking the Hippocratic oath, which is at the heart of how doctors understand their ethical obligations to their patients. So I knew it would be difficult to find a doctor willing to speak openly about breaching patient confidentiality. Moreover, because abortion indictments and prosecutions are unpublished, I lacked easy access to the names of doctors who served as witnesses in these cases. I caught a break here, although I didn't know why until later.

In 2002, Dr. Marvin Diaz (pseudonym) was a young attending physician working in the emergency room of a public hospital while training as an obstetrician.[30] There, he treated a woman named Karina Climaco, whose mother had brought her in; she was hemorrhaging and passing blood clots. Diaz examined Karina and found evidence of both uterine enlargement and placental tissue in her vaginal cavity. According to Karina, after the examination, Diaz called the police. Within hours of her admission to the hospital, police arrived at Karina's mother's apartment, searched her home, and found the cold body of a newborn baby.[31]

Karina was later convicted and imprisoned before being exonerated when her defense lawyers proved she had a spontaneous miscarriage. The case received considerable publicity, and I was able to review the transcript, where I found Diaz's name.

After a number of false starts, I found Diaz's contact information. At first, he insisted I had the wrong person; his surname is common in El Salvador. I persisted, though, and after some back-and-forth, he agreed to meet with me. I didn't understand why until I got to his office.[32] There was a Jewish candelabrum on his otherwise empty desk.

Surprised, I asked, "What's this for?" There are no more than a hundred Jews living in El Salvador.[33] Diaz responded that he was a Converso, descended from a long line of Jews who ostensibly converted to

Catholicism during the Spanish inquisition of 1492, and who survived by hiding their religious identity and practices.[34] He said he'd guessed I was Jewish from my name. He had guessed correctly, although I'd never considered my surname, invented at Ellis Island two generations ago, to be particularly Jewish.

"That's why I agreed to meet you," he told me. We chatted a little in broken Hebrew and, oddly moved, I turned to the conversation at hand.

Diaz remembered the sequence of events around the reporting differently than Karina had: "It was her mother who found out about the baby when she noticed blood underneath the bed, and it was the mother who pressed charges. In any case, all we did was come and perform some tests to figure out if the woman had been pregnant. It didn't mean we were going to call the police, but somehow the police got there at that moment."[35]

"Would you have reported her, though?" I asked.

"No," he answered, "we are supposed to protect what our patients tell us and we do."

"Even though the law says that you have to report it?" I asked.

"Yes," he answered. "And I have to be sincere with what I am about to say. In El Salvador, the law is not applied to everyone, but rather only to certain individuals. For example, in private hospitals, things are done where no one really knows what happened except for the doctor and the patient."

Diaz is now in private practice; his office is in the same neighborhood as Rosario's. I wanted to probe Diaz's comfort level with the outright ban on abortion.

"How does it feel as a doctor to see a ten-year-old girl, pregnant as the result of incest?" I asked.

"The law here is very strict," he replied. "It says that you can never terminate a pregnancy. There is never an extenuating circumstance. . . . In my medical view, I'd say it was worth it to allow her to have that baby. I've seen people for whom it was hard during the pregnancy because of situations like those, but when the baby is born, the woman's life is completely transformed. I've seen women who come to me and, well, yes, they do need support, and that's what they don't have here. You can have a difficult situation, but as long as you're supported, you will continue to go forward. You'll be able to overcome any obstacle."

My conversation with Diaz shook me at many levels. It was oddly refreshing to meet someone who supported the abortion law. He was not troubled by the law's failure to make exceptions in "hard" cases like incest, which after all have nothing to do with the fetus's moral status. Instead, he was bothered by the hypocrisy that permits wealthy women to evade the law.

Diaz saw abortion as murder.

Yet, even though he supported the abortion ban, Diaz was unwilling to acknowledge that he'd ever divulged patient confidences, even in the past. He did not want credit for having alerted the police about Karina's dead baby. Instead, he gave me a flimsy story about how it might have been her mother who called the police.

What bears noting is that both Diaz and Rosario portrayed medical confidentiality as a commodity. Rich women buy their privacy from private doctors. Poor women arrive at the country's public hospitals too broke to go anywhere else. They lack the funds to ensure their secrets will be kept private.

The story of how abortion is prosecuted in El Salvador begins with this reality: doctors at public hospitals call the police and poor women are prosecuted.

POOR, INNOCENT WOMEN
ACCUSED OF ABORTION CRIMES

It helps to remember Diaz's patient, Karina, as we move from the subject of detecting abortion to considering the third consequence of banning abortion in El Salvador: innocent women were prosecuted and convicted of abortion-related crimes.

Karina was reported to police on suspicion of illegal abortion after Diaz treated her in the emergency room of the public hospital. She was hemorrhaging, and the size of her uterus plus the presence of a placenta (also referred to as the afterbirth) left no doubt that she had been pregnant. Where was the baby?

Cases like hers make up over 50 percent of the cases brought against women for abortion.

The Typical Abortion Prosecution in El Salvador

At first, it's hard to see why the crime of abortion would generate cases like Karina's, which involve a dead full-term fetus. The answer lies in what we already know. First, it is hard to detect early abortion. Second, when there is physical evidence that a woman has recently delivered a baby, doctors naturally may suspect foul play. Because there is evidence to support their suspicions, they are more willing to notify the police.

The comprehensive study of all abortion-related prosecutions in the decade between 2001 and 2011 found 129 cases in which women were investigated for abortion-related offenses.[36] That is a lot, if one pictures each prosecution in all its complicated, intimate messiness. But honestly, I was surprised to find that even in a country unequivocally committed to enforcing criminal laws against abortion, there were seldom more than ten or twelve prosecutions a year.

More puzzling still was the fact that close to half of these investigations ultimately did not involve the crime of abortion at all. Instead, these investigations and arrests involved fetuses at or beyond seven months' gestation at the time of their deaths.[37] These are hardly the sort of cases that come to mind when one thinks about making abortion a crime.

These late-term cases wind up playing a larger and larger role as abortion investigations work their way through the Salvadoran criminal justice system. Not all abortion investigations turn into cases that get prosecuted, of course. More often than not, prosecutors opt not to pursue criminal charges. Some cases do move forward, though, and at this point, we see the most startling pattern emerging in the abortion prosecutions: they aren't about abortion at all.

Of the forty-nine Salvadoran women arrested for abortion, only thirteen ultimately were convicted of that crime. Salvadoran law distinguishes between abortion and homicide, treating as homicide any case involving a fetus beyond seven months' gestation. Thus, if it turns out the fetus was beyond seven months' gestation, the charges against the woman are elevated from abortion, which is punishable by two to eight years imprisonment, to homicide, which carries a maximum sentence of fifty years in prison. Of the forty-nine women originally charged with abortion, thirty-six were convicted of aggravated homicide.

The typical abortion prosecution in El Salvador doesn't look at all like what I'd expected. Rather than involving women who obtained early, illegal abortions through the black market, the cases involve women accused of deliberately killing their newborns after delivering them at home.

These cases evoke a visceral revulsion with which I am familiar. The facts behind these prosecutions aren't all that different from some of the cases in the United States involving mothers who kill their children. Here, too, the cases involved mothers who denied or concealed their pregnancies, unattended births, or babies who died after being delivered in toilets. Here, too, the mothers were charged with homicide.

But in these cases in El Salvador, the only crime the mothers seem to have committed is being desperately poor and pregnant, and losing a baby after delivering it at home.

I'll confess that I did not feel much sympathy for these women at first. Perhaps their doctors violated confidentiality, but surely the possibility that a woman has killed her newborn merits a police investigation at the least.

Munoz, the Salvadoran defense lawyer, persuaded me I was wrong.[38] In case after case, the Salvadoran criminal justice system has wrongly convicted poor women of homicide when the only evidence against them was that they had a late miscarriage.

To help me understand the connection between abortion laws and the criminalization of miscarriage, in March 2012 Munoz took me to meet Christina, a former client.

From the Hospital to the Prison: Christina's Story

We visited Christina at her grandmother's home in El Transito, a village two hours outside San Salvador. She began her story at the point when she was seventeen and expecting her second child. Several months into her pregnancy, she and her three-year-old son left El Transito and moved to San Salvador, living in the second bedroom of her mother and stepfather's apartment so that Christina would be close to the public hospital when her baby came.

It was Saturday, October 23, 2004. Earlier that week, Christina and her mother had shopped for new linens and baby clothes, having decided to spend money on the baby rather than on a baby shower. As her mother prepared to leave for work, Christina mentioned that she'd had diarrhea earlier that morning. Neither she nor her mother was alarmed, though. Christina had had stomach problems regularly since her appendix burst, about a year before, and her baby wasn't due for another month or so.

After dinner, when her mother returned from her shift at the tortilla factory, Christina mentioned that her stomach was upset. She lay down on the bed she shared with her three-year-old son. She felt sick, but it didn't feel as if she was having contractions; she knew because she remembered how they'd felt.

Several hours later, she got out of bed and told her mother she couldn't sleep. Her mother made her some tea with sugar.

In the middle of the night, Christina awakened with an urge to go to the bathroom. She sat up in bed and felt a sudden, tremendous pain. The apartment was small, so she managed to get to the bathroom by dragging herself, one hand on each wall. The pain was so intense that she felt she was suffocating. The last thing she remembers is struggling to push open the metal bathroom door.

She woke up in a hospital bed where a woman stood over her demanding, "*Y el bebé?*" ("And the baby?"). As she emerged from the fog of anesthesia, three guards stood at her bedside, asking, "What's your name? Where do you live? How many months pregnant were you?" She kept falling asleep, and they kept shaking her awake, saying, "You have to answer us."

Over the course of long hours of interrogation, she learned that her baby had died. After getting a call from the doctors, police had searched Christina's mother's apartment and found the body in the mess of blood and towels left behind when her mother dragged Christina to the neighbor's waiting truck so they could drive her to the hospital.

Christina had experienced what doctors call "precipitous labor and delivery," in which there is a sudden onset and rapid progression of the birth process.[39] Doctors don't always know why this happens, but one expert on the subject, Dr. Anne Drapkin Lyerly, a professor and obstetrician at the University of North Carolina, offered several explanations for what might have caused Christina's miscarriage.

"My first guess," she said, "involves infection. The fact that she had ongoing gastrointestinal problems is a common sign of infection. In pregnant women, such infections can spread to the amniotic sac, leading to precipitous delivery and/or miscarriage."[40]

Lyerly noted that a quick pathology investigation of the placenta would have revealed the presence or absence of infection. In Christina's case, no such examination was performed. It's not clear whether the government would have paid the costs for such testing, given Christina's impoverished status and her reliance on a public defender. It's not even clear that doctors or prosecutors bothered to preserve her placenta as forensic evidence. The issue is moot, though, as Christina's lawyer never made the request.

Instead, after two or three days at the hospital, Christina was arrested on suspicion of abortion and was transferred, handcuffed and still bleeding, to the police station just outside the women's prison in the city of Ilopango. After a week of interrogations and after the coroner determined that the fetus was beyond seven months' gestation, Christina was charged with homicide.

At her preliminary hearing, the prosecutor argued that Christina must have known she was in labor because she had already had a child. Once a woman experiences labor pains, he claimed, she cannot mistake them for any other sort of pain. Christina killed her child, the state alleged, by not telling someone she was in labor.

The presiding judge told the prosecutor to respect Christina's loss. He dismissed the case for lack of proof.

Fifteen days later, the prosecution claimed it had "new evidence," although Christina's defense team never learned what it was, and Christina's case was reopened. She was assigned a new public defender, whom she didn't meet until the day of her preliminary hearing. Once again, the state had charged her with *homocidio culposo*—our version of manslaughter. The crime carried a potential sentence of two to eight years. This time, the judge let the case go to trial.

At trial, her new lawyer failed to object when the judges decided to convict Christina of a far more serious crime than the one with which she had been charged: *homicidio agravado*, or aggravated homicide. The judges justified this heightened penalty by referencing the innocence of the victim, and by once more invoking the notion that, as an experienced mother, Christina must have known she was in labor.

Christina was convicted on the theory that, by failing to get medical help, she caused her baby's death. Aggravated homicide (*homicidio agravado*) carries a much higher penalty than manslaughter (*homicidio culposo*), and Christina was sentenced to thirty years.

I asked Lyerly what she thought of the state's claim that Christina must have known she was in labor.

"There's no logic to the court's position," she said.

> There was no reason why she should have known it was labor, and a lot of reasons why she shouldn't have—her history of gastrointestinal trouble actually means she was unlikely to know it was different; women deliver precipitously all the time; vaginal birth changes the musculature such that later deliveries tend to be much faster than first-time births. And given that she was a month away from her due date, she was more likely to think she was not in labor.[41]

Inside Ilopango, the women's prison, Christina met eight or nine women convicted of abortion-related crimes. Amid the hundreds of women imprisoned in the crowded women's cells of Ilopango, they stuck together.

Like all prisons, Ilopango had a social hierarchy. According to Christina, the drug traffickers and mass-murderers were treated the best. The other inmates applauded them. The worst treatment, by contrast, was reserved for those who had killed their children. "*Te comiste a tus hijos*" ("You ate your children"), they called out in passing to her and to the others incarcerated for abortion-related offenses.

After almost two years in prison, one of the other abortion inmates introduced Christina to Munoz, who was her lawyer. Munoz quickly spotted the judicial error in Christina's case. In El Salvador, as in the United States, judges are not permitted to revise the charges against a criminal defendant. Only the prosecutor can determine what crimes to charge.

Munoz submitted a motion seeking a new trial, arguing the court had overstepped its bounds by convicting her of a crime with which she had not been charged. The state quickly responded, offering to release Christina for time served. Christina was happy to go home to her son and her family, and opted not to seek a new trial and the chance to clear her name.

For Munoz, Christina's case was just one among a score of similar cases, one in which justice came relatively easily.

Late Miscarriages, Wrongful Convictions, and Implications for the Abortion Ban

In El Salvador, the battle over the abortion ban increasingly focuses on cases like Christina's. The problem of wrongful convictions in such cases emerged as a surprise finding of the 2009 conference between Nicaragua and El Salvador, convened by opponents of the abortion bans in both countries. Few in attendance anticipated that they would work on cases of women who never wanted to terminate their pregnancies in the first place. Yet the stories told by defense lawyers like Munoz made it clear that, in El Salvador, cases like Christina's had become commonplace.

To be sure, before the 1998 ban, women were convicted of homicide in cases involving dead newborns. But those cases did not originate in calls to police from public hospitals involving women who had had late-term miscarriages. Instead, they involved babies whose bodies, when found, showed signs of having been born alive.

At first, abortion-rights activists struggled over whether to work on this type of case, rather than strategizing ways to overturn the ban. After all, they had joined together with a specific goal: persuading the government to make exceptions to the ban. The activists call themselves the Agrupación Ciudadana por la Despenalización del Aborto Terapéutico Ético y Eugenésico (Citizens Group for the Decriminalization of Ethical, Eugenic and Theraputic Abortion), or the Agrupación Ciudadana, for short. Their wordy name reflects their goal of reinstating the abortion law that governed the country prior to 1998: a ban with the exceptions for cases involving rape, incest, fetal anomaly, or threats to maternal life or health. The group comprises lawyers, academics, students, and activists, who write grants to fund their work, which originally consisted of social media publicity and street-level activism, such as parades and protests.[42]

As I learned from one of the group's founders, Morena Herrera, many felt disturbed by cases like Christina's and worried they were a distraction from the battle over the abortion law.[43]

Eventually, though, the Agrupación Ciudadana dedicated itself to defending these women and to protesting the pattern of wrongful convictions.[44] Its lawyers undertook an investigation of the cases of all the women incarcerated on abortion-related offenses.

On April 1, 2014, the Agrupación Ciudadana submitted seventeen petitions to the legislative assembly, each of which demanded a legal pardon for a woman serving a sentence for an abortion-related homicide. The seventeen cases included every Salvadoran woman then incarcerated for abortion-related homicide.[45]

According to Munoz and his colleagues, there was *not a single guilty woman* among those who had been imprisoned for these crimes since 1998. It is a stunning claim. Yet the facts behind their cases are so similar as to be interchangeable. If it could happen to one woman, why not seventeen?

Each of the seventeen women was serving a sentence of between thirty to forty years. The majority were poor, uneducated, and young; over a quarter were illiterate and over half had not made it past third grade.[46] All had experienced obstetrical complications at some point during their pregnancies, resulting in late miscarriages. They gave birth unattended. Their newborns were stillborn or died shortly after birth. The women bled so heavily that they sought care at a hospital, where they were arrested.

The Campaign for the 17, as it is known in El Salvador, has had surprising success. On January 22, 2015, the legislative assembly announced its decision to pardon Guadalupe, one of the seventeen women.[47] It was one of the only pardons issued by the government in years, owing in part to the fact that in order to pardon a crime, the state must acknowledge its own error.

Scarcely a month later, the Agrupación Ciudadana secured another victory, this time for a woman who had been incarcerated after her doctor reported her to police for a suspected abortion. She had been sentenced to thirty years in prison for having brought about the death of her five-month-old fetus. In April 2015, after she had served fifteen months in prison, the judge found that her doctor had violated the obligation to maintain patient confidentiality and, in addition, that the prosecution had failed to prove that the baby had been born alive.[48] In May 2016, a third woman—Maria Teresa Rivera—was released after serving four years of a forty-year sentence, when the state acknowledged lack of evidence of live birth or criminal intent.[49]

These cases are travesties. It is almost too painful to imagine what it feels like to go into labor suddenly, alone, far from the hospital. To be carried to the hospital, hemorrhaging and in pain, having lost the pregnancy. To arrive there only to be accused of killing your baby, by a state that never had evidence the baby was born alive, let alone that you intentionally killed it.

It is hard for a legal system to admit that it got things wrong. So these exonerations are a tribute to the Salvadoran legal system, as well as to the Agrupación lawyers. Yet these victories remain exceptions.

The 2014 legislative assembly rejected the pardons of the remaining fourteen women, in some cases without comment, in other cases giving explanations such as "risk of recidivism due to poor social status and lack of education."[50]

The Agrupación Ciudadana continues to fight, but it seems that for every woman whose freedom it has secured, there are several more women newly convicted. By 2015, Las 17 had become twenty-four, which was the grand total of the original seventeen, minus three, for the women exonerated, and plus eight for the newcomers. Munoz and the other Agrupación lawyers know all the newly convicted women. The facts of their cases are familiar by now. But the work of overturning their convictions proceeds slowly, case by case.

ASSESSING THE CONSEQUENCES OF BANNING ABORTION

What are we to make of what has happened in El Salvador under the abortion ban? The effort to assess the law's consequences feels like a charged, partisan endeavor. At the end of the day, it seems that abortion exists in a world in which, as Friedrich Nietzsche observed, "There are no facts, only interpretations."[51]

I can't tell you how to interpret the story I've told you. But I can assure you that it would be largely the same story, any place around the globe.

Abortion Will Still Happen

No one ever claimed that banning abortion would eliminate it. What's surprising is that there is no evidence that banning abortion reduces the abortion rate. It is possible, of course, that the ban makes a difference at the individual level, leading some women to keep their unwanted pregnancies, rather than having abortions.

But we know that there can't be millions or even thousands of such women, because if there were, then we would see higher birth rates in countries with abortion bans than we do in similar countries with more permissive laws. We don't. El Salvador's birth rates are no higher now than they were before the ban, in 1998. Nor are they significantly different from those of their neighbors with more permissive abortion laws: Honduras, Costa Rica, and Panama.

Banning Abortion Has an Impact on Women and Girls

When abortion is illegal, it is unsafe. In El Salvador, scores of women die every year from illegal abortions.[52] They aren't the daughters of the elite, whose money helps them find safe, private ways to end their unwanted pregnancies. They are the women who live far from cities, in cinder-block homes with dirt floors and no running water. They are the women who continue to use coat hangers in the age of the Internet because they cannot afford to purchase abortion drugs online.

In addition, banning abortion changes the lives of girls, who, because they cannot get an abortion, become mothers as teenagers. El Salvador has one of the highest rates of unwed teen motherhood in the world; a Pan American Health Organization report noted that one in four births in El Salvador is to women ages fifteen to nineteen.[53]

In El Salvador, having a child at age fourteen isn't simply a cause for shame in the eyes of a religious community. It also increases the odds of a life lived in crushing poverty, of marginal education and employment, of vulnerability to the violence and chaos that scores the lives of the poorest Salvadorans.

Some girls, faced with that prospect, opt to kill themselves. Government statistics reveal that three out of eight maternal deaths in El Salvador are the result of suicide among pregnant girls under nineteen.[54] Many of these girls have suffered rape and sexual abuse, and are silenced by the shame of these humiliations, in addition to the stigma of pregnancy.

Across the globe, one finds similar trends. Where abortion is illegal, there are high rates of medical complications and deaths due to illegal abortion. There are high rates of teen pregnancies. Pregnant teens commit suicide.

For opponents of the abortion ban, each of these trends is a clear indictment of the law.

For the ban's supporters, though, I imagine these indirect consequences on the lives of women and girls are viewed as part of a picture that includes other lives—those that begin at conception and that the law must therefore acknowledge and protect.

The Law Won't Catch the Women It Targets

The most intense condemnation of abortion typically is reserved for women whose motives seem entirely selfish. The wealthy, married woman for whom a baby is inconvenient or the woman who has an abortion because she wants to be able to wear her bikini. The women whom Mayora, an outspoken supporter of El Salvador's ban, decried as "wanting an abortion for any reason, or for no reason at all."[55]

What we learn from El Salvador is that the law can't catch such women. Illegal abortion no longer has to involve "abortion doctors." Ready access to abortion drugs and the fact that abortion is almost always indistinguishable from miscarriage mean most privileged women who have early abortions will escape detection, even when things go wrong and they wind up in the hospital.

What is true for El Salvador will be doubly true in wealthier countries, where women will have many more options for ending an unwanted pregnancy in a relatively safe, discrete way.

The Law Will Catch Innocent Women

The law will catch women who arouse their doctor's suspicion. In El Salvador, the women accused of abortion are among the poorest women in the country. They seldom know the doctors they meet at the public hospitals where they get care. And in most cases, their doctors understand very little about them. Their doctors don't know anyone who lives as these women do—with outhouses, dirt floors, no running water. These women are so poor and marginal that their doctors find it hard to understand their responses to crisis. Their world is so unfamiliar that it becomes possible for doctors, and later prosecutors and judges, to project their own fears onto it, inventing motives for crimes in the process.

To the woman in labor who fell down the steep path to the latrine, they impute the intention to conceal her delivery and kill her child. She must have wanted the child to suffocate in the muck so that she could avoid the burden of raising it on her own, with no husband and no money.[56]

The lucky ones have lawyers who spend years undoing the errors that led to their convictions. But there is no way to undo the harm brought on by a state that took a woman in crisis, having arrived at a hospital hemorrhaging and in pain, having given birth alone, having lost a child, and treated her like a criminal.

It is tempting to say these cases will not arise in the United States. Surely, our defense lawyers would protect the rights of the wrongly accused, insisting that the state prove the woman's guilt rather than being able to presume it.

But here, too, doctors can be suspicious of women who live on the margins of society, of those they meet only in the emergency rooms of public hospitals.[57] The consequences of making abortion a crime include a pattern we've already seen, in the context of prosecutions of women for ingesting illicit drugs during pregnancy. As I discuss in detail in chapter 5, these prosecutions have disproportionately targeted poor, black women, many of whom were seeking prenatal care at public hospitals. Ban abortion and that pattern will intensify. The hospital will increasingly become the site of a crime scene investigation, and poor women will be the suspects.

CONCLUSION

We saw in the first chapter how abortion opponents look to the law to reinforce their moral vision. In this chapter, we see the pragmatic limitations of the law.

The conceit of the law is that the moral stance and the practical consequences will move in one direction. Can we honestly say this is true about the abortion ban?

At best, the results are ambiguous. It is a law whose only tangible benefit beyond its moral message is hypothetical: there must be some women whom the law deters, even if there aren't enough to cause a rise in birth rates.

Are these hypothetical lives saved enough to offset the consequences we've seen in El Salvador?

I can't make that calculus for you, but make no mistake: these consequences will follow us as we turn to the question of restricting abortions in the United States.

We'll be tempted to ignore them, because they play no part in our pitched battle over abortion law. But if we keep them in mind, they'll permit us to see the shallow and misleading nature of our abortion war.

THREE

THE REDDEST STATE: OKLAHOMA'S LONG BATTLE OVER ABORTION LAW

The best place to watch the US battle over abortion law play out is in a state where a strong majority identifies as pro-life, and lawmakers are determined to pass laws opposing abortion. I wanted to understand the way abortion opponents viewed the law. Did they look to the law for moral condemnation, as I'd seen abortion opponents do in El Salvador? How might things change, in their eyes, were abortion to be banned?

I couldn't hope to learn how the pro-life movement viewed abortion laws without leaving my home, in the blue state of California. And so, in 2013, I went to Oklahoma.

As most Oklahomans will proudly tell you, it is a really, really red state. After Democrats lost every single county in the state in the 2008 and 2012 presidential elections, Oklahomans laid claim to being "the reddest state in the country."[1] In 2016, Republican Donald Trump won over 65 percent of the vote. His Democratic opponent Hillary Clinton earned less than 30 percent.

Oklahoma caught my eye when I first began thinking about visiting a red state because of the pace at which Oklahoma passed its pro-life legislation. In less than a decade, it brought its abortion laws right to the limits of what was permissible under federal law as dictated by the US Supreme Court. This fervor has earned Oklahoma top ratings in the Americans United for Life's annual legislative report card for over a decade.[2]

Oklahoma also has the virtue of being home to several law schools, which meant I had a place to begin seeking contacts. The Oklahoma City University Law School, located blocks from the capitol, has alumni serving throughout state government. I reached out to former dean Lawrence Hellman, who, along with Professors Arthur LeFrancois and Andrew Spiropoulos, introduced me to lawmakers, lobbyists, doctors, and activists at the forefront of the state's battles over abortion law.

I rented a house in a modest neighborhood in Oklahoma City and moved in for the hot summer months of 2013. And I started listening.

WHEN OKLAHOMA WAS A DEMOCRATIC STATE

In 1973, Oklahoma was a solidly Democratic state. Not only did the people vote Democratic in national elections, Democrats held both chambers and the governor's office. The largest religious organization in the state, the Southern Baptist Convention, supported legalized abortion.[3]

Anyone hoping to understand abortion politics in Oklahoma must sooner or later reckon with the impact and the legacies of two men: Tony Lauinger and Bernest Cain. Since 1973, Lauinger has devoted himself singularly to the cause of ending legalized abortion. He's never held office, yet even the legislators I met spoke of the bills Lauinger introduced, the laws he got passed, and the thickly powerful pro-life coalition he commands.

From 1978 to 2006, Lauinger's nemesis was state senator Bernest Cain. In his capacity as chair of the Senate Human Resources Committee, working at the behest of the Senate president pro tempore, Cain spent close to thirty years preventing antiabortion bills from reaching the Senate floor. His district was the most liberal in the state, which insulated him from the increasingly socially conservative statewide electorate. By keeping pro-life bills stalled in his committee, he single-handedly kept Oklahoma from passing laws that restricted access to abortion.

By the end of his time in office, Cain was playing a frenzied game of whack-a-mole. Both state houses were filled with legislators elected on promises to end legalized abortion. The backlog of antiabortion bills was legion. Districts had swung so far to the right that his fellow Democrats no longer thanked him for protecting them from the political fallout they would have faced, had they been forced to cast a vote their constituents might have viewed as "pro-abortion." Whether for reasons of moral conviction or political expedience, most Democrats and Republicans wanted to pass laws restricting abortion.

But our story begins decades before then, back in the days when abortion had just become legal.

Building a Pro-Life Movement in Oklahoma: 1973–2004

Lauinger was alone when, in 1973, he began fighting against legalized abortion. He was a Catholic in a state where 60 percent of the population was Southern Baptist and only 4 percent was Catholic.

In an article in the National Right to Life Committee (NRLC)'s *World Magazine*, Lauinger's entry into antiabortion activism is described: "In 1972, he was preparing to become a father for the first time. He reveled in being able to feel his baby kicking inside his wife's womb. When the Supreme Court legalized abortion, several months after his daughter's birth, he felt like he'd been hit in the face by a four by four."[4]

Born into exceptional wealth, Lauinger was thirty in 1972, when he felt called into service in response to *Roe v. Wade*.[5] He began by founding Tulsans for Life, an affiliate of the NRLC. By 1978, he was president of Oklahomans for Life and a member of the NRLC's board of directors.

It is hard to remember a time when the battle over abortion was not at the center of our public discourse. Kristen Luker's 1984 book, *Abortion and the Politics of Motherhood*, is a masterful history of antiabortion activism in the years immediately following *Roe*.[6] Her book helps set the context for understanding Lauinger's work.

Luker's research on pro-life activism in the years following the Supreme Court's *Roe* ruling documents a movement built largely by individuals who were shocked by the court's decision. They had interpreted the relative silence about abortion as a collective agreement that the fetus was a person, and that abortion ends the life of a child.[7] United by their shared opposition to abortion on moral grounds, yet lacking political experience or community-organizing backgrounds, early pro-life activists gained a foothold in faith-based communities.

In the context of religious communities, Lauinger forged an alliance that is central to the power of Oklahoma's pro-life movement. By the early 1980s, Lauinger was working to mobilize Oklahoma's largest faith-based organization to join him in fighting against legalized abortion.

In order to explain the way pro-life politics evolved in Oklahoma, I have to say a bit about the centrality of organized religion in public life. God is ubiquitous in Oklahoma. That's silly, of course, because for those who believe in God, by definition, God is everywhere. But in Oklahoma, unlike California, God is really out in public. God surfaces not only in clichéd billboards and bumper stickers but also in casual conversations.

I feel pretty grounded in my faith as a Jew. I'm not put off when others make reference to God when describing their lives, the decisions they've made, or the way they've coped with adversity. There was something foreign to me, though, about the way so many Oklahomans spoke of a personal relationship with God and of the need to live, and to pass abortion laws, in accordance with God's dictates.

To the extent that I was going to understand what folks meant when they invoked God in our conversations about abortion and the law, I knew I needed to understand more about the Southern Baptist Convention. There are many different types of evangelical communities in Oklahoma, and I don't mean to suggest that the Southern Baptists speak for all of them. It's just that the Southern Baptists are by far the largest: 60 percent of Oklahomans identify as Southern Baptists.

So, on a hot July morning in 2013, I traveled to the state headquarters of the Southern Baptist Convention to meet with Dr. Anthony

Jordan, its executive director. The five-story office building on Oklahoma City's north side houses an organization that represents over 1,830 churches in Oklahoma. It publishes a paper with the third-largest circulation in the state, a weekly called the *Baptist Messenger*.[8] In a sense, one might see Jordan as the voice of the state's majority.

Jordan's involvement with abortion politics didn't begin until 1985. That year, he was asked to preach at a statewide conference for Baptist pastors. He was invited to speak about any moral issue. Because he and his wife had struggled with infertility, he had a personal connection to the issue of adoption, and to the way in which legalized abortion reduced the number of babies put up for adoption. He decided to preach about abortion.

He began by listing his reasons for opposing abortion, which included both medical and biblical sources. But the speech took a personal turn when he mentioned a recent news story about the discovery of sixteen thousand body parts found behind an abortion clinic in California. "At that point," he said, "I asked my wife to bring up our five-month-old adopted daughter. 'When I read about the trash heap,' I told the crowd, 'it bothered me even more so because this little girl. . . . If it hadn't been for the Baptist Children's Home opening their doors to her Catholic mother, she could have been in a trash heap.'

"The entire room, including me, was in tears," he said. His eyes were wet even now, remembering the moment.

In the wake of that speech, Jordan and the Southern Baptist Convention joined forces with Lauinger and the Oklahoma Right to Life organization. Together, they developed a series of projects and initiatives. Foremost among the public demonstrations is the annual Rose Day rally, which began in the mid-1970s when two Catholic women brought roses to their state legislators to mark the anniversary of *Roe v. Wade*. This small gesture evolved into a yearly event that by 2016 saw an estimated twenty thousand Oklahomans converge on the state capitol, each bearing roses for their lawmakers. Today, Oklahoma's Rose Day is one of the nation's largest annual pro-life gatherings.[9] In the early years, pro-life legislators invited the activists into the state house, letting them sit on the floor during their rally. In recent years, the crowd has been so big it fills the Senate floor and both legislative galleries. The rally features speakers ranging from the governor to national pro-life leaders. Roses are everywhere.

On a more quotidian level, the church began offering support, along with ministry, through pregnancy resource centers. Jordan's church created Hope Pregnancy Center, one of the first in the state. It is staffed by volunteer community members and funded by donations and by the state of Oklahoma, through its sponsored "Choose Life" license plate program. The center, along with several hundred similar centers around the state, offers pregnancy tests, ultrasounds, and aid to women facing unplanned pregnancies. Jordan explained the mission of these centers, "We offer to stand beside the woman, supporting her through parenting training, placement of her baby with adopted family, if they wish. We support her either way."

The Southern Baptist Convention's work is not limited to rallies and counseling. Indeed, its most significant impact may be the mobilization of a powerful voting bloc. Under Jordan's leadership, the Southern Baptist Convention publishes election brochures that list candidates' positions on abortion. Jordan told me that he couldn't vote for a pro-choice candidate today, and his voting guides help similar-minded voters follow suit.

With at least nine hundred thousand members identifying as Southern Baptists, Jordan confidently noted, "We're organized and we can move." They've developed an alert system, dividing the state into districts to get out the vote. With a phone call, his office can mobilize forty-two separate organizations.

Until 2004, all that mobilization had little effect on the statewide abortion laws. "We had the numbers," Jordan noted. "I knew where people stood on the abortion issue in my constituency. I knew the number of churches, the number of Catholics, and the number of nondenominational Christians. But the Capitol wouldn't move."

I knew why. I'd already had lunch with Senator Bernest Cain.

Block That Bill: The Career of Senator Bernest Cain

Over lunch in a crowded restaurant where suited patrons stomped off the March rain and greeted one another with cheery backslaps and clasped handshakes, former state senator Bernest Cain told me about his relationship with God.[10]

"It's always been a religious deal to me," he said. "I knew my work at forestalling abortion bills was only a holding pattern. I never looked at it as a success; I never celebrated my victories. It had to be dealt with spiritually. I've done what I've done because I've worked to be true to my faith as a Unitarian.

"The hypocrisy of wealthy Republicans aggravates me," he said. "I think they've gotten away with making abortion a litmus test, more so than gay rights, because of class and gender. Abortion affects poor women, not men." Having seen firsthand which women were most affected when El Salvador banned abortion, I knew all too well what Cain meant.

What he said about gay rights made sense to me too. It's not that the battle for gay rights was easily won, but think of the speed with which activists were able to secure those rights. In the face of AIDS, in an era in which the president took years to acknowledge that millions of gay men were dying, activists got the Food and Drug Administration to accelerate the drug approval process. Two decades later, they had won rights ranging from freedom from discrimination to the right to marry.

The triumph of gay rights is a reflection, as Cain suggests, of the relative power of privileged gay men compared to poor women of color. Gay men (and women) vote. Political candidates ignore or insult them at their peril. By contrast, the women most affected by abortion policies aren't organized into a voting bloc. Many aren't even old enough to vote. Women's options, when facing an unwanted pregnancy, depend upon their financial resources. We saw it in El Salvador, and we see it here. Those with money have better options than those without. And the poorest women are unlikely to command the ear of a senator.

Cain paid an enormous price for his commitment to protect abortion rights. Although Cain is most proud of work he did on other issues—child support and aid to the elderly poor—he is remembered and reviled for his stance on abortion. By the end of his three decades in office, he feared for his life.

"Some of these people hated me," he said. Six years after leaving office, he still feels the burden of his legacy. "I made a lot of enemies, which limits my ability to serve as a retiree and a volunteer."

Cain never campaigned on a reproductive rights platform. He didn't even think about abortion during his first campaign, back in 1978:

My opponent was a John Birch–type incumbent who wanted to fire gay teachers. She voted against the Equal Rights Amendment.

I'd left the Baptist church a few years before, after spending a summer in 1972 working as a missionary in Center City, Philadelphia. I was in my third year of Baptist Bible College in Texas. I'd had a hard year because I'd begun to question the notion that the Bible is the word of God. I'd already decided that virgins didn't have babies. And then, in Philly I saw girls from the ghettos, black and Italian young girls. I came home worried that their lives were ruined as a result of having babies so young.

By the end of that year, they kicked me out of Bible College. I finished school at the University of Oklahoma, where I later got a law degree and completed the course work for a PhD in political science. I was working at the university in education, setting standards for county governments. The issues that mattered to me then embarrass me now: mandatory minimum sentences and capital punishment. I favored them both. And I also felt strongly about protecting the civil rights of gay teachers.

The gay community organized around my campaign. I won by 175 votes. There was a big fight over seating me; it was such a close election. After that first race, though, I knew how to organize. I walked door-to-door, precinct by precinct. I held my seat even after the Right to Life turned poor churchgoing whites into Republicans. Even after 1986, when Tony [Lauinger] started mailing my constituents at election time saying I was for killing babies.

OKLAHOMA'S RED SHIFT

Everything about abortion law in Oklahoma began to change between 2004 and 2006, the final two years of Cain's tenure.

As Jordan of the Southern Baptist Convention put it, "In 2004, politics finally began to reflect the true nature of Oklahoma." It was and remains a state in which a large majority of the public identifies as social conservatives.

The Law

In September 1990, Oklahoma voters passed a term-limits law, State Question 632, limiting service in the state legislature to twelve years. The consequences of this amendment to the state constitution weren't felt until 2004, when the first group of lawmakers termed out. Certainly the most obvious change was the rapid shift in political control over the House, first, and then the Senate, from Democratic to Republican hands.

Professor Andrew Spiropoulos explained how it had happened: "Term limits plus the candidacy of Barack Obama turned the state red almost overnight," he said.[11] Spiropoulos knew firsthand how Oklahoma suddenly went "pro-life." In 2005, he took a two-year leave of absence from his job teaching law at Oklahoma City University in order to serve as the Oklahoma State House Policy Advisor. In that capacity, he was in charge of helping the new Speaker of the House determine and implement the Republican agenda.

Abortion was a big part of the Republican agenda because of the central role it played in unifying constituents within the Republican coalition. Spiropoulos said, "Urban Republicans always needed a coalition of rural voters to win here, and these rural voters are pro-life and 'pro-marriage.'" (He clarified that by "pro-marriage," he actually meant anti–gay marriage.) The pro-marriage issue won't sustain the coalition, he conjectured, because more libertarian urban Republicans will defect. Hence, abortion has become the central unifying issue for Oklahoma's Republican Party.

In spring 2006, a bill requiring minors to obtain parental consent became the first antiabortion provision signed into law. It was quickly followed by a bevy of laws, including provisions barring the use of state funds or public facilities to provide abortions, mandating ultrasounds, banning abortion after twenty weeks' gestation, restricting the prescription of RU-486, and prohibiting insurance companies from offering abortion coverage.[12]

Spiropoulos attributed the extraordinary volume of abortion laws passed as a response to Cain's having blocked the laws for so long:

> The most important consequence of Cain's single-handed thwarting of majority sentiment is that he created such an intense blockage in the system and waves of resentment that, when the Republicans took over, it exploded in a flood of new laws. If Cain had not blocked everything, a few of the laws would have passed over the years and, arguably, there wouldn't have been such a rush to pass everything but the kitchen sink—there would have been new pro-life legislation, but the efforts would have been more measured.

Now I understood how Oklahoma had suddenly emerged as a pro-life legislative powerhouse.

None of the laws Oklahoma passed were new. They simply passed every measure enacted by other pro-life states, along with the occasional model bill drafted by Americans United for Life.

The laws cover a broad range of issues. Some of the laws, such as a ban on sex-selective abortion, are plainly symbolic. Women seeking abortions in Oklahoma, as in other states, need not provide a reason for terminating their pregnancies. There is no way to enforce this provision.

Other laws have had a direct impact on the delivery of reproductive health care in the state. For example, one state law forbids the use of public funds or facilities for the provision of abortion services. This law bars doctors at the University of Oklahoma hospital—the state's leading health-care center—from providing abortions for any reasons other than rape, incest, or medical necessity. The ban's most dramatic consequences are seen in cases involving poor women, who learn, typically halfway through their pregnancies, that their fetuses have severe anomalies.

Consider what happens when a poor woman finds out that her fetus has trisomy 18, a condition that causes severe developmental delays due to an extra chromasome 18. As anomalies go, it's fairly common—one in 2,500 pregnancies, and one in 6,000 births. Most of the time, the woman miscarries. For those who survive, life is precarious and profoundly limited. Only 10 percent will reach their first birthday. Those who live require full-time, institutionalized care.[13]

Yet unless this pregnant woman has money to pay for a private abortion—which by mid-trimester, when these anomalies typically are discovered, will cost thousands, rather than hundreds, of dollars—she must continue her pregnancy.

Nor is the impact of these new abortion laws limited to the poorest Oklahomans. Indeed, one of the men I interviewed remarked that the laws already have affected him personally. When he and his wife were expecting their first child, his wife's obstetrician advised them to do their routine twenty-week ultrasound at eighteen weeks, earlier than called for by the national standard of care. Because state law now bans abortions after twenty weeks, the doctor worried that waiting would risk their ability to terminate the pregnancy in the event the tests revealed a serious fetal anomaly.

Abortion Lawmakers: Moral Visionaries and Movement Politicians

I wanted to talk with the lawmakers. It seemed like the best way for me to understand what sort of expectations were behind this firestorm of new abortion laws. Did the legislators think the law could deter abortions? Were they persuaded that a speech from a doctor about fetal pain would cause some women to rethink their decisions? Or did they see the law as serving more symbolic purposes? Would they have agreed with Jordan of the Southern Baptist Convention, who said, "It may be tempting to postulate that the laws don't matter; that it's impossible to legislate morals. But no, you can legislate morality."

Although he had never held office, Lauinger's name was at the top of my list of people I wanted to interview. My conversations with Spiropoulos confirmed my sense that Lauinger played a central role in setting the state's antiabortion legislative agenda. Spiropoulos offered to call Lauinger on my behalf to tell him that I was "safe" and to ask him to meet with me.

When Lauinger didn't return my e-mails, I asked Spiropoulos if he'd reach out again. He did. Then, with only weeks to go before my visit, I left two voice messages at Lauinger's office. Finally, I found a residential listing under his name in Tulsa and left an apologetic message, introducing myself and all but pleading for the chance to meet him.

Mostly, I wanted to know what animates someone like him to devote his life to fighting to make abortion illegal. Pro-life men populate clinic protests, their red faces hurling epithets at cowering patients. But Lauinger didn't stand in the rain with a Bible and a placard. He was universally described as "courtly" and "gentlemanly."

To me, he seemed like the wizard behind the curtain. He was the unelected man who, from his home in the suburbs, waged a decades-long battle to change abortion law. And if victory was measured in numbers of laws passed, he seemed to be winning.

"Why the law?" I wanted to ask him. "What is it you believe will be changed when *Roe* falls?"

But Lauinger didn't return my calls or messages, so I never got to ask him. I learned later that, in addition to ignoring my entreaties, he also framed the scope of my interviews in Oklahoma. A week before my first visit to Oklahoma, Lauinger had sent e-mails to a long list of pro-life leaders around the state. One of the men I interviewed later read Lauinger's e-mail to me. Lauinger had written to him as an "ally," telling him that he and his assistant had declined my request to meet with them. He encouraged this man to do the same.

"She is pro-abortion," he wrote, and as proof, he included a link to an online petition I'd signed in 2007, decrying the threats to civil rights and to public health policy posed by forcing pregnant women to undergo testing for illegal drugs. He continued, "Long experience has taught me that there's nothing to be gained by helping gather intelligence from behind enemy lines from seemingly well-meaning academics." Now I understood why three Republican legislators had written to cancel our meetings, telling me they were too busy to reschedule.

In the end, I was left with a small but interesting cross-section of folks to interview. There were four former legislators and two sitting lawmakers, one who is widely viewed as the furthest right member in the State House of Representatives, and the other, the furthest left in the State Senate.

It was a rich pool in spite of Lauinger's interference. Two of the former lawmakers were pro-life Republicans; both had served for at least two terms and both had been in office during the recent shift in power. Because I wasn't looking to survey a large group of lawmakers, but rather to learn how they understood the role of law, the combined experiences and perspectives of those I interviewed proved to be plenty.

The Moral Visionary

Many of my interviews about abortion law in Oklahoma began with a preface, offered palms up and with an unwavering gaze: "I believe that abortion is the taking of a human life." If someone starts from that premise, it seems obvious why they would favor a complete ban on abortion. The law should not permit women to terminate their pregnancies any more than it should permit women to kill their two-week-old newborns. The law governing abortion should mirror the law governing homicide.

I went searching for a lawmaker who held these beliefs. I found State Representative Mike Reynolds.

Elected in 2002, Reynolds proudly told me that he's considered "the most outspoken member of the legislature."[14] He's passionate in his battle against the corruption he believes permeates much of state politics. He's crusaded against tax policies and other political stratagems that serve the interests of the four billionaires who "essentially control the whole state," including the newspapers and other media outlets that they own. That said, he is clear about what really matters to him.

"The stuff about corruption is games," he said. "The only thing I've ever cared about is saving unborn children."

I was a little surprised Reynolds still wanted to meet with me, given how many of his colleagues had canceled our interviews. "Ten o'clock will be perfect," he told me. "We can meet at H&H. That way, you can stay for lunch at the High Noon Club. It's every Friday. We have all sorts of speakers. Half the Republican caucus will be there, and sometimes the lieutenant governor and the governor come, too. The only rule of membership is, if you have to ask what time it meets, you can't come."

He laughed playfully and asked if I needed directions. I assured him I could find it on my own, and indeed, it was hard to miss. The H&H Shooting Sports store is like a small fluorescent city. It's home to the country's first National Shooting Sports Foundation's five-star indoor shooting range, which boasts thirty rifle lanes, twelve pistol lanes, and six air-gun lanes.

Reynolds met me at the door. A tall, fit man in man in his mid-sixties, he greeted me with twinkling eyes. Together, we passed through scores of aisles with shoulder-high shelves bearing crossbows, arrows, knives, shotguns, rifles, and pistols. An astonishing array of taxidermy stared down at me from various posts on the walls and atop the shelves— bears, large antlered deer, and smaller mammals, the names of which I must have learned in grade school.

"I've never been any place like this," I said, as we worked our way through the maze of weaponry. "And I've been to some pretty wild places."

"Thought so," he said, smiling.

Reynolds had first noticed the abortion issue in 1992, when the news covered the story of Dr. Nareshkumar Patel: "He was practicing, or murdering, in Warr Acres, Oklahoma. He was caught burning fetal remains in a Shawnee field. I organized a protest at his two clinics. And then I rented a 225-square-foot office in the same complex as his Shawnee clinic. We used it to intervene and counsel women going to Patel's clinic. I was dragged into legislative office ten years later because of my frustration with political corruption in the state, not because of abortion laws. The problem with abortion is more cultural than legal. Mothers and women are taught to see the unborn child as a thing. It's a cultural change that's needed, not a legal one. That doesn't mean that the pro-life movement won't do everything possible to change the law. But the culture also has to change."

"You were in office during this past decade," I noted, "when the state went from a Democratic to a Republican majority. Has that shift changed the way you view your job?"

"I'm not into coalition building," Mike responded. "I stand up for what I believe is right. I don't fight every battle, just the ones I run into." He laughed. "Seriously, though, I've only had five bills passed by the legislature in eleven years, and three of them were vetoed. I tend to spend my energy killing bad laws. I'm more afraid of doing the wrong thing than of not doing the right thing."

He went on: "The so-called pro-life movement is worried about pragmatics. Tony [Lauinger] takes slow, measured steps. He has his own sense of how to do things. Even though we both want the same outcome. . . . When I was first elected, Tony called me about a bill. He spoke for twenty-six minutes before he asked me what I thought. He's killed bills behind my back. And now, the Republican leadership has turned against me. They've cut me out of committee assignments. There are folks running against me, raising dirt about my past."

As Reynolds and I chatted, drinking water at H&H's 4U Café, our conversation veered into the personal. Reynolds spoke with remorse about things he'd done in his youth. There were tears, even though nothing he described struck me as unusual or even particularly blameworthy. The difference was that over the course of time, he had developed a new sense of the meaning and purpose of his life. He regrets not having been a better person. And he lives now with the conscious intent to be the best person he can be.

Reynolds didn't go "off the record" with me when he spoke of his family, his faith, or his past. He is not a man who worries about the political implications of his personal beliefs.

He believes life begins at conception. He grieves that so many oral contraceptive users don't understand that the Pill doesn't merely prevent ovulation, but also stops a fertilized egg from implanting. I disagreed with him, explaining that the vast majority of hormonal contraceptives *do* work by suppressing ovulation so that the egg never ripens and there is nothing to fertilize, but he dismissed my interruption.

"I didn't know this fact until recently," he said. "It pains me enormously. It's why I supported the Personhood Act in both 2010 and 2012. Tony [Lauinger] argued against it this past term because he was afraid of failure. There were pro-business issues that worried the people from national, and they were calling the shots. Tony went to the Republican leadership and killed the bill. With Tony, it's always 'my way or the highway.'"

At high noon, we walked across the store to the paneled event room at the back. The stuffed animal heads gazed down from the walls, watching with feigned indifference. The room was already crowded when we arrived. The women all wore suits, as did around half of the men. The others wore flannel shirts and cowboy boots.

Reynolds steered me toward a tightly coiffed woman in her late fifties. "Hey Sally," he said, "I'd like to introduce you to Michelle Oberman."

Representative Sally Kern, who a week earlier had abruptly canceled our appointment, turned and took my hand. "Oh yes, I've heard your name. . . ." Suddenly she dropped my hand, her pink-lipsticked lips almost disappearing as she swung away from me.

The Pro-Life Movement Politician

I'll confess that I was as smitten as I was dumbfounded by my conversation with Reynolds. Like him, I aim to live in accordance with my moral compass. Like him, I feel badly when I fall short of the mark, which is often. Like him, I have a hard time understanding those whose lives seem out of sync with their professed moral sensibilities.

At the same time, I was troubled by his moral vision and, even more, by his willingness to use his office to impose it on others. He was convinced he had the truth, and he understood his election as a mandate to align the law with that truth. He had no patience for lawmaking by consensus and compromise. He was a political gadfly.

I gathered that the majority of his colleagues who had canceled their interviews with me belonged to what he termed "the so-called pro-life movement." And over the course of my time in Oklahoma, it became pretty obvious who controlled that movement.

Reynold's comments about the negative consequences of his rift with Lauinger over the Personhood Bill in 2012, when Lauinger changed his position and opposed the bill, weren't entirely surprising. He wasn't the only one to suggest that "with Tony, it's always 'my way or the highway.'" Nor was he the only one to allude to the power Lauinger had to influence which bills were introduced, whether they progressed, and even which legislators were denied key committee assignments. Or worse.

Former Democratic Representative Ryan Kiesel remarked that Lauinger could "use the fear of retribution in a way no one else can."[15] He recalled the 2010 debate over the Personhood Bill—the one that Lauinger supported, not the one he later lobbied against: "Tony sent letters to all the legislators saying that a vote against the bill would 'put their seat in jeopardy.'"

In spite of Lauinger's efforts to keep those in his pro-life network from talking with me, I found a solution in my interview with a former Republican legislator. He asked me not to use his name, so I'll call him Tom Smith.[16] Smith served over fifteen years in both the state House and Senate, and anticipates a run for higher office in the future. Hence, his desire for anonymity.

Smith ran for office on a job-creation platform, an interest he pursued over the long course of his career in public office. That said, Smith also noted that he is active in the Southern Baptist church. "I knew I was pro-life when I ran for office," he said. "I campaigned as such, and my voting record is perfect."

When I asked Smith how he understood the purpose of abortion law, his response was layered. The foundation was familiar: a core moral belief that abortion was murder, and a belief that the law should reflect this conviction. He said, "The purpose of the law is to stop abortion. To send a moral message. To get the message out via the law, to spark a debate in the population. The government's responsibility is to give people education. It is up to the government to tell them that abortion is wrong. It's not an acceptable solution."

Like Reynolds, Smith saw the law as somehow communicating to a hypothetical woman facing an unwanted pregnancy. The law sends her a message that abortion is wrong. But unlike Reynolds, Smith was a career politician. He had his own set of priorities that were unrelated to abortion. He was happy to show his loyalty to the pro-life cause by supporting the party's abortion agenda. He was able to list the issues, yet he had given little thought to the question of what might happen if the agenda actually became law. Indeed, I was struck by the lack of details in Smith's vision for what might happen if abortion became a crime.

Smith said the ideal replacement for *Roe* would be a law just like the one that existed in most states before *Roe*. (And, incidentally, just like the one that El Salvador had before the ban in 1998.)

"I'd favor making it a crime," he said, "but not under all circumstances. Maybe it would be banned entirely after the first twelve weeks. Or maybe it would allow abortion in the first twelve weeks only in cases of rape and medical necessity and fetal anomaly. And I think the doctors and the state would have to be serious about enforcing these exceptions. If a woman wanted an abortion on the grounds of rape, then they should make sure she actually filed criminal charges."

Yet Smith tossed out the alternatives as if they were interchangeable, like competing options in a political platform: "Make it a crime." "Keep it legal for the first twelve weeks." "Exceptions for rape." My sense that he was speaking in slogans, rather than actually thinking about how a change in abortion laws might work, was underscored by his list of the exceptions he'd permit to an abortion ban.

The list itself wasn't a surprise; he'd simply reverted to familiar old state laws. But the way he talked about closing the "maternal health exception" caught my attention. Many of the pro-life individuals I met talked about the need to close the maternal health loophole, inferring that, before *Roe*, women had obtained abortions by fabricating claims of mental distress or threatening suicide if they were denied an abortion.

I have not found any data confirming this claim, but I was struck by how often it was invoked over the course of my interviews in Oklahoma and elsewhere. It suggests the power of the pro-life movement to shape the imagination of its members, thereby dictating the terms of the legal landscape.

Lawmakers as Moral Messengers

For all their differences, what Reynolds and Smith had in common was a shared vision of the purpose of abortion law: the law is intended to make a moral condemnation. For example, here's how Smith responded when I asked him about why he would permit abortion at all, given his convictions: "What is it about rape that makes it OK for a woman to have an abortion? Do you see abortion as somehow less of a murder in those cases?"

"These exceptions reflect my value system," Smith explained. "'Judge not lest you be judged.' I'm OK with saying to a woman that abortion is wrong, but I'd leave room for a remedy in these cases."

Smith was far from the only person I met who spoke of an unwillingness to judge women who seek abortion under circumstances they viewed as extenuating. What interests me is the tacit willingness to pass judgment on women who seek abortion under all other circumstances.

Both Smith and Reynolds were relatively uninterested in my questions about the law's likely impact. When I asked Smith how abortion laws should punish violators, and about whether the law would actually deter abortion, these details struck him as secondary concerns. He was resigned to the idea that women would attempt to break the law.

"Well, I'd predict there would be a lot of girls and women who would travel," he said. "Those who could afford to would go someplace else. And there would be medicine abortions. It's hard to stop that from happening."

He seemed nonplussed by these shortcomings; the fact that some people would break the law was not a reason for legalizing the practice. From his perspective, the purpose of the law was to send a clear message about the wrongness of abortion.

MOVEMENT POLITICS AND
ABORTION'S LEGISLATIVE AGENDA

I learned three things when I asked people what would happen if *Roe* were reversed and abortion could once more be outlawed. The first was that the terms of the debate would likely be set by the pro-life movement, rather than by individual, impassioned lawmakers. The second was that those who identified as pro-life wouldn't yet have a consensus about how the law should look. Finally, I learned that this lack of consensus wouldn't stop the movement from demanding unwavering loyalty from its members.

Lauinger taught me each of these things.

Lessons from Lauinger

Due to Lauinger thwarting my efforts to meet with pro-life lawmakers, I learned that the pro-life movement in Oklahoma is run by elite outsiders, not by elected officials and not by community organizers. With a single e-mail, a never-elected activist could police the ranks of state officials against an outsider like me. More interesting was the way lawmakers anticipated that Lauinger and the Right to Life movement would shape the legislative agenda if *Roe* fell and abortion became a crime.

One of the questions I asked everyone I met was what they thought would happen in Oklahoma if *Roe v. Wade* fell.

Ryan Kiesel, who had served ten years in office fighting for reproductive rights, had a cynical response:

> The right doesn't want to win. They don't want *Roe* to fall. Opposing *Roe* is their template for running for office. It's their political touchstone. It avoids the need to talk about anything else. If that's taken away from them, they're going to have to deal with splits in coalition.[17]

Smith's prediction evoked similar concerns about fragmentation. "If *Roe* falls? I've honestly never considered it," he said. He paused for a moment, then added, "There'll be a huge fight on the right. The activists on the far right will want a complete ban, but the majority would want the exceptions I mentioned (rape, incest, life of the mother). The game of politics will dictate which exceptions make it into the law, because the control of special interests over this issue will be profound. It's not enough to please the 90 percent who identify as pro-life. You'll lose office because the 10 percent who are more extreme will organize to defeat you. That's what happened to Kris Steele."

Several of the people I interviewed in Oklahoma had mentioned former House Speaker Kris Steele in this tone, as if he'd somehow fallen from grace. Jordan of the Southern Baptist Convention invoked Steele as an example of a politician who was "maybe too collaborative," noting that he was "certainly seen to have been less reliable on pro-life issues." Democratic Senator Constance Johnson was more candid in her assessment. "Kris Steele had his lunch fed to him," she said, "because they didn't think he was conservative enough. He started to question Tony Lauinger. That was his sin."

Through the story of what happened to Steele I came to understand both the way in which pro-life movement elites set the agenda for lawmakers and the remorseless manner in which they punish those who deviate from the lockstep obedience they demand from members.

Kris Steele's Story

Former Oklahoma House Speaker Kris Steele's office is literally on the other side of the tracks, in an old brick building on the torn fringes of Oklahoma City. He runs an organization called The Education and Employment Ministry (TEEM). It provides job training, counseling, and housing for a lucky few of the hundreds of women who are released from Oklahoma prisons each year. Steele founded the nonprofit after he left office in 2012.

"We have the highest number of female inmates per capita in the world," Steele told me as he ushered me into the conference room, swinging his lame leg with grace. "They're here for drug-related crimes—theft, passing bad checks, all secondary to addiction," he said. "And there's a 70 percent re-incarceration rate for their children. But it's impossible to pass even evidence-based sentencing reform without being called soft on crime."[18]

I pulled out my papers. Steele asked if I'd mind if his intern joined us.

"I've been so eager to talk with you," he said, cutting off my introductory thank-you. "It's like *The Big Sort*, you know?"

Embarrassed, I confessed that I did not.

Steele was referring to Bill Bishop's book, *The Big Sort*, which describes the increased homogeneity of American communities over the past four decades—precisely the era since *Roe v. Wade* was decided. The provocative 2008 book called attention to the fact that we increasingly live in communities that reflect our values, places where we seldom encounter those who hold different viewpoints on core issues.

Bishop and others demonstrate the forty-year migration into value-segregated communities by tracking the number of counties that give landslide victories to either Democratic or Republication candidates. He begins with the 1976 election—a close race even at the county level—when just over 26 percent of American voters lived in counties that voted overwhelmingly for a particular candidate. By 2004, an equally divided electorate revealed a different pattern: 48.3 percent of Americans lived in "landslide" counties—places where the victors won by a margin of 20 percent or more. By 2012, over half of Americans lived in such communities.

The result, according to Bishop, is not simply a cultural sorting, but also an intensification of our differences. Citing research by social psychologists, he explains how, as people hear only their own beliefs reflected and amplified by those around them, they become more extreme in their thinking.

It suddenly hit me: I was as much a mystery to Steele and his intern as they were to me. How often did they meet someone who self-identified as a "liberal Democrat"? Somewhat self-consciously, I turned to my questions.

"Could you tell me about how you got involved with the abortion issue in Oklahoma?"

"As an ordained minister, my faith shapes my beliefs," Steele began.

I wondered when he became a minister; he looked no more than thirty years old.

"I'd been active in the pro-life movement prior to entering legislative service," he told me. "I was used to sharing my convictions, having lots of conversations, doing grassroots work on the issue."

"When did you join the House?"

"I was a representative from 2000 to 2012," he said, "and I served as speaker during the last two years. I was in the House when it turned Republican. You can skip most of your questions, I bet, because my record shows it: I'm a conservative, pro-life Republican."

"What was your goal in terms of abortion law reform?" I asked. "What sort of laws did you want to pass?"

Steele answered, "If you call a law *pro-life* in Oklahoma, it passes. No one has time to read all the bills, so the debate is reduced to, 'If you're pro-life, you'll support this bill.' Take the 'Safeguards for IVF' bill. It banned compensation for donating eggs. Somehow the money triggered fearmongering about women's exploitation, and we thought it was OK to bring the government into the lives of infertile couples. It was hard, in retrospect, to see how the bill was pro-life. Perhaps it was just pro-Catholic.

"It was my biggest regret in office—voting 'yes' on that bill," he added. "I only understood when one of my loyal constituents confided in me that his two precious children would not exist had they been unable to pay their egg donor."

"After that vote," Steele continued, "I realized the complexity of these issues and I started working for systemic change. I spent two years revamping Medicaid so it was a transparent, efficient, well-run program. It's the thing I feel most proud of."

I learned later, from those to Steele's right and left alike, that he'd responded to his constituent's story by campaigning against the 2010 in vitro fertilization bill in the State Senate. He succeeded, and the bill was voted down.

Steele left government in 2012, when he had reached the term limits, but my conversations with others suggested there was a more complicated story behind his departure.

One senior Republican lobbyist, speaking anonymously, tied Steele's fall from grace to the 2010 Personhood Act—the one Lauinger supported. "When Steele kept the 2010 Personhood Bill from reaching the House floor," he said, "he took the blame, even though the entire caucus voted with him."

Steele told me that out-of-state advocates had been pushing the 2010 Personhood Bill, wanting to use Oklahoma as a test case: "We already had a law saying life begins at conception. Why did we need one saying 'Constitutional rights attach at conception'? It's not possible to give the unborn the right to vote, so it seemed redundant to me."

In one of his final acts as House Speaker, Steele facilitated the 2010 Republican caucus's vote not to schedule the Personhood Bill for a hearing. He told me that the majority of the caucus had supported his decision to defer consideration of the bill, noting that it made sense in view of the proximity of the controversial vote to the general election. But in its aftermath, he alone took the blame for having scuttled the pro-life bill.

After the bill died, Steele said, "Church folk sent e-mails to me saying things like, 'I wish you'd never been born.'"

Lessons from Steele's Story

What are we to make of the way pro-life advocates regarded Steele's opposition to a single bill—one that the movement itself rejected in the very next legislative cycle—as a sign that he was not "reliably pro-life"?

The story sheds light on the ways in which single-issue advocates achieve their goals. It is a great example of what happens in state legislatures in response to many highly charged issues. Those who care most deeply are willing to invest time and money to influence their lawmakers. Those whose interests are more diffuse don't bother to raise their voices or to advocate loudly for a contrary position unless and until they too begin to care deeply about the issue.

It's called public choice theory, and it takes as its starting point the observation that, on any given issue, there are those who care deeply about it, and those who don't care as much. In the abortion context, those who are most motivated to make legislators hear their voices are those who believe that abortion is murder and should be banned. Their sense of urgency fuels the pro-life movement, giving it an outsized influence on the legislative process.

There's no real way to know whether their position on abortion is a majority view, but it turns out that that question is almost irrelevant. Their viewpoint will continue to hold sway until it offends the sensibilities of enough of those holding a contrary view that they, in turn, are prompted to mobilize in opposition. This phenomenon is precisely what Kiesel and Smith meant when they referred to the political battles likely to ensue should *Roe* fall.

I was amazed at how much admiration and heartache I felt for Steele. Amazed because his views on abortion were, at least in one sense, more extreme than anyone else I interviewed. He alone was comfortable endorsing the prosecution of women for abortion. "I'd expect there to be punitive consequences for blatant offenders of the law," he said, without hesitation. "Of course, I'd also incentivize carrying to term, but the core function of government is to protect its citizenry, so there must be consequences for those who break abortion laws."

What drew me in was the extent to which Steele expressed compassion for women facing an unwanted pregnancy. Smith had shrugged off the likelihood that women with enough money would evade the law by traveling. He seemed untroubled by the way the law would have a disproportionate impact on poor women. To him, the question of whether the law would stop abortions was almost beside the point.

Steele's response was different.

"Of course," he said, as we ended our conversation about abortion laws, "the best way to lower abortion rates is to deal with what causes women to want to abort in the first place."

Alone among the pro-life lawmakers and activists I met, Steele has direct experience working with poor women. Like the others, he wants the law to send the message that abortion is wrong. But only he seemed ready to acknowledge how little a change in the law will do to stop women from seeking abortions.

CONCLUSION

As I left Oklahoma that summer, I realized I'd learned a lot about the connection between morality, symbolism, and abortion laws. The message that abortion should be a crime was so pervasive that I suspected most Oklahomans no longer noticed it. At first I felt as though I couldn't escape it. It was on the billboards: "Abortion stops a beating heart." It was on the counter in the gym, where they sold Plexiglas photo key chains that said, "It's a life, not a choice" around the edges. It was there on the "I survived *Roe v. Wade*" bumper stickers on the trucks I passed on the highway.

After a while, I got used to the signs and the emblems. Images of fetuses became part of the landscape, like American flags or the crimson and cream of the University of Oklahoma Sooners. The pro-life messages were so ubiquitous that they faded into the background. But it's not a tranquil background. Instead, these messages generate an ominous sense that things are awry, and that it's on each of us to put them right again.

The mystery is how making abortion illegal will put things right. The battle over abortion law seems utterly disconnected from Steele's observation that "the best way to lower abortion rates is to deal with what causes women to want to abort in the first place." Doesn't everyone agree with him?

Oklahoma's ambitious body of abortion-restrictive laws is a testimony to the belief that the law matters. And if nothing else, the epic battle over abortion suggests that both sides share that belief: we take it for granted that changing abortion laws will change things in the lives of women facing unplanned pregnancies.

We've seen, both in El Salvador and in Oklahoma, how the law has become a vehicle for voicing moral opposition to abortion. And we've seen enough in El Salvador to know that banning abortion won't stop it from happening. We are now ready to investigate how and why abortion laws matter here in the United States.

The next chapter examines US abortion laws and policies, as well as those governing reproductive health care and motherhood in general. By illuminating the ways in which existing rules shape women's lives, we gain insight into how and how much abortion laws actually matter.

FOUR

THE ABORTION-MINDED WOMAN AND THE LAW

We've seen how abortion opponents have come to look at the law as a means of underscoring their belief that abortion is immoral. But the law is a tool; enforced, it has practical consequences. This chapter explores those consequences, considering the question of whether and how the law affects pregnant women who are considering abortion.

To think meaningfully about the issue, it helps to see the world through the eyes of such women. We must be clear about why a woman might consider having an abortion.

The largest research study into the question of why women choose abortion—it surveyed twelve hundred abortion patients—found most women cite not one, but several reasons: 74 percent said having a child would interfere with education, work, or their ability to care for dependents; 73 percent said they could not afford a baby now.[1]

The women are telling us something that is hiding in plain view: motherhood is really expensive. What's interesting about the costs of motherhood is that most of the costs actually could be reduced, if a government chose to do so. The price of being a mother is not foreordained. There is no "neutral" policy that dictates how much of the cost of mothering should fall on the individual mother. Instead, a country sets the price via a constellation of laws and policies: housing, day care, food, health care, education, and so on.

In order to understand how abortion laws work, we must also understand the impact of laws and policies that determine the costs of motherhood. You might picture a pregnant woman balanced on a scale, with abortion on one side and motherhood on the other. To understand the impact of changing the one side, you have to know what's on the other.

I knew I wanted to understand, up close, the sorts of things that really matter to women who are struggling over whether to terminate their pregnancies. The starting place for thinking about the laws and policies that influence women facing unwanted pregnancy was to spend time with those who are trying to influence actual women. This chapter begins with an extended interview with a group of pro-life advocates who think it's possible to sway those considering abortion. Indeed, they've spent the past four decades trying to do so.

After hearing their stories, the chapter considers the backdrop factors, economic and social, that might make a woman more or less inclined to carry a pregnancy to term. By examining these default norms, from child care to jobs and housing, we are able to see how the societal policies we take for granted shape the decisions of women facing unplanned pregnancy.

Then, with this background in mind, the chapter turns to an examination of the abortion laws and regulations enacted in the years since abortion became legal. Specifically, it considers the ways in which these laws and policies shift the balance, tilting women away from abortion.

In the end, we come away with a surprisingly clear, if troubling, sense of how the law can shape the decisions made by abortion-minded women.

LOBBYING AND LOVING THE ABORTION-MINDED WOMAN

One of the first organized responses of abortion opponents in the years following *Roe* was to open counseling centers that catered to women in "crisis" over an unplanned pregnancy. These centers aim to reach what they call "abortion-minded women," offering advice and varying degrees of support in the hopes of convincing a woman to carry her pregnancy to term.

There's a lot of controversy surrounding these centers. Abortion-rights advocates accuse them of false and misleading practices, like deliberately locating near abortion clinics or neglecting to mention that their center does not provide abortions or even abortion referrals. Pro-life advocates respond that they're enhancing women's choices by helping them find the support they need in order to keep their pregnancies. Even the name of these centers is controversial. Supporters call them "pregnancy care centers," while opponents employ the term historically used in the clinics' advertisements—"crisis pregnancy centers."

Regardless of the controversy, these faith-based counseling centers exist in far greater numbers than abortion clinics. Every day, they see women who are struggling in response to an unplanned pregnancy. And because they're endeavoring to persuade them not to have abortions, they know all about the things that make a woman consider having one.

Birth Choice of Oklahoma's main office is on the far south side of Oklahoma City. The red brick building sits alone on a stretch of a busy four-lane highway. Baby shrubs mark the lot's perimeter. With yellow Doric columns and three doorways topped with cheery porticos, it's like a mansion crossed with a strip mall.

I couldn't figure out which door was the entrance. The few cars in the otherwise empty lot were crowded near the smallest entrance, but there was no sign. Small piles of dirty snow flanked the sidewalk as I walked in the crisp March air. I approached the biggest door. Still no sign, but I peered through the glass window and saw a waiting room. A woman with long brown hair held her toddler in a worn armchair. She looked up, noticed my leather briefcase, my interview blouse and pearls, and glanced away as I raised my hand in a half wave.

When I had told people back home about my plan to visit a crisis pregnancy center, they'd joked about my needing a bulletproof vest. Would I pretend to be neutral, they'd wanted to know, or even pro-life?

I'd sent an e-mail to Barbara Chisko, the executive director, mentioning the names of two prominent pro-life advocates who had referred me to her: "I believe your long commitment to Birth Choice gives you a unique perspective on the law and its limitations, in terms of impacting women's responses to unplanned pregnancy."

Before I'd even explained my project, my background, and the questions I had, she wrote back, "Would love to meet with you." We spoke by phone and I think I said enough about why, as a law professor from California, I needed to travel to Oklahoma to better understand pro-life culture and its connection to the law. I didn't hide my position on legalized abortion, but later I wondered whether I'd been clear enough.

The young receptionist led me through a short hallway and across an empty dining room into a cozy pastel living room. Three women stood to greet me. I circled the group, shaking hands, smiling and saying my name, and took a seat on a soft floral sofa. A toddler with hair like corn silk sat on the floor across from me, playing with a plastic truck. The women looked at me expectantly.

"I want to thank you for being willing to meet with me," I said, hoping I seemed comfortable and relaxed. "It's hard to find people who will speak openly about abortion, and I come from such a blue state, if you know what I mean. I don't know very many people who are pro-life. And I don't know any pro-life activists."

"Let's begin by introducing ourselves," suggested Chisko, in the silence that had suddenly grown loud. Sitting in an armchair to my right, she pointed with her open palm to the pretty, spry woman who sat next to me on the couch.

In her late fifties, Katie Gordy was one of four Birth Choice founders. "I've done debates and abortion clinic confrontations for the Right to Life," she said. "But I hate all that. I'm a specialist in post-abortion counseling. I've been volunteering with Birth Choice since 1973. And I've been president of our board for the past fourteen years."

Rae Merchant walked into the room as Gordy was speaking. The drive down from the north-side clinic, which she's directed for thirty-four years, was slower than usual.

"I have eleven children," she offered when Gordy finished. "Eight are adopted and three are my biological kids. I've been a foster parent to 180 newborns. It all flows together for me," she said, lifting her hands and shrugging. "Adoption, foster care, parenting. That said, Birth Choice is my heart."

"It's because there's no shaming here," said Chisko. "No judgment. Women come in and we love on them. No shame, just love." She laughed.

"I think people connect in their brokenness," Gordy added quietly, looking down.

"I'm doing pregnancy tests now on women whose mothers I helped years ago," said Merchant. "We listen with a nonjudgmental ear. We work on offsetting this quick-fix society. We help them understand that abortion won't fix things."

It was the first time I'd heard the term "quick-fix society," but I didn't need a translation. I thought about the women I'd met in the Ohio Reformatory for Women when I was studying mothers who killed their children. My coauthor and I had asked them why they hadn't terminated their pregnancies. The chaos in their lives was profound and long-standing. They must have known a new baby would make their lives even harder.

"My family doesn't believe in abortion. That's murder," many replied without irony. Indeed, most hadn't intentionally killed their children. Instead, their babies' deaths were almost predictable by-products of their grim circumstances.

"I know what you mean about the quick fix," I said, and told them about the mothers I'd met in prison.

Typically when I speak about their crimes, I can sense the disgust these mothers evoke in others. Their situations may have been terrible, but their crimes seem too heinous to merit sympathy, let alone empathy.

The women all started to speak at once.

"I suspect the majority of those women may have had previous abortions," said Chisko.

Merchant offered a different theory, saying, "I've observed in my work with women who abuse their children that a lot of them wanted to have kids, but then their kids failed to meet their expectations."

From across the room, Ellen Roberts spoke for the first time. Sitting on the floor next to her small son, Roberts was at least twenty years younger than the rest of us. She tucked her chin-length chestnut hair behind an ear and said, "Working here, I've learned that it's not their bad choices that have landed the women at our door, but rather God's grace that kept me from being in their situations."

Conversation began to flow as the personal merged with the professional. We all had stories to share.

A woman in a pink polo shirt walked into the living room, calling, "Time for lunch, ladies."

She walked over to me. "Hi, I'm Ruth Blakely," she said, extending a firm hand. "Another one of the four founders. Nice to meet you."

We moved into the dining room, taking seats around the big square table. From the galley kitchen tucked behind the far wall, another woman stepped out to join us.

"This is my daughter and our accountant," said Chisko, with a broad smile.

With Roberts's son in his highchair, we were eight in all. Without hesitation, I bowed my Jewish head as Chisko said grace.

With the exception of Roberts and Barbara's daughter, these women all were veterans of 1973. Each dated her entry into pro-life activism to learning, in church, that abortion had been legalized.

"I couldn't believe that women would tear apart their own babies. Or that they could be coerced into doing so," said Chisko. "You know, doctors have a way of telling women what they think is best. And our clients . . ."

"People judge our clients," Merchant interrupted. "Especially those on welfare. 'Why do these women keep having babies?' they ask. The common denominator is the desire to be loved. Even a 'lowlife' wants to be loved. We all crave intimacy."

"The four of us met at a church event," Chisko began, sitting back in her chair. "We signed up to volunteer with the Right to Life. They suggested we put ads in the paper for 'crisis pregnancies.' But they left after four months, leaving us with one phone line and a folding chair.

"We offered a training session for volunteer counselors and a hundred and eighty people showed up. But only twenty stayed on as regular volunteers. We just didn't know what we were doing. We had a burning desire to help people, to meet them where they are. I myself had just had a miscarriage. At that time, pro-life simply meant 'don't murder your baby.' We felt our job wasn't to evangelize or proselytize. Just live life as you should. Be a model. At first, we were part of 'Birth Right,' an international group. But by the 1980s, the organization set rigid rules: no shelters, no clinical services, just administer pregnancy tests and give out baby clothes. Just persuade the women not to abort their babies."

"They like to shame women," said Merchant. "In Lawton's clinic, they have a life-size cardboard Jesus in the lobby."

"Birth Choice's priorities are shaped by the belief that the best place for a child is with mom," Chisko added.[2]

I was beginning to understand what Roberts had meant when she'd said, earlier that morning, that there were "two kids of pro-life people. People who are pro-life and people who are antiabortion."

"The antiabortion folks are really difficult to work with," Roberts remarked. "They use our clients to fight their fight. But they never come to fight our fight."

The women's passion for supporting the poor surprised me. I thought social conservatives typically blamed the poor for not working harder to change their circumstances. It was the Democrats who supported welfare, minimum wage laws, and a bigger safety net. Yet these women, like everyone else I'd met in pro-life Oklahoman circles, were Republicans.

I didn't really know whether they were exceptions to the norm among social conservatives, though, because I couldn't remember the last conversation I'd had with a social conservative.

"How did Rose Home come to be?" I asked. Several of the pro-life religious and political figures I'd interviewed had mentioned Birth Choice's shelter for pregnant women.

"It was through an adoption agency referral, back in our crisis pregnancy clinic in 1986," said Chisko, setting her fork down. "The woman had had several prior pregnancies that ended in abortion or adoption. She'd planned to relinquish her current pregnancy, but slowly she changed her mind."

Chisko sighed and looked at Gordy, Merchant, and Blakely, shaking her head and smiling. "She needed help parenting and she needed money. The adoption agency billed her thousands of dollars when she pulled out. Volunteers made it work. An attorney friend of ours made the bill go away. When this woman spoke at our twenty-fifth-anniversary dinner, she thanked us. 'You taught me how to trust,' she said."

Chisko's voice cracked and her eyes were wet.

Gordy continued for her, "At first, we tried to serve our clients by finding them jobs and housing. But our clients weren't always well received."

"There were some angel donors for Rose Home," Chisko said, gesturing around the room, which could comfortably have held another three dining tables.

"We opened Rose Home in 1986," she continued. "We've had a woman stop in at thirty-five weeks' gestation. Terrified of the health-care system. A twelve-year-old girl in foster care was gang-raped. She was being pushed by the state to have an abortion. She didn't want it, so I helped arrange to take her into federal jurisdiction, where a federal judge gave Birth Choice custody of her. We brought her home and eventually we helped her get money so she could be reunited with her mom and move to a safer neighborhood."

The story rang a bell. It had gotten a lot of national press. I remember cringing at the thought of how a twelve-year-old rape victim had been manipulated into carrying to term. I didn't share this memory with the women.

Only later did I wonder why I was so sure this twelve-year-old girl I didn't know would have been better off having an abortion than carrying to term.

Roberts described how Rose Home chooses its residents:

> We see three hundred to four hundred women a month here at Birth
> Choice, plus another hundred or so at the north-side clinic. We
> do blood workups, check blood pressure and weight. We help the
> women get covered by Sooner Care and make prenatal referrals to
> St. Anthony's. If they're ineligible for insurance, we provide their
> prenatal care.
>
> Some of our clients are struggling with domestic violence, or
> they're couch surfing or living out of a car. We screen for these issues
> and offer housing to those who truly have no place else to go. We can't
> accept severely mentally ill clients, which is a real problem. There's
> nowhere to send these women. They have to be violent before they
> qualify for housing in a state group home. But we can't handle them
> at Rose Home.

Because many of the women are fleeing violent relationships, the
shelter's location is undisclosed. They can bring their children with
them, so long as they are under age five.

The residents almost always qualify for public assistance, which
helps with funding. In weekly meetings with their caseworkers, the
women articulate goals and plan their futures. They receive mental
health counseling, drug abuse treatment, and vocational training. They
get help making court dates, as many have open cases for abuse and
neglect. There are quarterly meetings and ongoing support services even
after they leave Rose Home.

"How many women live in Rose Home?" I asked.

"We can house five women at a time. And up to thirteen children,"
Roberts answered.

"Doesn't it break your heart, having to turn away so many needy
women?" I asked no one in particular.

"It's cheaper to have an abortion than to have a baby," Merchant said.

"There's no doubt that the bottom line encourages abortion," Chisko added. "Even though there aren't enough young people to pay for older people. Dr. Wilke's *Handbook on Abortion* spotted this issue, as did Paul Marx's *The Death Peddlers*," Chisko continued. "And it's true. The majority of our clients need food and clothes. But they're not at Birth Choice for resources. They come because we help them feel worthy, cared for, and trusted."

The rhetoric was new to me. I hadn't thought about the way the high costs of raising a child are an incentive for abortion. It's so obviously true.

Don't get me wrong—the long interview wasn't entirely a "kumbaya" moment, as we say in my family. Some of the things said left me stunned in disbelief. Like when Merchant said, "So many of our ills—violence in the world, weather phenomena, Obamacare—are all tied to abortion."

When I asked whether they would support a complete ban on abortion, telling them briefly about Beatriz's case, Chisko answered without hesitation: "I learned early on that if a woman is healthy enough to get pregnant, she's healthy enough to go to term." She recalled a woman with a heart condition who'd been advised to terminate. The woman had refused, and according to Chisko, she had her baby and is alive today.

She believed that Beatriz did not need an abortion to survive. Indeed, she sees Beatriz's survival as proof of her point.

But when it came time to say goodbye, I mostly felt awed by what I'd witnessed there. The women of Birth Choice had aligned their moral compasses with a keen eye to the needs of the most vulnerable women in society. I loved them for it.

"If the law changes," I asked, "If *Roe* falls and abortion becomes illegal, will Birth Choice still be here?"

"We'll be here no matter what," Chisko answered. "Women are always going to get pregnant and they're always going to struggle."

DEFAULT NORMS: THE CONTEXT IN WHICH U.S. WOMEN MAKE ABORTION DECISIONS

One of the most important things I learned from the women at Birth Choice was to view the decision to keep or to end a pregnancy from the perspective of a woman struggling to decide. In order to understand the impact of abortion laws, we must first consider the backdrop against which such decisions take place. That backdrop is easiest to see when one focuses on the experience of the most vulnerable women. The women at Rose Home.

Of course, the backdrop is there for everyone, not just for poor women, and not just in the context of abortion. There are norms and policies that shape and constrain our options in life. The backdrop norms informing decisions about abortion consist of our policies regarding motherhood and parenting. We mostly regard these policies as neutral. But when we see their impact on the most vulnerable women, we understand how one's circumstances circumscribe the "choices" one actually has.

What Makes a Woman Consider Abortion?

"What makes a woman consider having an abortion?" I asked Samara Azam-Yu, executive director of Access Women's Health Justice in Oakland, California.

"Women have been making hard choices forever," she answered. She works with the poorest women in the state, helping them arrange travel from small towns throughout northern and central California to San Francisco in order terminate unwanted pregnancies.

> There are people who spend their life savings, travel hundreds of miles to get procedures, and then don't even have the money to get home. California has the highest poverty rate in the US. The economy crashed in 2008, and years later, the people I serve are running on fumes. Abortion is not really a "choice" for the women who call us for help. A baby will push the family deeper into poverty.

After seven years of working with women living on the thin edge of despair, Azam-Yu has almost as little patience for the rhetoric of "choice" as she does for that of "life." The way she sees it, abortion decisions arise out of desperation.

Azam-Yu said, "There's a Native American nurse at an abortion clinic in San Francisco who put it this way. She said, 'If you have twins and it's a bad year, you have to put one in the badger hole.'"

Until I met both Azam-Yu and the women at Birth Choice, I hadn't realized the extent to which, by thinking and talking about abortion in hypothetical terms—the rape victim, the unwed teenager, the fetus with Down syndrome—we distort reality. We erase the complex network of factors underlying a woman's decision to end her pregnancy.

A woman faces the surprise of an unplanned pregnancy as if on the tracks, with a locomotive barreling toward her. The only variation lies in how many other trains are coming at her from other directions.

Azam-Yu and the Birth Choice founders see the most vulnerable women in society, the ones who, even before they got pregnant, spent their days trying to avoid incoming trains—housing, food insecurity, abusive relationships, addiction.

Azam-Yu told the story of a client she'd recently helped:

One woman came by bus from Arcata, in the far north of the state. She found someone to watch her kids for two days. Access Women's Health Justice paid for the six-hour bus ride to San Francisco. Found her a place to stay the night. One of our volunteers drove her to the UCSF clinic. She got there, and was meeting with the pre-abortion counselor. After around half an hour she said, "I'm so sorry. I've changed my mind. Now that I've had time to think about it . . ."

Azam-Yu's work with Access Women's Health Justice has one approach to helping poor women resolve unplanned pregnancies. Birth Choice has another. Their clients are one and the same, though. So many things weigh on these women as they confront their pregnancies that it's hard to know how best to help them.

"There's so much chaos in our clients' lives," Azam-Yu said, after telling me about the woman who'd changed her mind about having an abortion, "that choices aren't real until they are actually confronted with them."

I want us to bear this woman in mind as we consider the way laws and policies set the ground rules and expectations for motherhood. She helps make visible the ways in which our policies about motherhood set the context in which women respond to an unplanned pregnancy.

Motherhood's Default Norms

Think back to Chisko's observation that "the bottom line encourages abortion." She was calling attention to the costs associated with having a child. When asked their reasons for seeking abortion, women make reference to many such costs. Work, school, ability to care for others, and money—each factor is affected by policies; each reflects governmental priorities. Consider an obvious example: there is no paid maternity leave in the United States. And there's no subsidized day care. Yet the majority of women in the country must work in order to support their households. These policies reflect a position that the costs of caring for children are a private responsibility, rather than a public obligation.

These policies seem neutral. But upon reflection, and certainly from the perspective of the most vulnerable women, we can understand these policies as reflections not only of governmental priorities, but also as factors that influence whether poor women will opt to have children.

In many countries worldwide, including most of Western Europe, governments pay families a monthly allowance for each child they are raising. Day care is affordable, as is health care. Both are government subsidized. Workers are guaranteed several months paid maternity leave. In some countries, mothers receive a year off from work, with pay, after having a baby. These policies are meant to encourage childbearing over abortion by offsetting the costs of having a child. These countries want more children.

Like Western Europe with its child allowances, the United States has a fertility policy. We know how much it costs to have a baby; we know

how much it costs to raise a child. And for the most part, we refuse to
subsidize that cost.

You might argue that we're simply remaining neutral, allowing families to make their own private decisions about when and whether to have
children. But what is the place from which "neutrality" is measured?

Let me make my point clear by telling you about California's fertility policy. Like many states, until 2016, California had a "family cap"
law as part of its welfare provisions.[3] If you have a child within the first
year after enrolling, you don't get any additional support from the state.

Lawmakers around the country from both political parties support
family caps as necessary disincentives for women who otherwise might
have babies simply to increase their monthly income. Former president
Ronald Regan called them "welfare queens," and for almost forty years,
the fear of lazy women having babies in order to live off the social dole
has animated our collective imagination. Their choices seem like a form
of reproductive blackmail.

Azam-Yu's organization, Access Women's Health Justice, waged a
ten-year battle against California's family caps. She recalled one of its
former clients, Melissa Ortiz, who testified in a legislative hearing about
the impact of the cap on her family. Ortiz was supporting four children
on just $516 a month in aid:

> When we first had the twins, the only person in my family getting aid
> was my oldest son. We didn't have money to buy them car seats to get
> home [from the hospital]. . . . We didn't have money to pay for diapers,
> wipes, shampoos, and toiletries. . . . I had to go to charities, wait in line,
> and hope that the charities had diapers that day. . . . I am constantly
> trying to pay just enough to not have [the utilities] shut off. . . . I am
> trying my best to be a great mom. I do not need to be punished for
> deciding to have children.[4]

In an era of bitter partisan animosity, family caps enjoy rare bipar-
tisan support. In spite of the enormous wealth separating the United

States from countries like El Salvador, US mothers like Ortiz have to ration their babies' diapers in much the same way that I witnessed in El Salvador.

Having a baby in the United States is expensive. And the government is comfortable with the high price point.

"No one who's at all savvy will say they don't want poor women to have children, because that sounds eugenic," Azam-Yu said. "But they will say, 'There's no money in the budget for that.'"

I don't mean to suggest that only poor women struggle when confronted with an unplanned pregnancy, or that money is the only factor that shapes a woman's response. Instead, I have described their struggles because they are so basic that they make it easy to see how policy choices (not to subsidize maternity leave, housing, day care, or even diapers) constrain American women's mothering choices.

Once we recognize the costs of having children as constraints on motherhood, we can more readily see the context in which all women find themselves when facing an unplanned pregnancy. If we broaden the lens now to include all women, rather than only the poorest women, we can see the ways in which women who are better off have more options. Without a doubt, as we move up the socioeconomic ladder, these backdrop policies have less force. If she has a good job, a place to live, a strong relationship, or family ties, a woman has options, even if the government does not offset the costs of having a child.

A woman whose basic needs are met has time to think about her options. She can consider her best response to the train coming down the tracks. This does not mean that the train ceases to exist, though.

Abortion is not the result of a simple yes/no calculus. Rather, it's the product of weighing competing costs. On one side of the scale are the costs of motherhood. On the other are the costs associated with abortion—costs that are largely determined by the legal regulations and restrictions on abortion.

REGULATING ABORTION:
HOW DO ABORTION LAWS WORK?

In order to understand how the law shapes the cost of abortion, it is important to recognize the significance of both criminal laws and civil laws and regulations. The Supreme Court's 1973 decision in *Roe v. Wade* barred states from making it a crime to have an abortion before viability. It left states free to regulate abortion, though, just as they would any other health procedure. And they did.

Abortion Laws as Nudges and Shoves

When the US Supreme Court determined that women had a constitutional right to abortion, and that states could not make abortion a crime, the Supreme Court tipped the balance away from motherhood and toward abortion. Before the decision, abortion was illegal in forty-eight states. After, it was legal in fifty. The law changed the balance; once abortion became legal, it became easier for women to choose abortion over motherhood.

Pro-life lawmakers have been working to tip the balance back ever since.

Behavioral economists talk about the complicated ways laws can influence human behavior, creating incentives or disincentives that cause humans to alter their default course of action.[5] Professor Dan Kahan describes how lawmakers try to shape human behavior by drafting laws that operate as either "gentle nudges" or "hard shoves."[6]

As an example, he cites the way the law responded to the alarming findings of the 1964 surgeon general's report, which for the first time linked smoking to cancer. Rather than banning smoking, which would have generated intense conflict because so many Americans smoked cigarettes, the law proceeded with gentle nudges: first, it included warning labels on packages; then the law banned cigarette advertisements on television. Only decades later, after the norms regarding smoking had shifted, did the law employ a "hard shove" by banning smoking in public areas.[7]

To understand how abortion laws work, we might see them as ways of nudging or shoving a woman toward or away from abortion. The very first congressional battle over abortion after *Roe* was decided is a great example of how abortion laws are intended to shift the balance—to nudge the pregnant woman away from abortion and toward motherhood.

Congress passed the Hyde Amendment in 1976, prohibiting the use of federal dollars for abortions, except in cases of rape, incest, or medical necessity.[8] The law was important for symbolic reasons: abortion opponents didn't want their tax dollars to be spent on abortion. But lawmakers also saw in the law an opportunity to tip the balance away from abortion. Here's how Representative Henry Hyde explained his law's goals: "I certainly would like to prevent, if I could legally, anybody having an abortion: a rich woman, a middle-class woman or a poor woman. Unfortunately, the only vehicle available is the . . . Medicaid bill."[9]

It worked. Researchers later demonstrated the impact of restricting federal funding. They studied abortion rates between 1974 and 1988, examining what happened when the federal government and some states banned taxpayer funding for most abortions. When states denied public funding, they saw a 5 percent decline in abortion rates.[10] The impact of denying funding is particularly stark among the poorest women. The study found that, without funding, 22 percent of abortions that would otherwise have occurred did not take place. By refusing to pay for poor women's abortions, a state can get thousands of women to have babies instead of abortions.

In the first twenty years following *Roe*, states with pro-life majorities explored other ways of using abortion regulations to tip the balance away from abortion. They passed laws requiring pregnant teens to obtain parental consent, and laws requiring patients to wait a day or two between requesting an abortion and actually getting one.[11] Proponents saw the regulations as responsive to state goals of protecting health and life. Opponents decried the laws as obstacles to a woman's ability to exercise her constitutional right. Legal battles ensued in almost every state as lawmakers tested the limits of their power to regulate abortion.

Eventually, the Supreme Court had to resolve the disputes by letting states know how far they could go in their attempts to nudge women away from abortion. In 1992, the Supreme Court decided *Planned Parenthood v. Casey*, creating the "undue burden test":[12]

> Unless it [imposes an undue burden] on her right of choice, a state measure designed to persuade her to choose childbirth over abortion will be upheld if reasonably related to that goal. Regulations designed to foster the health of a woman seeking an abortion are valid if they do not constitute an undue burden.[13]

For pro-life lawmakers, *Casey*'s "undue burden" test was an invitation to pass laws intended to dissuade abortion-minded women. At first, pro-life states moved slowly, with most states focusing on issues like waiting periods. Starting in 2004, the pro-life group Americans United for Life launched a model legislation project. It drafted a broad set of antiabortion laws, including provisions banning abortion after twenty weeks on the grounds that the fetus could feel pain, and restricting the settings and the providers for abortions. The group encouraged pro-life states to enact whole slates of antiabortion laws, keeping track of its successes with a national pro-life "report card" system.

Some of these model statutes are plainly unconstitutional, as they have the effect of completely curtailing abortion. One state, for instance, passed a law revoking the medical license of any doctor performing an abortion.[14] But most of the laws work at the margins—nudging rather than shoving women away from abortion.

How Much Do Abortion Laws Tip the Balance?

There is surprisingly little consensus about whether and how much these abortion laws and regulations matter. We simply don't know how often laws requiring things like waiting periods or ultrasounds tip the balance, leading a woman to choose to carry to term rather than abort her pregnancy.

At the national level, there's a bitter dispute about whether restrictive abortion laws lead to lower rates of abortion. Since 2008, abortion rates have been declining all over the country.[15] The leading pro-life economist says this decline proves the laws are working to deter women from having abortions. The pro-choice economists respond that he's wrong, because abortion is declining throughout the country, including in states without pro-life laws.[16]

For our purposes, though, the question is not necessarily how often or how much the laws deter abortion. What we want to know is how the law might tip the balance away from abortion.

Sociologist Sarah Roberts has undertaken a deep inquiry into how abortion restrictions affect women's actual decisions. After Utah enacted a seventy-two-hour waiting period, one of the longest in the country, Roberts surveyed five hundred women who sought abortions in Utah. Her study found that the waiting period had an impact on women's decisions, but in a surprisingly indirect manner:

> The 72 hour waiting period and two-visit requirement did not prevent women from having abortions, but it did burden women with financial costs, logistical hassles, and extended periods of dwelling on decisions they had already made. The wait also led some women to worry that they would not be able to obtain abortion drugs, and pushed at least one beyond the clinic's gestational limits for abortion.[17]

Roberts found no evidence suggesting that the three-day waiting period led women to change their minds about abortion. But it is clear that the law had an impact on the woman contemplating abortion: it increased the costs of having an abortion.

Laws restricting abortion by banning insurance coverage or requiring waiting periods don't target any particular set of pregnant women. The laws are neutral on their face. Yet poor women disproportionately feel the impact of these laws.

Take, for example, a hypothetical low-income single mother in Wisconsin. In recent years, that state enacted a law requiring a twenty-four-hour waiting period, and another law banning the use of telemedicine by abortion providers. The state has only three abortion providers, all in Madison or Milwaukee. The abortion procedure itself costs, on average, $593. For a single mother in rural Wisconsin, though, the actual costs are much higher. To the cost of the procedure, she must add the costs triggered by the waiting period and the distance she must travel. Gas, lodging, child care, and missed work add up, so that in the end, an abortion actually costs her $1,380.[18]

In the end, abortion laws aim to nudge women away from abortion by raising the costs of getting one. And the women most likely to be nudged away from abortion because of the costs are those who are poor. Ironically, and to my mind most cruelly, these are the same women who were nudged toward abortion because of the high costs of motherhood.

Our policies on both ends of the scale leave poor mothers so constrained by their options that it is hard, in good faith, to see either motherhood or abortion as a "choice."

CONCLUSION

From a distance, we can see that the abortion laws in the United States are not different in kind from those in El Salvador. El Salvador's ban on abortion works by raising the costs and risks associated with terminating a pregnancy. Wealthier girls and women in El Salvador are better able to offset these costs; they have access to private doctors, and they can travel. They are more insulated than their poorer sisters from the hard shove of the abortion ban.

Likewise, US policies and regulations governing motherhood and abortion are simply ways of pushing a woman one way or the other as she contemplates her response to an unplanned pregnancy. There's the dramatic push of making abortion legal (or criminal). And there are the gentle pushes offered by the Birth Choice women. No life-size cardboard Jesus to shame them. Instead, perhaps, a life rope. Health insurance, housing, help finding work, the prospect of being reunited with children lost to foster care.

The behavioral economists speak of nudges and shoves, distinguishing laws that work indirectly and gradually (the nudges) from those that directly penalize a given activity (the shoves). But when it comes to abortion, this dichotomy between nudges and shoves does not fully capture the impact of the law on pregnant women. Not all nudges are alike. Or rather, what feels to one woman like a gentle nudge is a hard shove to another.

Let's be honest about our abortion policies. Rather than nudging a poor pregnant woman by giving her incentives to choose motherhood, contemporary US abortion laws work by constricting her options. Whether for reasons of fiscal constraint or a belief that abortion is morally abhorrent, our antiabortion laws are cheap. They show no love for the abortion-minded woman. Instead, they work to tip the scales toward childbirth by simply raising the costs of abortion.

The real challenge for abortion laws is yet to come. Pro-life lawmakers cannot be content with laws that merely nudge women toward childbirth or away from abortion. They've been elected on a platform that affirms that life begins at conception and regards abortion as murder.

There is a pent-up demand for the harder shove of making abortion illegal.

The final chapter of this book examines the changes that will be set in motion in the event that *Roe* is reversed and states are once again free to make abortion a crime.

FIVE

AMERICA AFTER *ROE*

Of the many things dividing the United States, none seems more salient than the divide between pro-life and pro-choice forces. At the heart of the dispute is an assumption that, if *Roe* is reversed and abortion becomes illegal, things will change.

We talk about banning abortion as if we all understand how things will change if abortion becomes a crime. On both sides, we invoke naive generalities and obsolete references when imagining post-*Roe* America. The coat hangers, staple features of pro-choice protesters, suggest that women will die if abortion becomes illegal. And the pro-life slogan, "Stop abortion now," seems to assert that making abortion illegal will stop women from having them.

These vague suggestions do not serve us well. Rather, they impede clear thinking about what will happen if states are permitted to make abortion illegal. A variety of legal issues will be set in motion by permitting states to criminalize abortion, many of which arise from the fact that, even without *Roe*, abortion will remain legal in many states around the country.

After considering how *Roe*'s demise would alter, but not halt, women's access to legal abortion in the United States, I turn to the issue of abortion law enforcement. Making abortion a crime is actually more a question than an answer. If abortion is a crime, who are the criminals?

As we reflect upon the way in which laws against abortion matter, the experiences of other countries have much to teach us. You already know a good deal of these lessons, having taken this journey with me. You'll remember Beatriz, whose illness and doomed fetus illuminated the ways in which symbolic laws get tested by hard facts. You've met Christina and the other Salvadoran women serving long prison sentences for crimes they did not commit.

Questions of abortion law enforcement are clear: who will we target for punishment, and who will we actually catch? The choices we face, as we look to abortion crimes, are surprisingly obvious, and the consequences are as disturbing as they are predictable.

ABORTION LAWS IN THE ABSENCE
OF A CONSTITUTIONAL RIGHT

Judging from how we fight over *Roe*, you might think that if *Roe* were overturned, it would be impossible to get a safe, legal abortion in the United States. The truth is otherwise: those with enough time and money will find it easy to obtain a legal abortion, regardless of the laws in their home state. This is because abortion will remain legal in many US states, regardless of the Supreme Court's position on the matter.

Let me explain. Back in 1972, every state had its own laws about abortion. Most states made it a crime, but included some exceptions, such as in cases where the mother's life or health was at risk. A few states—New York, Washington, California, and Hawaii—had recently legalized abortion, permitting it for any reason, before viability. Rather than "legalizing" abortion, the Supreme Court's 1973 decision in *Roe* effectively told the other forty-six states they needed to do so, too.

Talk about the law making a hard shove! By finding that a woman has a constitutional right to privacy under the Fourteenth Amendment, the court overturned the criminal laws of forty-six states.[1] Any decision that reverses *Roe* must begin with a reconsideration of the scope of the constitutional right to privacy.

Roe v. Wade used the concept of fetal viability as the outer limit on a woman's right to privacy. A woman has a broad right to abortion, as a matter of her private choice, before the point at which the fetus is viable. If the fetus is not yet capable of living outside the woman's body, abortion is permissible. If the fetus could survive independently, however, she can no longer abort it.

There was no axiomatic reason for picking viability as the dividing line, though. The court might just as easily have drawn the line earlier or later in pregnancy. And in the absence of *Roe*, a state might well choose some other cutoff point along the gestational path. Indeed, several states have passed laws banning abortion any time after one can hear a fetal heartbeat. Although these laws cannot currently take effect because *Roe* still protects a woman's constitutional right to abortion, they hint at how some states might want to restrict abortion if *Roe* falls.

Even if the Supreme Court reverses itself and decides that the Constitution no longer protects a woman's right to abortion, though, it still will need to set limits on how states frame their abortion laws. For example, it is clear that no state could ban abortion completely. No state could force a woman to continue a pregnancy that poses a threat to her life because the Constitution guarantees a woman's right to life. Unlike in El Salvador, where the country's constitution declares a right to life from the moment of conception, nothing in our Constitution recognizes an absolute "right to life" for the fetus. And there's little chance of this changing any time soon: Constitutional amendments are exceptionally hard to pass, requiring approval not just by both houses of Congress, but also ratification by a majority vote in three-quarters of the states in the country.[2]

If the Supreme Court reverses *Roe*, then, the open question is how far the court will allow states to go. Will it narrow a woman's privacy right to some earlier point in pregnancy, or will it jettison the privacy right altogether, permitting states to dictate the circumstances under which abortion will be allowed?

It's worth playing out the tape on the most extreme case, just to see how much it would matter. Let's imagine that the Supreme Court goes so far as to permit states to ban abortion except when a woman's life is at risk. How many states would subsequently enact such bans?

When I asked a pro-life Oklahoman state senator what would happen if *Roe v. Wade* were reversed, he sighed and said, "It will be a bloodbath on the right." Pro-life communities will be forced to reckon with the disparate views of their constituents, the vast majority of whom want to keep abortion legal in cases of rape, incest, and fetal anomaly. If *Roe* falls, there will be a furious battle over how to frame the crime of abortion.

But not all states will be fighting. Perhaps the most important thing to remember when thinking about America after *Roe* is that not all states will choose to criminalize abortion. Even without *Roe*, abortion will remain legal in as many as half the states. This fact often gets lost in the contentious debates over the Supreme Court's rulings on abortion. In a number of states around the country, the Supreme Court position doesn't make a difference. Many states are safely pro-choice, with judicial decisions interpreting state constitutions as protecting a woman's right to privacy, and large majorities favoring legalized abortion.[3]

If *Roe v. Wade* is reversed, it is clear that the battle over abortion laws will not end. Instead, while pro-life states struggle to determine the scope of laws restricting abortion, elsewhere, abortion will be legal. As a result, it is fair to say that the most significant barrier to abortion, in a world without *Roe v. Wade*, will be wealth: how much will an arbortion cost and how far must one travel in order to get one?

ACCESS TO LEGAL ABORTION IN A POST-*ROE* AMERICA

We already know what happens when abortion becomes a crime. Women with money get abortions by traveling to places where it is legal. Remember what I told you about Chile, where I met Marina, who told me, "The rich women fly to Miami. Women like me stay here."[4]

"Abortion tourism," as it is known, happens here, too. In 1972, the year before *Roe*, when abortion was legal in only four states, a review of medical records shows that 40 percent of abortions were performed on women who came from out of state.[5] Even today, when abortion is legal in all fifty states, women travel in order to avoid local abortion restrictions. For example, in 2014, New Mexico's Department of Health data revealed that around 20 percent of the forty-five hundred women who got abortions there came from out of state.[6] And with a number of states now banning abortion after the twentieth week of pregnancy, many women face legal barriers to abortion when second trimester tests reveal a severe fetal anomaly. In such cases, women often travel to states like California or Colorado, where the law permits abortions, on limited grounds, through the twenty-eighth or even thirtieth week of pregnancy.[7]

If abortion remains legal in even one state, it will be available to any woman who can get to that state. This guarantee is built into the structure of our federal system, through the Constitution's Privileges and Immunities Clause, which forbids a state from treating citizens of other states in a discriminatory manner.

Nor can states readily stop their own residents from leaving home in order to get an abortion. The Constitution guarantees the right to travel freely between the states; a state cannot stop a woman from leaving home, even if it knows she's intending to evade its laws.[8]

In effect, if abortion becomes a crime, there will be two laws: one for those who can afford to travel and one for those who cannot. No one believes that women will stop having abortions, simply because they are illegal.

A BLACK-MARKET ABORTION'S PREDICTABLE CONSEQUENCES

Abortion rights sympathizers use the symbol of the coat hanger to call to mind the thousands of women who died from illegal abortions in the years before *Roe v. Wade*. In the decades leading up to the legalization of abortion, an estimated five thousand American women died that way, every year. Make abortion a crime, and the assumption is that we will once again see hospitals filled with women dying from illegal abortions.

A different story emerges when one takes a close look at the mortality rates in countries worldwide today in which abortion is either banned or permitted only to save the mother's life. Consider Latin America, where the vast majority of countries have restrictive laws against abortion. There are approximately 4.6 million illegal abortions in Latin America every year. In 1990, researchers estimated an abortion mortality rate of 30 deaths per 100,000 live births. By 2008, the rate had dropped to 10.

Think of it this way. In 1972, the United States experienced 5,000 abortion-related deaths in a population of 200 million. Today, there are 600 million people in Latin America. At 1972 rates, we'd expect to see 15,000 women dying from illegal abortions every year. Instead, in 2016, there were around 900 deaths.

I want to be clear: the risks of dying from illegal abortion haven't dropped everywhere in the world. In Africa, abortion-related deaths remain high; it's the cause of at least 9 percent of all maternal deaths. As many as 16,000 African women die from illegal abortions every year.[9] But in the world's more industrialized nations, the rate of deaths from illegal abortions has dramatically declined.

Why the difference? Experts point to widespread access to abortion drugs throughout Latin America (and indeed, throughout much of the world, with the exception of Africa). For example, consider the case of Brazil. Exact figures are impossible to determine, as is always the case where abortion is illegal, but experts believe that somewhere between 500,000 and 1 million pregnancies are terminated in Brazil each year. Around half of them are induced using abortion drugs and the rest are performed in clandestine clinics. Between 2003 and 2009, as abortion drugs became easier and easier to procure, the number of women hospitalized from complications from illegal abortions fell by 40,000.[10]

For any woman with a smartphone and money, illegal abortion today is far less risky than it was in 1972. That is to say, the risks of illegal abortion vary by class, age, education level, geographic location, and race.

As a result, we already know what illegal abortions will look like in the United States, in the event that abortion becomes illegal. Remember what we saw in El Salvador: women who live in cities and are educated enough to determine how long they've been pregnant and how to procure the right dose of Cytotec that can end their pregnancies without detection. The medical risks—uncontrolled bleeding and infection from an incomplete abortion—are readily treated. With 25 percent of all pregnancies ending in miscarriage, losing a pregnancy is so commonplace that, in the vast majority of cases, doctors will have no way of knowing whether a woman deliberately ended her pregnancy.

But the risks of illegal abortion vary. A wealthy woman can readily identify and buy unadulterated drugs or access to a well-trained physician. A poor woman will struggle to find accurate information and safe abortion providers. A pregnant teenager living in a Salvadoran village might have a smartphone; almost everyone there does. But chances are that she'll have a harder time safely ending her unwanted pregnancy because she'll be poorer, less educated, and farther away from the cities where she might buy abortion drugs. Even if she finds money to pay for the bus and the abortion drugs, she's less likely than her more educated peers to know how far along her pregnancy is, or how to navigate the black market to find a safe abortion provider.

But we need not look to El Salvador to imagine how the black market in illegal abortion will work here. The United States already is experiencing an increase in illegal abortions. As we saw in chapter 4, with the growing number of regulations governing abortion providers, the costs of accessing abortion have increased. One consequence of increasing the time and money required to get a legal abortion is a rise in the number of women attempting to terminate their pregnancies on their own. A 2015 study by Dr. Dan Grossman confirmed this trend. He surveyed Texas women having clinic-based abortions and found that 7 percent of them had first tried one or more times to terminate their pregnancies on their own.[11]

Hospitals, too, are seeing signs of this trend. For example, in 2015, a Tennessee woman named Anna Yocca attempted to give herself an abortion with a coat hanger in a bath tub. She was twenty-four weeks pregnant. Worried about the excessive bleeding she immediately experienced, Yocca went to the emergency room. She later was charged with attempted murder. A few years earlier, a Tennessee woman's attempt to induce an abortion with a coat hanger led to a life-threatening infection, forcing doctors to perform a hysterectomy.[12] Three recent cases involve women accused of having shot themselves in the belly in an effort to end their pregnancies.[13]

If women already are opting to attempt to end their pregnancies on their own, surely they will continue to do so in greater numbers if abortion becomes illegal and thus even harder to access. And as greater numbers of women attempt to self-abort, we will see an increase in the number of women seeking emergency care after self-abortion.

We already know, having seen what happened in El Salvador, that any effort to enforce laws against abortion will focus on what happens in the emergency room. It is at the emergency room bedside that we can begin to consider the answers to the questions of when and how abortion crimes will be enforced.

THE QUESTION OF ENFORCEMENT

If abortion is a crime, who is the criminal? Will we punish the woman who has an abortion or her doctor? What if there is no doctor involved? How much of our criminal justice resources are we willing to spend on enforcing abortion laws?

The question of how and when abortion will be prosecuted is one of the most intensely disputed issues in our contemporary abortion debate. Abortion rights advocates often assume that, if abortion becomes illegal, women will be targeted. Their position is bolstered by occasional pro-lifers' assertions that "there would have to be some sort of punishment for women," as President Donald Trump said while on the campaign trail in 2016.[14]

But most antiabortion advocates reject this position, explaining that, even if abortion is illegal, women will not be targeted. Rather than seeing women who have illegal abortions as criminals, they see them as abortion's "second victims."[15]

Instead of punishing women, pro-life movement leaders assert that when abortion becomes a crime, abortion doctors, not women, will be punished.[16] Indeed, the official pro-life position labels the suggestion that women could be prosecuted for illegal abortions "pro-choice propaganda." Clarke Forsythe, general counsel of the pro-life advocacy group, Americans United for Life, is emphatic on the subject: "Pro-life legislators and pro-life leaders do not support the prosecution of women and will not push for such a policy when Roe is overturned."[17]

The truth is that both sides are right. As we'll see, abortion laws historically and today typically are not enforced against women but, rather, against those who provide illegal abortions. Nonetheless, in recent years, hundreds of US women have been prosecuted for crimes stemming from their own attempts to terminate their pregnancies.

Prosecuting Abortion

I was surprised to learn how rarely abortion laws are enforced in places where it is illegal. Indeed, it was my desire to understand the scarcity of prosecutions in Chile—despite the ban, there are only a handful of prosecutions a year, mostly against doctors—that inspired this book. Throughout history, and around the world today, abortion-related prosecutions are few and far between.

Professor Leslie Reagan has written a comprehensive history of how the United States enforced its laws against abortion in the years before 1973. In it, she documents a pattern of occasional, local efforts at cracking down on illegal abortion, accompanied by a general tendency to look the other way.[18] And although law enforcement strategies varied over time, the targets for prosecution were almost never women. Instead, the so-called "abortionists" were charged with the crime.[19] However, unless a woman died, these doctors seldom were arrested and even more seldom convicted.[20]

It wasn't that prosecutors could not have charged women with illegal abortion. Most state laws were general, making it illegal for anyone to bring about an abortion. In fifteen states, laws explicitly penalized women who solicited or submitted to an abortion.[21] Some states even made it clear they wanted to target women, enacting laws against "self-abortion." For example, an 1869 New York law criminalized a woman's participation in her own abortion.[22] Even today, there are no fewer than four states with laws on the books that forbid "self-abortion."[23]

Despite the fact that prosecutors could have prosecuted women for having illegal abortions, though, there is no evidence that they did so. In the century or so when abortion was illegal, US historians have found only two cases involving women charged with abortion-related crimes—one in 1911 and another in 1922.[24]

The same pattern prevails throughout the world today in countries where abortion is illegal. Abortion prosecutions are rare. One finds occasional crackdowns, rather than consistent enforcement. There was one in 2007, in Mato Grosso do Sul, a remote state in Brazil, in which officials subpoenaed ten thousand medical records from two decades of practice at a notorious abortion clinic and sentenced three hundred women to perform community service for having committed the crime of abortion.[25] Between 2009 and 2011, several conservative states in Mexico intensified abortion prosecutions, seemingly in response to Mexico City's decision to legalize abortion.[26] Typically, these spikes in prosecution are local, rather than part of a national or even a regional policy or plan. For the most part, prosecutions focus on abortion providers, rather than on the women who seek them.

El Salvador is the exception among countries because it has enforced its abortion laws primarily against women, rather than against their doctors. That's what led me to go there. Law enforcement agents have toured the country's hospitals, urging doctors to report women they suspect of having deliberately ended their pregnancies. Even so, prosecutions are rare. There are, on average, only twelve abortion-related prosecutions a year.[27] And as we saw in chapter 2, most of those cases wind up involving women whose babies die during childbirth. They are not really abortion cases at all.

When abortion is a crime, women are seldom prosecuted. But seldom is not the same as never. A close look at the cases that do get prosecuted, both in the United States and abroad, reveals a striking pattern: they are cases in which there is no doctor to blame.

Which Women Are Prosecuted?

Pro-life advocates explain the decision not to prosecute women by positing that the woman who commits an abortion on herself is not the perpetrator, but the "second victim" of the crime. As notions go, it is not a particularly compelling one.

The claim that women are victimized by abortion might be borne out in a narrow set of cases. A woman looking for love puts her trust in a bad man who leaves her pregnant and alone. One can see this narrative at work in the following excerpt, from pro-life Amherst College jurisprudence professor Hadley Arkes:

> On the one hand there may be a young, unmarried woman, who finds herself pregnant, with the father of the child not standing with her. Abandoned by the man, and detached from her family, she may feel the burden of the crisis bearing on her alone, with the prospect of life-altering changes.[28]

The problem with the "second victim" exception to abortion prosecutions is that not all women fit the pattern. Not all women who have abortions look like victims, or at least not like the sort of victims Arkes might recognize.

Life typically is more complicated than a morality play, after all. Sometimes there are many men or no man in particular. Sometimes the woman is on drugs. Sometimes she ends her pregnancy on her own; there is no doctor to blame. Unsurprisingly, as the narrative shifts, so too does the extent to which the woman is perceived as a second victim of abortion.

So long as there is a doctor or a faithless lover in the picture, it is possible to understand the crime of illegal abortion as having two victims, with the doctor or the absconding lover emerging as the only criminal. What happens, though, when there is no third party involved?

In recent decades, law enforcement officials have charged hundreds of US women with crimes relating to pregnancy or abortion. This is true even though abortion is legal. Pro-choice advocates see these prosecutions as evidence that it will become routine for states to charge women with abortion crimes if abortion becomes illegal. Pro-life advocates object, insisting that these prosecutions involve extraordinary facts—not simple illegal abortions—and therefore the women involved merit punishment.

The dispute is complicated because the cases aren't necessarily straightforward. Regardless, one fact unites almost all the prosecutions to date: these are cases in which there are no doctors to blame for the harm done to the fetus. And it turns out that, without a third party to blame, the law sees the women not as second victims but, rather, as criminals.

A 2013 article offered the first systematic investigation into cases in which officials have endeavored to restrict and punish pregnant women for harming their fetuses. Authors Lynn Paltrow and Jeanne Flavin identified and analyzed 413 cases from 1973 to 2005.[29] Drawing their data from a thorough review of newspaper articles and court dockets, and including only cases that were fully adjudicated by the time of publication, their study offers an overview of the range of ways in which the legal system has targeted pregnant women.

Some of the cases they found seem unrelated to abortion, such as those targeting women accused of using drugs or alcohol while pregnant. Indeed, most of the interventions they identified concerned women who sought not to terminate, but rather to continue their pregnancies. The women in these cases typically were restrained, and even prosecuted, for behaving in ways that risked harming their fetuses. But many of the cases Paltrow and Flavin identified did involve women who were prose-cuted for illegally ending their pregnancies. The truth is that, around the country today, women are being prosecuted for having illegal abortions.

You might wonder how a woman can be prosecuted for illegal abor-tion, if abortion is legal in the United States? The answer lies in the fact that we regulate abortion, as we do all health procedures. Abortion is only legal when it is performed in compliance with these regulations. At the very least, this means that to be legal, an abortion must be per-formed by a licensed doctor. Therefore, a woman who ends her preg-nancy on her own can be understood to have had an illegal abortion.

Paltrow, a lawyer who has for decades been defending women ac-cused of illegal abortion and other pregnancy-related crimes, notes that, between 1973 and 2013, at least 413 women were prosecuted for illegal abortions.[30] These cases range from alleged illegal abortions to claims arising out of miscarriages, stillbirths, or perceived risks taken while pregnant and thought to have contributed to the death of the fetus.[31] Women have been prosecuted in cases of fetal demise in nineteen differ-ent states, and not only for illegal abortion, but for a variety of related crimes as well.[32]

The prosecutions stand in stark contradiction to the claim that women will not be punished for abortion because they are "abortion's second victims." The common thread in these cases is that they almost always involve women who acted on their own, rather than with the help of an abortion provider. With no one else to be the "perpetra-tor," a prosecutor might see the woman not as a victim, but instead as a criminal.

The facts underlying many of these prosecutions testify to the ways in which abortion regulations already restrict abortion access, lead-ing desperate women to attempt unsafe abortions. If these sorts of self-abortion cases are arising while abortion is still legal, then we are sure to see more of them if and when abortion becomes illegal. As such, it's helpful to examine one such prosecution in detail, so we can better understand how the law can be invoked to punish a woman suspected of having illegally terminated her pregnancy.

In July 2013, Purvi Patel was charged with two crimes relating to the death of her fetus. A disclosure here: I followed the case closely not only because it interested me, but also because my spouse was her appellate defense lawyer.

Patel was unmarried and living with her parents, who were devout Hindu immigrants, when she became pregnant. She worried about how her parents would respond to her violation of their norms surrounding premarital sex and out-of-wedlock pregnancy. These concerns were intensified by the fact that she had been having an affair with a married coworker.

Estimating that she was at most three months' pregnant, Patel determined to end the pregnancy without her parents' knowledge. After learning that a trip to the nearest abortion clinic would take over three hours and that she would need to return twice in order to have the procedure, Patel found an online advertisement for abortion pills, sold by an overseas pharmacy. She ordered the drugs, and when they arrived two weeks later, she took them.

It turned out that her pregnancy was far more advanced than she'd thought. After ingesting the pills, Patel delivered a one-and-a-half-pound baby of approximately twenty-five to twenty-six weeks' gestation in the bathroom of the home she shared with her parents.

She arrived at the emergency room, hemorrhaging and having lost 20 percent of her total blood volume. After several hours of emergency surgery, she awoke surrounded by police officials, who questioned her about the whereabouts of her missing fetus. When authorities located the body, the state of Indiana charged Patel with both felony child neglect and feticide. After trial, she was sentenced to twenty years in prison.

There is a stark contrast in the ways in which the pro-choice and pro-life media responded to Patel's conviction. The pro-choice world was outraged by Patel's prosecution, asserting that she was innocent, and that she had been sentenced for having a miscarriage.[33] By contrast, the pro-life world saw Patel as a monster:

> [W]hat happened here wasn't just an abortion. . . . Granted, the line between legal abortion and criminal feticide isn't a bright one. Both kill a child whose existence is disagreeable to someone. But someone who seeks out an abortionist at least has the excuse that a professional the law says she can trust lied to her and withheld key information about what abortion really was.[34]

Those who supported Patel's conviction worried that pro-choice advocates would use the case "as a golden opportunity to push the meme that pro-lifers are secretly clamoring to throw post-abortive women in jail."[35] They insisted that the facts were otherwise, pointing to the fetus's gestational age and the illegal drugs as distinguishing factors.[36]

On appeal, the Indiana appellate court overturned Patel's conviction for feticide, finding that feticide laws did not apply to pregnant women, but only to third parties. However, the court upheld her conviction on the lesser charge of neglect of a child.[37]

The debate over Patel's case has much to teach us about how women might come to be prosecuted if abortion becomes a crime. Prosecutions will be reserved for exceptional cases—those in which the woman does not seem like a second victim to the prosecutor. And the most important factor in determining whether a woman will be seen as abortion's second victim is whether there is someone else to view as the perpetrator.

Consider how we might have responded to Patel if, rather than taking illegal abortion drugs, she had been given an abortion by her best friend Fay, a medical technician who had advised Patel about buying the drugs. If Fay had performed an abortion on Patel, I suspect the law would have viewed Fay, rather than Patel, as the perpetrator. How could she have preyed upon her trusting, vulnerable friend? How did she overlook the possibility that Patel's pregnancy was too far along? She jeopardized Patel's life.

With Fay cast as the perpetrator, it would have been possible to see Patel as a second victim, as an innocent woman whose life was endangered at the hands of the real monster. If there is a moral justification for punishing a woman who induces her own abortion, but not one who hires another to do so for her, it is not clear to me.

The second and more important lesson we learn from Patel's case is that individual actors, rather than official policies, determine whether and how the law is enforced. The decision to report Patel to the police, the decision to prosecute her for a homicide offense—these were judgment calls made by individual doctors and prosecutors.

Paltrow and Flavin's forty-year study of pregnancy crimes demonstrates that Patel's case was not unique in this regard. Instead, these cases demonstrate a dramatic pattern of selective law enforcement. Although women have been charged with pregnancy-related crimes in forty-four states and the District of Columbia, more than 50 percent of these prosecutions were in the South. One state, South Carolina, accounts for 93 of the 413 cases.[38] Further analysis shows that "in individual states, cases tend to cluster in particular counties and sometimes in particular hospitals":

> [I]n South Carolina thirty-four of the ninety-three cases came from the contiguous counties of Charleston and Berkeley. Staff at one hospital, the Medical University of South Carolina, initiated thirty of these cases. In Florida twenty-five of the fifty-five cases took place in Escambia County. Of these, twenty-three came from just two hospitals: Sacred Heart Hospital and Baptist Hospital. In Missouri twenty-six of the twenty-nine cases came from Jackson County. Of these, twenty cases came from a single hospital: Truman Medical Center.[39]

This pattern of prosecution—one hospital, one county—speaks to individual crusaders, rather than careful policy making. And the resulting cases expose the most profound problem with this individualized exercise of legal power: it is unmistakably biased against the most marginalized women in society.

Paltrow and Flavin found that almost 60 percent of the 413 cases in their study involved poor women of color. Needless to say, this rate far exceeds their representative share of the population.[40] In spite of overwhelming evidence demonstrating that pregnant women of all races and classes abuse drugs at similar rates, 84 percent of these prosecutions were brought against minority women charged with having used an illegal drug.[41]

Where are the white women?

For decades, doctors and prosecutors have used the force of law to sanction poor pregnant women and, particularly, poor women of color.[42] We saw this pattern in El Salvador, where the women prosecuted in relation to abortion are overwhelming poor, uneducated, and rural. And we will see more of it here, among poor minority women, as we intensify abortion restrictions.

If history is any indication of what to expect should abortion become illegal, we will need to append an asterisk to the promise that women won't be punished for abortion. The truth is, wealthy women will not be punished.

Poor women may be prosecuted, though—particularly minority women who seek care at public hospitals after attempting to end their own pregnancies. There won't be many such prosecutions; most doctors will opt to maintain their patients' confidentiality.

But we can be sure we will see some cases growing out of this scenario. We already have.

CONCLUSION

We started this chapter by recognizing the underlying questions one must ask about making abortion a crime: Will it stop abortions? If not, who will the law target, and who is it likely to catch?

We've seen the answers to these questions, hiding in plain view: abortion will remain legal in some states and, where it is not, illegal abortion will be prevalent.

We've seen enough to know that abortion prosecutions will be rare, and they will be set in motion not by an overarching policy but, rather, according to the moral sensibilities of individual actors. We've seen how these individual actors will tend to target the most marginalized women in society.

I haven't yet mentioned the indirect consequences of banning abortion. There is more that we can predict will happen as a consequence of making abortion a crime. First, we're likely to see a rise in births to teenagers. Compared to adults, teenagers are less likely to use contraception, and they are slower to recognize that they are pregnant. Once they are pregnant, teenagers have a hard time accessing illegal abortions. In addition to being younger, less educated, and more vulnerable in general, teens typically lack the money and the mobility necessary to get abortions on their own.

In El Salvador, the consequences of the abortion ban fall disproportionately on teenage girls. The country has one of the highest teen pregnancy rates in Latin America. Even as teen pregnancy rates are dropping in the United States and elsewhere worldwide, El Salvador's rates are rising. A 2014 National Family Health Survey report notes that 23 percent of Salvadoran women ages fifteen to nineteen have had a child before age eighteen.[43] There are serious long-term costs associated with teen motherhood, for the mother and child, and for society at large. Teen mothers are disproportionately likely to drop out of school. They are more likely than older mothers to raise their families in poverty, with negative consequences for the entire family's health, education, and long-term stability.

Nor is teen motherhood the only consequence of the abortion ban for adolescent girls. In addition, where abortion is illegal, one finds elevated rates of suicide among pregnant teens.[44] In El Salvador, hundreds of pregnant girls commit suicide every year.[45] Indeed, suicide is the highest cause of death among the country's pregnant girls.

There is every reason to believe we will see similar patterns among US teens in places where abortion becomes illegal. Although we are a wealthier country, the factors driving El Salvador's teens to pregnancy, motherhood, and even suicide would be the same here. Here, too, teenagers will struggle to identify options when faced with an unplanned pregnancy. Here, too, teens are prone to catastrophic thinking. We can predict with certainty the news stories we're likely to read, in places where abortion is illegal: rates of births to teens will rise, and on occasion, some of our poorest, most isolated pregnant teens will feel there is no way out but death.

So, what are we to make of these facts? How are we to weigh the significance of what we know will and won't happen, if *Roe* falls and states can make abortion a crime?

It is important to remember Beatriz's case in considering our answers. Those who morally oppose abortion derive an intangible, yet vitally important benefit from a law that reinforces their view. The law plays a significant role in helping to express collective values—to set as ideals, if not as norms, the things we hold to be true.

We saw the lengths to which El Salvador was willing to go in order to defend the principles embodied in its abortion ban. By permitting Beatriz to end her pregnancy, but only in self-defense—only when the threat of her death became imminent—El Salvador stayed true to its position that a fetus has the same rights as any other human being.

For many, many Americans, the idea that the law makes abortion legal, without qualification, is anathema. They will not rest easily until the law is aligned with their moral position.

In addition to resting more easily, abortion opponents believe that banning abortion may also have some deterrent effect on abortion rates. As we've seen, there's no evidence in the aggregate to support the claim that banning abortion reduces abortion rates. Indeed, we've seen that abortion rates are actually higher in countries where it is illegal than in countries where abortion is legal. Still, it stands to reason that, by banning abortion, some women who otherwise would have aborted will carry their pregnancies to term. We just don't know how many.

Which brings us back to Cass Sunstein's admonition against fanaticism: The true test of a law's validity lies in assessing not simply its message but also its impact.[46]

Is it worth it to you?

I can't answer that question. But I am absolutely certain that you need to do so. It's at the center of the only meaningful conversation to be had about abortion laws.

PARTING THOUGHTS ON LEAVING BEHIND THE ABORTION WAR

As I put this journey behind me, I'm struck by my feelings of nostalgia. I'll miss the conversations. I'll miss hearing the stories.

For it's clear that's what I've been doing all along. Collecting stories. The stories people told me about how they thought about abortion and abortion laws felt surprisingly private. They were personal, like secrets.

Our abortion battle is so constrained by slogans that we almost never get to talk about the ideas that underlie our positions, the things that lead us to care about the abortion issue in the first place. By this, I mean the big questions: what we make of sex, motherhood, love, the purpose and meaning of life.

I will miss the way, time and again, strangers moved me to tears. How I sat in the gigantic gun store with Oklahoma senator Mike Reynolds and heard him speak of his faith that life begins at the moment of conception. How I cried when he described the guilt and the pain he felt about his wife's use of contraception that prevented implantation, causing the fertilized eggs to pass, month after month. He didn't persuade me to change, or even to reconsider, my position on legalized abortion. But he helped me see the world, for a time, through his eyes.

You see, before this journey, it's not just that I didn't understand how pro-life advocates thought about abortion laws. It's also that I had come to view pro-lifers in broad generalities, as if they were two-dimensional objects, not subjects.

And unlike subjects, it's easy to dismiss objects with contempt.

I'm reminded of a favorite passage from George Orwell's Spanish Civil War memoir, *Homage to Catalonia*, in which he recalls catching sight of a Fascist soldier on a dawn reconnaissance mission. The man was holding up his pants as he ran, and Orwell couldn't bring himself to shoot him. "I had come to Spain to shoot Fascists," he said, "but a man who is holding up his trousers isn't a 'Fascist,' he is visibly a fellow creature."[1]

The most painful moment in my journey still stings, years later: it was when I learned how Tony Lauinger had characterized me. "She is pro-abortion," he'd said. "Long experience has taught me that there's nothing to be gained by helping gather intelligence from behind enemy lines from seemingly well-meaning academics."

Everything Lauinger said about me is pretty much true, although I bristle at the label "pro-abortion." I'm an academic, I'm pro-choice, and I suppose that this project, like all of my work, might therefore be seen as coming from behind enemy lines.

So it is puzzling, at first, to understand why his words made me feel as if he'd kicked the breath out of me. It's because he'd rendered me two-dimensional. I can't recognize myself in his description of me. He'd reduced me to a set of categories, to an object that he could regard with distrust and contempt.

We pay a moral price for dehumanizing other human beings. Contempt and distrust corrode our ability to connect. They prevent us from recognizing ourselves in one another. They keep us apart.

We pay a practical price, too. Our mutual contempt leaves us locked in debate over the question of whether abortion should be legal. And as we've seen, that question is not serving us well. It's distracting us from the better question of how we think things will change if abortion is illegal.

That's the question I would have liked to ask Lauinger.

To be sure, abortion laws have symbolic importance. Both sides in the abortion war care deeply about the messages sent by laws governing abortion. The pro-life world's outrage that abortion legalizes killing is matched by the pro-choice world's insistence upon the full legal autonomy of women. Honestly, I don't see how we'll ever resolve our ideological differences.

In the meantime, though, our blinkered focus on whether abortion should be legal distracts us from the plight of the women and children most affected by our abortion laws. You met them in chapter 4 during journeys through Oklahoma and California: they are the most marginalized women in the country. Another child will thrust them deeper into poverty, but an abortion does little to lift them out of it. The war over abortion law draws our gaze away from them, relieving us of the obligation to notice, if not to reset, the odds against them.

I think back on former Oklahoma House speaker Steele's comment that "the best way to lower abortion rates is to deal with what causes women to want to abort in the first place." It was a wistful observation, an afterthought to our conversation, yet it was also a point of complete agreement between us—a blue-state, pro-choice feminist and a red-state, pro-life minister.

What would it look like to design a policy around the idea that no one should have to choose abortion because she is too poor to have a child? It would cost billions of dollars. Yet, we routinely spend such sums on the war over abortion's legality. Might it be worth it to try something different?

I dedicated this book to the women at Birth Choice of Oklahoma, and to those at Access Women's Health Justice because they share core values that transcend our endless war over abortion. Both organizations understand how the deck is stacked against poor women and their children.

I have a fantasy that, if I could just get them in the same room, talking about their clients, they'd see one another as kindred spirits. Maybe they'd forge an alliance. The battle over abortion law would rage in the distance, but in the living room, plans would be made to launch a new way of harnessing our power for the good.

The hardest thing would be learning to listen to one another, for deep listening is the prerequisite to any meaningful conversation. It will take extraordinary patience to look past the trappings of our abortion team allegiances. But we don't need to abandon our respective teams to sit together and recognize our shared goals.

And in that hard-won conversation, we would not take long to realize that this fight over abortion laws is not the only battle women face. It's not even the most important one.

ACKNOWLEDGMENTS

My deepest thanks to those who have helped me along the way. To my editors at Beacon Press: Alexis Rizzuto, who saw the potential, and Rachael Marks, who brought it home, helping me hear my own voice and knowing precisely when to praise effusively and when to pause. Thanks also to the production team for continual and kind support.

To Santa Clara University and its Jesuit mission, which provided for all my needs: time, money, students, and intellectual freedom.

To Peter Handler and Ariella Radwin, more midwives than readers. You coaxed my stories out of me, comforting me when the telling grew hard, listening so closely you understood what I wanted to say long before I figured out how to say it.

To all those I met on my journey. Thank you for trusting a stranger with your stories. It was a gift to sit in intimate, earnest conversation. So different from the distorted rhetoric with which we fight our abortion war. Whether or not you're mentioned, every conversation I had helped shape my understanding of the stories I've told herein. Your vision helped clarify my own. I carry you with me, and am grateful for the company.

To those in El Salvador, heroic in the face of struggles larger than any I've known. In particular, to the Agrupación Ciudadana por la Despenalizacion del Aborto, without whom I never would have taken this journey. To Hermana Peggy O'Neill and Centro Arte Para la Paz, for sheltering my body and feeding my soul. To the lay midwives of

Suchitoto, "Las Estrellas," Angeles, Darlyn, Johanna, Vilma, Zulema, and Yanira, for being my teachers.

To the folks at Oklahoma City University Law School, who opened doors and minds, most notably my own. In particular, I am indebted to Lawrence Hellman, Arthur LeFrancois, Andrew Spiropoulos, and Dr. Eli Reshef.

To Trisha Cobb, for deep insight and superb research assistance.

Thanks also to those who read drafts: Felice Batlan, Khiara Bridges, Suzanne Carey, Paula Dempsey, Father Paul Goda, Ed Goldman, Liz Klein, Art LeFrancois, Rachel Marshall, Lynn Morgan, Hanna Oberman, Sarah Roberts, Carole Joffe, and Andrew Spiropoulos. And to those who helped workshop my ideas: Tracy Weitz, Carole Joffe, and the Bixby Center for Global Reproductive Health, my colleagues at Santa Clara University Law, my students in Abortion & the Law (spring 2015), Chicago-Kent College of Law faculty workshop, American Bar Foundation workshop, and 2017 anthropology students and faculty at Mt. Holyoke College and Smith College.

Finally, to my friends and family. To Kathy Baker, Dina Kaplan, and Sarah Delson, for helping me shout down my demons. And to Larry Marshall, Rachel Marshall, Shlomie Marshall, Jaclyn Marshall, Yoni Marshall, Liz Klien, Hanna Obermen, and Noa Oberman, for letting me make abortion "table talk." I am so very blessed by your presence in my life.

So many have helped, in so many ways, over the years I've worked on this project that I'm sure I've forgotten some names. These omissions belong alongside the other mistakes I'm sure to have made in these pages. Unintentional, and mine alone.

NOTES

Introduction

1. David Foster Wallace, *This Is Water: Some Thoughts, Delivered on a Significant Occasion, About Living a Compassionate Life* (Boston: Little, Brown and Company, 2009).
2. Michelle Oberman, "Sex, Drugs, Pregnancy, and the Law: Rethinking the Problems of Pregnant Women Who Use Drugs," *Hastings Law Journal* 43 (1991–92): 505, http://digitalcommons.law.scu.edu/facpubs/518/.
3. M. Schäfer, B. Schnack, and M. Soyka, "Sexual and Physical Abuse During Early Childhood or Adolescence and Later Drug Addiction," *Psychotherapie Psychosomatik Medizinische Psychologie* (2000), http://www.ncbi.nlm.nih.gov/pubmed/10721277.
4. Michelle Oberman, "Eva and Her Baby (a Story of Adolescent Sex, Pregnancy, Longing, Love, Loneliness, and Death)," *Duke Journal of Gender Law & Policy* 16 (2009): 213–22, http://digitalcommons.law.scu.edu/facpubs/44/.
5. Indeed, it has become common for states to enact ten or more such laws in a single legislative session. Steven Ertlet, "States Pass More Pro-Life Laws Saving Babies from Abortions in Last 5 Years Than the Previous 15," LifeNews.com, January 4, 2016, www.lifenews.com/2016/01/04/states-pass-more-pro-life-laws-saving-babies-from-abortions-in-last-5-fives-than-the-previous-15/. These new laws govern practices ranging from prohibitions on buying human eggs to mandating physician disclosure of misleading and often inaccurate information. Texas and Arizona have passed laws requiring doctors to tell patients that the abortion drugs they are about to take can be reversed, should they change their minds and decide to keep their pregnancy. This in spite of the lack of any medical evidence proving it is true. Rick Rojas, "Arizona Orders Doctors to Say Abortions with Drugs May Be Reversible," *New York Times*,

March 31, 2015, http://www.nytimes.com/2015/04/01/us/politics/arizona
-doctors-must-say-that-abortions-with-drugs-may-be-reversed.html. Other
states require doctors to tell patients that abortion is correlated with
elevated risks of breast cancer and suicide—findings lacking scientific
support and rejected by the relevant medical authorities. Guttmacher Institute, "Counseling and Waiting Periods for Abortion," *State Policies in
Brief (as of June 2013)*, http://www.guttmacher.org/statecenter/spibs/spib
_MWPA.pdf.

6. For a detailed recounting of her story, see Michelle Oberman, "Judging
Vanessa: Norm Setting and Deviance in the Law of Motherhood," *Wil-
liam and Mary Journal of Women and the Law* 15 (2009): 337–59, http://
digitalcommons.law.scu.edu/facpubs/498/.

7. Estimates range from sixty thousand to three hundred thousand abortions
annually. E. Prada and H. Ball, "Induced Abortion in Chile," In Brief,
Guttmacher Institute, 2016, https://www.guttmacher.org/sites/default/files
/pdfs/pubs/journals/IB_Abortion-Chile.pdf.

8. In the United States, legal induced abortion results in only 0.6 deaths per
100,000 procedures. Worldwide, unsafe abortion accounts for a death
rate that is 350 times higher (220 per 100,000), and, in Sub-Saharan Africa, the rate is 800 times higher, at 460 per 100,000. "Facts on Induced
Abortion Worldwide," In Brief, Guttmacher Institute, 2012, http://www
.who.int/reproductivehealth/publications/unsafe_abortion/induced
_abortion_2012.pdf. See also Department of Reproductive Health and
Research, World Health Organization, *Unsafe Abortion: Global and
Regional Estimates of the Incidence of Unsafe Abortion and Associated
Mortality in 2008*, sixth ed. (Geneva: World Health Organization, 2011),
http://www.who.int/reproductivehealth/publications/unsafe_abortion
/9789241501118/en/.

9. E. Koch, "Impact of Reproductive Laws on Maternal Mortality: The
Chilean Natural Experiment," *Linacre Quarterly* (2013), http://www
.melisainstitute.org/uploads/1/2/3/9/12398427/koch_2014_rev_chil
_obstet_79_5_351_en2.pdf.

10. Lidia Casas Becerra, "Women Prosecuted and Imprisoned for Abortion
in Chile," *Reproductive Health Matters* (1997), http://www.rhm-elsevier
.com/article/S0968–8080(97)90003–3/pdf. See also Lidia Casas and
Lieta Vivaldi, "Abortion in Chile: The Practice Under a Restrictive Re-
gime," *Reproductive Health Matters* (2014), http://www.academia
.edu/10146213/Abortion_in_Chile_the_practice_under_a_restrictive
_regime.

Chapter 1: Beatriz and Her Case

1. Guillermo Ortiz, perinatologist at La Maternidad Hospital, in discussion with the author, June 2014 (notes on file with author).

2. Penal Code of El Salvador 1998, Title 1, Crimes Related to Life, Chapter II, Crimes Related to Unborn Humans, Art. 133–139, http://www.oas .org/dil/esp/Codigo_Penal_El_Salvador.pdf; Soledad Varela, "Persecuted: Political Process and Abortion Legislation in El Salvador: A Human Rights Analysis," *Center for Reproductive Law & Policy* 27 (2001): 96n130, http://reproductiverights.org/sites/default/files/documents/persecuted1.pdf, http://www.reproductiverights.org/sites/default/files/documents/persecuted2 .pdf; "El Salvador," in UN Population Division Department of Economic and Social Affairs, *Abortion Policies: A Global Review* (June 2002), http://www.un.org/esa/population/publications/abortion/profiles.htm.

3. Guillermo Ortiz, author interview.

4. "Ectopic Pregnancy," Cedars-Sinai, https://www.cedars-sinai.edu/Patients /Health-Conditions/Ectopic-Pregnancy.aspx, accessed November 8, 2016.

5. Alejandro Guidos, MD, president of El Salvador's Association of Obstetricians and Gynecologists, in discussion with the author, June 2014.

6. Oswaldo Ernesto Feusier, "Pasado Y Presente Del Delito De Aborto En El Salvador," *Universidad Centroamericana "Jose Simeon Cañas"* (2016), 135n, http://www.uca.edu.sv/deptos/ccjj/media/archivo/95bbb4_pasadoy presentedeldelitodeabortoenelsalvador.pdf.

7. Loida Martínez and Suchit Chavez, "Salud aboga por aborto terapéutico a mujer enferma," *La Prensa Grafica*, April 17, 2013, http://www .laprensagrafica.com/Salud-aboga-por-aborto-terapeutico-a-mujer-enferma.

8. "Red Familia rechaza aborto de Beatriz," editorial, *La Pagina*, April 18, 2013, http://www.lapagina.com.sv/nacionales/80505/2013/04/19/Red -Familia-rechaza-aborto-de-Beatriz.

9. Carmen Rodriguez, "Mamá de Beatriz: 'No quiero que mi hija muera,'" *La Pagina*, May 14, 2013, http://www.lapagina.com.sv/nacionales/81629/2013 /05/15/Mama-de-Beatriz-No-quiero-que-mi-hija-muera.

10. Although there is no information about El Salvador's IML online, see this description of Colombia's IML: Medicina Legal y Ciencias Forenses, http://www.medicinalegal.gov.co/en/quienes-somos;jsessionid=2BB1C1 A65FC88B98BAA84D741EA0CC34, accessed May 31, 2017.

11. Jose Miguel Fortin Magana, MD, director of the Instituto de Medicina Legal, in discussion with the author, June 2014.

12. "El Salvador," Center for Justice & Accountability, http://cja.org/where -we-work/el-salvador/.

13. Pew Research Center, *Religion in Latin America: Widespread Change in a Historically Catholic Region* (Washington, DC: November 13, 2014), http://www.pewforum.org/2014/11/13/religion-in-latin-america/.

14. Paul Glader, "Christianity Is Growing Rapidly in El Salvador," *Washington Post*, April 8, 2015, https://www.washingtonpost.com/news/acts-of -faith/wp/2015/04/08/christianity-is-growing-rapidly-in-el-salvador-along -with-gang-violence-and-murder-rates/.

15. Xochitl Sandoval, MD, gynecologist, in discussion with the author, June 2014.

16. Alejandro Guidos, author interview. Guidos explained his association's opinion as a matter of scientific fact: "It's well known that a pregnant patient with Lupus is considered high risk, especially if she had preeclampsia in a prior pregnancy. So, taking all this into account, and finally because of the fetal abnormality, we published an opinion supporting the termination of pregnancy."

17. Christian Melendez, "La Sala de lo Constitucional recibió ayer el informe médico que había solicitado sobre la joven con lupus," *La Prensa Grafica*, May 8, 2013, http://www.laprensagrafica.com/iml—beatriz-puede -continuar-con-su-embarazo.

18. Fortin Magana, author interview.

19. Carmen Rodriguez, "Salud pone en duda resultados de Medicina Legal en caso de Beatriz," *La Pagina*, May 11, 2016, http://www.lapagina.com.sv /nacionales/81502/2013/05/11/Salud-pone-en-duda-resultados-de -Medicina-Legal-en-caso-de-Beatriz.

20. "El Presidente de El Salvador dice que la mujer que pidió aborto tiene el derecho a decidir," *Qué!*, May 13, 2013, http://www.que.es/ultimas -noticias/espana/201305132346-presidente-salvador-dice-mujer-pidio -efe.html.

21. Maria R. Sahuquillo, "Beatriz: Pido al presidente Funes que salve mi vida," *El Pais*, http://sociedad.elpais.com/sociedad/2013/05/30/actualidad /1369922985_768623.html; Karla Zabludovsky, "A Salvadoran at Risk Tests Abortion Law," *New York Times*, May 28, 2013, http://www .nytimes.com/2013/05/29/world/americas/pregnant-sick-and-pressing -salvadoran-abortion-law.html.

22. Adam Cassandra, "HLI President Calls on El Salvador Supreme Court to Protect Life," *Human Life International News*, May 16, 2013, http:// www.hli.org/2013/05/hli-president-calls-on-el-salvador-supreme-court -to-protect-life/.

23. "En defensa de nuestra soberania" (author's translation), elsalvador.com, May 8, 2013, http://www.elsalvador.com/opinion/editoriales/106401/en -defensa-de-nuestra-soberania/.

24. Amnesty International, *On the Brink of Death: Violence Against Women and the Abortion Ban in El Salvador* (2014), https://www.amnestyusa .org/sites/default/files/el_salvador_report_-_on_the_brink_of_death.pdf.

25. Nelson Rauda Zablah, "Magistrates Finalized 'Historic' Hearing to Resolve Abortion Petition," *La Prensa Grafica*, May 17, 2013, http://www .laprensagrafica.com/csj-da-un-plazo-maximo-de-15-dias-para-caso-beatriz.

26. Karla Aabludovsky and Gene Palumbo, "Salvadoran Court Denies Abortion to Ailing Woman," *New York Times*, May 29, 2013, http://mobile .nytimes.com/2013/05/30/world/americas/salvadoran-court-denies-abortion -to-ailing-woman.html?from=world.

27. Corte Suprema de Justicia, *Case BC*, Amparo 310–2013 at 10 (El Salvador).

28. Guillermo Ortiz, author interview.

29. Thomas Aquinas is credited with introducing the principle of double-effect in his discussion of the permissibility of self-defense in the *Summa Theologica* (II-II, Qu. 64, Art. 7). Killing one's assailant is justified, he argues, provided one does not intend to kill him. "Doctrine of Double Effect," *Stanford Encyclopedia of Philosophy*, revised September 23, 2014, http://plato.stanford.edu/entries/double-effect/, accessed May 31, 2017. See also "The Principle of Double Effect," Catholics United for Faith, November 1997, http://www.cuf.org/FileDownloads/doubleeffect.pdf, accessed May 31, 2017.

30. Jorge Ramirez, MD, chief assistant to the minister of health, in discussion with the author, June 2014.

31. Wayne R. LaFave, *Substantive Criminal Law* § 10.4, at 142, second ed. (St. Paul, MN: Thomson/West, 2003).

32. The fundamental right to life and enjoyment of health appear in the Salvadoran Constitution.

33. Corte Suprema de Justicia, *Case BC*, Amparo 310–2013, at 22 (El Salvador). "In the event of termination of the pregnancy after twenty weeks gestation, the aim is not to destroy the fetus, and that the medical team will take all necessary measures to ensure, as far as possible, extrauterine life."

34. LaFave, *Substantive Criminal Law*.

35. Corte Suprema de Justicia, *Case BC*, Amparo 310–2013, at 14 (El Salvador).

36. Karla Zabludovsky, "A Salvadoran at Risk Tests Abortion Law," *New York Times*, May 28, 2013, http://www.nytimes.com/2013/05/29/world /americas/pregnant-sick-and-pressing-salvadoran-abortion-law.html.

37. A zygote is the fertilized egg cell that results from the union of a female gamete (egg, or ovum) with a male gamete (sperm). In embryonic development, the zygote stage is brief and is followed by cleavage, when the single cell becomes subdivided into smaller cells. The zygote represents the first stage in the development of a genetically unique organism. *Encyclopaedia Britannica Online*, s.v. "zygote," https://www.britannica.com /science/zygote, accessed November 8, 2016.

38. Cass R. Sunstein, "On the Expressive Function of Law," *University of Pennsylvania Law Review* 144 (1996): 2021, 2031.

39. Ibid., 2045.

40. Ibid., 2047.

Chapter 2: Assessing the Impact of El Salvador's Abortion Ban

1. Penal Code of El Salvador 1998, Title 1, Crimes Related to Life, Chapter II, Crimes Related to Unborn Humans, Art. 133–139, http://www.oas.org /dil/esp/Codigo_Penal_El_Salvador.pdf.

2. Abortion being illegal, it is hard to get accurate information about the rates of abortion. The WHO bases its estimations on numbers of women hospitalized for abortion complications (where available) and information on the safety of abortion, as well as on findings from surveys of women and studies using an indirect abortion estimation methodology from countries where those were available. E-mail from Dr. Gilda Sedgh, Guttmacher Institute, to author, July 7, 2012 (on file with author). See article by Gilda Sedgh, https://www.guttmacher.org/sites/default/files/pdfs/pubs /journals/Sedgh-Lancet-2012–01.pdf.

3. A recent survey by the El Salvador Ministry of Health reported 19,290 between 2005 and 2008; other surveys put that number as the annual average. See Nina Strochlic, "On the Front Lines of El Salvador's Underground Abortion Economy," *Foreign Policy*, January 3, 2017, http://foreignpolicy.com/2017/01/03/on-the-front-lines-of-el-salvadors -underground-abortion-economy/?utm_source=Sailthru&utm_medium =email&utm_campaign=New+Campaign&utm_term=%2AEditors +Picks.

4. Vinod Mishra, Victor Gaigbe-Togbe, and Julia Ferre, *Abortion Policies and Reproductive Health Around the World* (New York: UN Department of Economic and Social Affairs, Population Division, 2014), http://www

.un.org/en/development/desa/population/publications/pdf/policy/Abortion
PoliciesReproductiveHealth.pdf, accessed January 24, 2017.

5. For an excellent history of abortion in pre-*Roe* America, see Leslie J.
   Reagan, *When Abortion Was a Crime: Women, Medicine, and Law in
   the United States, 1867–1973* (Berkeley: University of California Press,
   1996), http://ark.cdlib.org/ark:/13030/ft967nb5z5/. For an equally rich
   history of abortion doctors in pre-*Roe* America, see Carole E. Joffe, *Doctors of Conscience: The Struggle to Provide Abortion Before and After*
   Roe v. Wade (Boston: Beacon Press, 1995).

6. Tekoa King and Mary Brucker, "Pharmacology for Women's Health,"
   Journal of Midwifery & Women's Health 55 (2010): 394, doi:10.1016
   /j.jmwh.2010.05.005.

7. Mifeprex, *RxList*, http://www.rxlist.com/mifeprex-ru486-drug.htm,
   accessed June 2, 2017.

8. Beverly Winikoff and Wendy Sheldon, "Use of Medicines Changing the
   Face of Abortion," *International Perspectives on Sexual and Reproductive Health* 38, no. 3 (September 6, 2012), https://www.guttmacher.org
   /about/journals/ipsrh/2012/09/use-medicines-changing-face-abortion.
   The most widely available illegal abortion drug in Latin America is misoprostol (brand name is Cytotec), which is less effective than mifepristone
   (brand name is Mifeprex). Nguyen Thi Nhu Ngoc et al., "Comparing
   Two Early Medical Abortion Regimens: Mifepristone Plus Misoprostol
   vs. Misoprostol Alone," *Contraception* 83, no. 5 (2011): 410–17.

9. "Abortion Induction with Misoprostol Alone in Pregnancies Through 9
   Weeks' LMP," Gynuity, October 2013, http://gynuity.org/resources/read/
   misoprostol-for-early-abortion-en/, accessed August 30, 2017.

10. Anibal Faundes, "Use of Misoprostol in Obstetrics and Gynaecology,"
    *Latin American Federation of Obstetrics and Gynaecology Societies
    (FLASOG)* (Santa Cruz, Bolivia: Industrias Gráficas Sirena, April 2005),
    www.ibrarian.net/navon/paper/Translated_from_Spanish.pdf.

11. Donna Bowater, "Abortion in Brazil: a Matter of Life and Death," *Guardian*, February 1, 2015, https://www.theguardian.com/world/2015/feb/01
    /abortion-in-brazil-a-matter-of-life-and-death, accessed January 23, 2017.

12. See Bela Ganatra et al., "From Concept to Measurement: Operationalizing WHO's Definition of Unsafe Abortion," *Bulletin of the World Health
    Organization* 92, no. 155 (2014), doi: http://dx.doi.org/10.2471/BLT.14
    .136333 (discussing the definition of "unsafe abortion," in view of factors
    ranging from legal context to relative risks depending on access to trained
    health care providers and medical abortions).

13. According to the World Health Organization (WHO), Latin America and the Caribbean have the highest regional rate of unsafe abortions per capita in the world (31 per 1,000 women, aged fifteen to forty-four) and see an estimated 4.2 million unsafe abortions every year. See Department of Reproductive Health and Research, World Health Organization, *Unsafe Abortion*.

14. Alejandro Guidos, author interview. For a thorough discussion of these conflicting laws, see Heathe Luz McNaughton et al., "Patient Privacy and Conflicting Legal and Ethical Obligations in El Salvador: Reporting of Unlawful Abortions," *American Journal of Public Health* 96 (2006): 1932.

15. McNaughton et al., "Patient Privacy and Conflicting Legal and Ethical Obligations in El Salvador."

16. For a detailed history of the Hippocratic oath and its ongoing relevance, see Steven H. Miles, *The Hippocratic Oath and the Ethics of Medicine* (Oxford, UK: Oxford University Press, 2004).

17. Raphael Hulkower, "The History of the Hippocratic Oath: Outdated, Inauthentic, and Yet Still Relevant," *Einstein Journal of Biology & Medicine* 25/26 (March 2010): 43, https://www.einstein.yu.edu/uploadedFiles /EJBM/page41_page44.pdf.

18. El Salvador's Health Code 287 states that breaching [patient] confidentiality may result in oral reprimand, written reprimand, a fine, a five-year suspension or the loss of one's medical license. For US law requiring doctors to maintain confidentiality, see Health Insurance Portability and Accountability Act, Pub. L. No. 104–191 (1996), requiring health-care providers and health plans to have policies and procedures concerning use and disclosure of protected health information.

19. Breach of Professional Confidentiality Sect. 187.

20. See Republic of El Salvador, Criminal and Procedural Codes: Prison Law and Its Regulations, Editorial Jurídica Salvadoreña, 2001, Penal Code, Art 312.

21. See Republic of El Salvador, Health Code (with incorporated reforms), Criminal and Procedural Codes: Prison Law and Its Regulations, Editorial Jurídica Salvadoreña, 2001, Penal Code, Art 232. Doctors, pharmacists, nurses, and other health professionals must report unlawful criminal acts that they become aware of in the context of their professional relationship, *unless the information they acquire is protected under the terms of professional secrecy* (translation; italics added).

22. "Miscarriage," *Medline Plus*, reviewed by Cynthia D. White, MD, November 16, 2014, http://www.nlm.nih.gov/medlineplus/ency/article /001488.htm.

23. OBOS Pregnancy & Birth Contributors, "Miscarriage in the First Trimester," *Our Bodies, Our Selves*, April 9, 2014, http://www.ourbodiesourselves .org/health-info/miscarriage-in-the-first-trimester/.

24. As applied in homicide cases, the term *corpus delecti* has at least two component elements: the fact of death, and the criminal act or agency of another person as the cause thereof. "Homicide," *American Jurisprudence*, second ed., section 4.

25. Michelle Oberman, "Cristina's World: Lessons from El Salvador's Ban on Abortion," *Stanford Law and Policy Review* 24 (2013): 271, http:// digitalcommons.law.scu.edu/facpubs/794/; Tracy Wilkinson, "El Salvador Jails Women for Miscarriages and Stillbirths," *Los Angeles Times*, April 15, 2015, http://www.latimes.com/world/great-reads/la-fg-c1-el-salvador -women-20150415-story.html.

26. Another study confirmed the disproportionate reporting patterns by doctors treating patients at public hospitals, and suggested three possible explanations. First, public health institutions are more likely to treat indigent women and adolescents who often resort to unsafe, low-cost, and readily detectable abortion methods (e.g., insertion of foreign objects). Second, private-sector providers have an explicit profit motive to protect their individual patients' privacy and avoid legal inconveniences. Finally, because public health-care workers are subject to governmental oversight and are susceptible to shifting ministerial politics, they may be more fearful of reprisal if they do not comply with prevailing governmental ideology or policies. McNaughton et al., "Patient Privacy and Conflicting Legal and Ethical Obligations in El Salvador."

27. Dr. Bernadette Rosario (pseudonym), in discussion with the author, March 2014. Transcription and notes on file with author.

28. Ibid.

29. Samantha Artiga, "Disparities in Health and Health Care: Five Key Questions and Answers," Kaiser Family Foundation, August 12, 2016, http://kff.org/disparities-policy/issue-brief/disparities-in-health-and-health -care-five-key-questions-and-answers/.

30. Details of this case are drawn from the trial transcript, on file with author.

31. Ibid.

32. Dr. Marvin Diaz (pseudonym), in El Salvador, May 23, 2012, in discussion with the author. Transcription and notes on file with the author.

33. Jessica Alpert, "El Salvador Virtual Jewish History Tour," Jewish Virtual Library, http://www.jewishvirtuallibrary.org/el-salvador-virtual-jewish -history-tour#life, accessed May 31, 2017.

34. For a detailed history of Conversos in the Iberian Peninsula, see Norman Roth, *Conversos, Inquisition, and the Expulsion of the Jews from Spain* (Madison: University of Wisconsin Press, 2002); for an analysis of the effect of Conversos on Judaism and Christianity, see also Jose Faur, *In the Shadow of History: Jews and Conversos at the Dawn of Modernity* (Albany: State University of New York Press, 1992).

35. Dr. Marvin Diaz, in discussion with the author. In asserting that the defendant's mother pressed charges against her daughter, Dr. Diaz made the common mistake of confusing civil and criminal charges. Even if her mother had found the baby and called the police, as opposed to simply permitting them to enter and search her apartment, in criminal actions, it is the state that presses criminal charges.

36. Citizen's Coalition for the Decriminalization of Abortion on Grounds of Health, Ethics and Fetal Anomaly, El Salvador, "From Hospital to Jail: The Impact on Women of El Salvador's Total Criminalization of Abortion," *Reproductive Health Matters* 22, no. 44 (2014): 52–60, http://www.rhm-elsevier.com/article/S0968–8080(14)44797–9/fulltext.

37. Ibid. Of women arrested in abortion-related cases, 46.5 percent involved cases of advanced pregnancy and resulted in charges of simple or aggravated homicide.

38. Lauren Bohn, "El Salvador's 'Abortion Lawyer,'" *New York Times*, September 12, 2016, http://kristof.blogs.nytimes.com/2016/09/12/el-salvadors-abortion-lawyer/.

39. See Rebecca G. Stephenson and Linda J. O'Connor, *Obstetric and Gynecologic Care in Physical Therapy*, 2nd ed. (Thorofare, NJ: Slack, 2000).

40. Dr. Anne Drapkin Lyerly, associate professor of social medicine and obstetrics and gynecology, University of North Carolina, in telephone discussion with the author on August 2, 2012.

41. Ibid.

42. To get a sense of the scope of Agrupación Ciudadana activities, see its website, at https://agrupacionCiudadana.org/.

43. Morena Herrera, in discussion with the author, June 2014.

44. Citizens' Coalition for the Decriminalization of Abortion on Grounds of Health, Ethics and Fetal Anomaly, El Salvador, "From Hospital to Jail: The Impact on Women of El Salvador's Total Criminalization of Abortion."

45. The only women excluded were those whose cases were still on appeal, so their sentences were not yet final. Munoz, author interview.

46. Citizen's Coalition for the Decriminalization of Abortion on Grounds of Health, Ethics and Fetal Anomaly, El Salvador, "From Hospital to Jail: The Impact on Women of El Salvador's Total Criminalization of Abortion."

47. Liz Ford, "El Salvador Pardons Woman Jailed After Birth Complications Led to the Death of Child," *Guardian*, January 22, 2015, https://www.theguardian.com/global-development/2015/jan/22/el-salvador-pardons-woman-guadalupe-stillbirth-miscarriage-anti-abortion-laws.

48. Marisela Gloria Moran, "Seis mujeres libres de condenas por aborto," *Contrapunto*, September 20, 2016, http://www.contrapunto.com.sv/sociedad/ddhh/seis-mujeres-libres-de-condenas-por-aborto/1717.

49. "El Salvador: liberan a María Teresa Rivera, condenada a 40 años tras un aborto," *BBC World*, May 21, 2016, http://www.bbc.com/mundo/noticias/2016/05/160520_america_latina_salvador_liberan_maria_teresa_rivera_aborto_dgm.

50. Kathy Bougher, "Salvadoran Council Uses Poverty to Justify Keeping Las 17 in Prison," *Rewire News*, January 7, 2015, https://rewire.news/article/2015/01/07/salvadoran-council-uses-poverty-justify-keeping-las-17-prison/.

51. As translated in *The Portable Nietzsche*, ed. Walter Kaufmann (New York: Viking, 1954), 458.

52. Nina Strochlic, "On the Front Lines of El Salvador's Underground Abortion Economy," *Foreign Policy*, January 3, 2017, http://foreignpolicy.com/2017/01/03/on-the-front-lines-of-el-salvadors-underground-abortion-economy/.

53. Twenty-four percent of pregnancies occurred in women from fifteen to nineteen years old. The specific fertility rate of women from fifteen to nineteen years old was eighty-nine per one thousand. Seven of ten adolescents with sexual experience had a pregnancy, and 8.9 percent of this group had had a previous pregnancy. See Pan American Health Organization, "Health in the Americas: El Salvador," 2012, http://www.paho.org/salud-en-las-americas-2012/index.php?option=com_content&view=article&id=36%3Ael-salvador&catid=21%3Acountry-chapters&Itemid=145&lang=en.

54. Anastasia Moloney, "Rape, Abortion Ban Drives Pregnant Teens to Suicide in El Salvador," Reuters Health News, November 12, 2014, http://www.reuters.com/article/us-el-salvador-suicide-teens-idUSKCN0IW1Y I20141112.

55. Carlos Mayora, in discussion with the author, June 5, 2014.

56. This description is taken from the facts of "Manuela's case," which re-sulted in an appeal to the InterAmerican Court of Human Rights in Peru. She died in prison of cancer, which the prison doctors misdiagnosed and failed to treat. Charlotte Krol, "Are El Salvador's Extreme Anti-Abortion Laws Justified?," *Telegraph*, February 14, 2015, http://www.telegraph.co .uk/news/worldnews/centralamericaandthecaribbean/elsalvador/11412550 /Are-El-Salvadors-extreme-anti-abortion-laws-justified.html.

57. See Ferguson v. City of Charleston, 532 U.S. 67 (2001) (holding that a urine test conducted by the hospital in conjunction with law enforce-ment absent the patient's consent was a violation of the Fourth Amend-ment right to be free from unreasonable searches). The use of criminal sanctions in the public hospital setting disproportionately affects poor, minority women. See, generally, Dorothy E. Roberts, "Punishing Drug Addicts Who Have Babies: Women of Color, Equality, and the Right of Privacy," *Harvard Law Review* 104 (1991): 1419 (arguing that given the historical context of devaluing black mothers, prosecuting these women violates their equal protection and privacy rights regarding reproductive choices); Michele Goodwin, "Prosecuting the Womb," *George Washing-ton Law Review* 76 (2008): 1657, 1661 (describing how fetal drug laws are inconsistent, ineffective, and exempt reproductive practices by affluent groups that are equally risky to the unborn fetus).

Chapter 3: The Reddest State

1. See CNN Election Center 2008, http://www.cnn.com/ELECTION/2008 /results/individual/#mapPOK and Politico's 2012; Oklahoma Presidential Results, http://www.politico.com/2012-election/results/president/oklahoma/, last updated 11/19/12.

2. The AUL's Life List report card is compiled by looking at abortion-related measures by state. Four states earned AUL's 2017 All-Star Status for their implementation of legislation written by AUL. See AUL's 2017 Life List, http://www.aul.org/2017-life-list/.

3. Joshua Holland, "When Southern Baptists Were Pro-Choice," *Moyers & Co.*, July 2014, http://billmoyers.com/2014/07/17/when-southern-baptists -were-pro-choice/.

4. Edward Lee Pitts, "Successful State Strategies Saving Babies," *The World*, January 22, 2014, https://world.wng.org/2014/01/successful_state _strategies_saving_babies.

5. In 1910, Tony Lauinger's ancestor founded PennWell Corporation, a privately held company in the fifth generation of continuous family

ownership. The company today has over 600 employees across offices worldwide, with 343 at its headquarters in Tulsa. His family has endowed Georgetown University with a Library Fund to foster Catholic values through the acquisition of current and retrospective books, journals, periodicals, audio-visuals, computer archives, and other library materials supportive of the teachings of Magisterium on the issues of abortion, contraception, infanticide, homosexuality, assisted suicide, euthanasia, reproductive technologies, and other similar issues related to marriage, family, human sexuality, human life, and bioethics.

6. Kristen Luker, *Abortion and the Politics of Motherhood* (Berkeley: University of California Press, 1984).

7. Ibid., 128.

8. For details about the paper and its circulation, see http://www.baptist messenger.com.

9. Chris Doyle, "Rose Day at 25," *Baptist Messenger*, February 3, 2016, https://www.baptistmessenger.com/rose-day-at-25/.

10. Bernest Cain, in discussion with the author, July 2013.

11. Andrew Spiropoulus, in discussion with the author, June 2013.

12. See "Timeline: Oklahoma Abortion Legislation at a Glance," *Oklahoman*, November 4, 2013, http://newsok.com/article/3901078.

13. For a detailed overview of Trisomy 18, see http://www.trisomy18.org /what-is-trisomy-18/.

14. Mike Reynolds, in discussion with the author, June 2013.

15. Ryan Kiesel, in discussion with the author, June 2013.

16. "Tom Smith," in discussion with the author, June 2013.

17. Kiesel, author interview.

18. Kris Steele, in discussion with the author, June 2013.

Chapter 4: The Abortion-Minded Woman and the Law

1. Lawrence Finer, Lori Frohwirth, Lindsay Dauphinee, Susheela Singh, and Ann Moore, "Reasons US Women Have Abortions: Quantitative and Qualitative Perspectives," *Perspectives on Sexual and Reproductive Health* 37 no. 3 (2005): 110–18, http://www.guttmacher.org/pubs/psrh /full/3711005.pdf.

2. Adoption lurks in the corners of any serious conversation about abortion, and I recognized Chisko's tacit reference to it here. I don't discuss adoption in this book. In a world where abortion is legal, issues surrounding adoption—its regulation, its impact on all those involved—are only tangentially relevant. Were abortion to become illegal, relinquishing a

child for adoption would be the only legal way to avoid motherhood. In that world, adoption and its consequences would be at the heart of the conversation.

3. CBS/AP, "California to End Contentious 'Maximum Family Grant' Welfare Policy," *CBS SF Bay Area*, June 14, 2016, http://sanfrancisco .cbslocal.com/2016/06/14/california-end-contentious-maximum-family -grant-welfare/.

4. Jamelle Bouie, "The Most Discriminatory Law in the Land," *Slate*, June 17, 2014, http://www.slate.com/articles/news_and_politics/politics/2014 /06/the_maximum_family_grant_and_family_caps_a_racist_law_that _punishes_the.html.

5. Christine Jolls, Cass Sunstein, and Richard Thaler, "A Behavioral Approach to Law and Economics," *Stanford Law Review* 50 (1998): 471.

6. Dan Kahan, "Gentle Nudges v. Hard Shoves: Solving the Sticky Norms Problem," *University of Chicago Law Review* 67 (2000): 607.

7. Ibid., 626.

8. "Since the Hyde Amendment passed, only four states have voluntarily decided to use their funds to cover abortion. Another thirteen states are required to do so by court order, just as they would other forms of health care. Thirty-two states and the District of Columbia basically follow the Hyde Amendment as the congressman intended, with some small variations. One state, South Dakota, only pays for abortion when a woman's life is in danger, but not in cases of rape and incest—an apparent violation of federal law." See John Light, "Five Facts You Should Know About the Hyde Amendment," *Moyers & Company*, January 25, 2013, http:// billmoyers.com/content/five-facts-you-should-know-about-the-hyde -amendment/.

9. Tribune News Service, "Democrats Seek Repeal of Ban on Federal Funding of Abortion," *Chicago Tribune*, August 16, 2016, http://www .chicagotribune.com/news/nationworld/ct-abortion-federal-funding-ban -20160816-story.html.

10. Rebecca Blank, Christine George, and Rebecca London, "State Abortion Rates: The Impact of Policies, Providers, Politics, Demographics, and Economic Environment," NBER Working Paper No. 4853 (September 1994), http://www.nber.org/papers/w4853.

11. Post-*Roe* laws from "Timeline of Abortion Laws and Events," *Chicago Tribune*, http://www.chicagotribune.com/sns-abortion-timeline-story. html: "1976—Congress passes the Hyde Amendment, banning the use of Medicaid and other federal funds for abortions. The legislation is

upheld by the Supreme Court in 1980. 1979—A Missouri requirement that abortions after the first trimester be performed in hospitals is found unconstitutional. Another law mandating parental consent is upheld. 1981—In *Bellotti v. Baird*, Supreme Court rules that pregnant minors can petition court for permission to have an abortion without parental notification. 1983—The court strikes down an Akron ordinance that requires doctors to give abortion patients antiabortion literature, imposes a 24-hour waiting period, requires abortions after the first trimester to be performed in a hospital, requires parental consent and requires the aborted fetus to be disposed of in a human manner. 1989—In *Webster v. Reproductive Health Services*, a law in Washington State declaring that 'life begins at conception' and barring the use of public facilities for abortions is found unconstitutional. It marks the first time the Supreme Court does not explicitly reaffirm *Roe v. Wade*. 1992—In *Planned Parenthood v. Casey*, the court reaffirms *Roe*'s core holding that states may not ban abortions or interfere with a woman's decision to have an abortion. The court does uphold mandatory 24-hour waiting periods and parental-consent laws."

12. *Planned Parenthood of Southeastern Pennsylvania v. Casey*, 505 U.S. 833 (1992).

13. Ibid., 878.

14. Niraj Chokshi, "Abortion Doctors Would Lose Medical Licenses Under New Oklahoma Bill," *Washington Post*, April 23, 2016, https://www .washingtonpost.com/news/morning-mix/wp/2016/04/23/this-is-our-proper -function-oklahoma-advances-measure-to-revoke-licenses-of-doctors-that -perform-abortions/?utm_term=.40a7b2951ca9.

15. The Data Team, "The Abortion Rate in America Falls to Its Lowest Level since Roe v. Wade," *Economist*, January 18, 2017, http://www.economist .com/blogs/graphicdetail/2017/01/daily-chart-16.

16. See debates between Michael New, Marshall Medoff, and Christopher Dennis; Michael New, "Analyzing the Effect of Anti-Abortion U.S. State Legislation in the Post Casey Era," *State Politics and Policy Quarterly* 11 (2011): 28–47; Marshall Medoff and Christopher Dennis, "Another Critical Review of New's Reanalysis of the Impact of Antiabortion Legislation," *State Politics & Policy Quarterly* 14, no. 3 (2014): 207–27; Marshall Medoff, "Biased Abortion Counseling Laws and Abortion Demand," *Social Science Journal* 46 (2009): 632–43, https://www.infona .pl/resource/bwmeta1.element.elsevier-141efa1a-29c3–3dfa-83f9–73903 a82b670/tab/summary.

17. Sarah Roberts, David Turok, Elise Belusa, Sarah Combellick, and Ushma Upadhyay, "Utah's 72-Hour Waiting Period for Abortion: Experiences Among a Clinic-Based Sample of Women," *Perspectives on Sexual and Reproductive Health* 48 no. 4 (2016): 179–87, doi: 10.1363/48e8216.

18. Erica Hellerstein and Tara Culp-Ressler, "Pricing American Women out of Abortion, One Restriction at a Time," *ThinkProgress*, February 25, 2015, https://thinkprogress.org/pricing-american-women-out-of-abortion-one -restriction-at-a-time-c545c54f641f#.jzr6c8z64.

Chapter 5: America After *Roe*

1. Jeffrey Antevil, "Supreme Court Rules on Roe vs. Wade in 1973," *New York Daily News*, January 21, 2015, http://www.nydailynews.com/news /national/supreme-court-rules-roe-v-wade-1973-article-1.2068726.

2. Constitutional Amendment Process, National Archives, August 15, 2016, https://www.archives.gov/federal-register/constitution. For a time, the pro-life movement threw its support into campaigning for such a change in the form of the "Human Life Amendment." Although the Republican Party's platform continues to support the Human Life Amendment, the movement has had little traction in Congress. It has been decades since Congress even considered the issue. See the Human Life Action website for an account of activity on the Human Life Amendment, https://www .humanlifeaction.org/sites/default/files/HLAhghlts.pdf.

3. Pete Williams, "Abortion Could Be Outlawed in 33 States if *Roe v. Wade* Overturned: Report," *NBC News*, January 23, 2017, http://www.nbc news.com/news/us-news/report-abortion-could-be-outlawed-33-states-if -roe-v-n710816.

4. "Marina," in discussion with the author, 2009.

5. Seth F. Kreimer, *The Law of Choice and Choice of Law: Abortion, the Right to Travel, and Extraterritorial Regulation in American Federalism* (1992), Faculty Scholarship Paper, 1336fn9, http://scholarship.law.upenn .edu/faculty_scholarship/1336.

6. See Colleen Heild, "New Mexico Becomes Abortion Magnet," *Albuquerque Journal*, March 20, 2016, https://www.abqjournal.com/743253/more -women-coming-to-nm-for-abortions.html.

7. See Kate Sheppard, "Why This Woman Chose Abortion—at 29 Weeks," *Mother Jones*, July 25, 2011, http://www.motherjones.com/politics/2011 /07/late-term-abortion-29-weeks-dana-weinstein; also see Molly Hennessy-Fiske, "Crossing the 'Abortion Desert': Women Increasingly Travel out of Their States for the Procedure," *Los Angeles Times*, June 2, 2016, http://

www.latimes.com/nation/la-na-adv-abortion-traveler-20160530-snap
-story.html.

8. Compare with Mark D. Rosen, "Extraterritoriality and Political Hetero-
geneity in American Federalism," *University of Pennsylvania Law Review*
150 (2002): 855, http://scholarship.law.upenn.edu/penn_law_review
/vol150/iss3/2. Rosen argues that the law actually permits states to regulate their citizens' out-of-state activities for the purpose of ensuring the
efficacy of constitutional state policies, and that state's determinations
to regulate citizens' extraterritorial conduct is actually only a policy
decision.

9. Alan Guttmacher Institute, "Abortion in Africa: Incidence and Trends,"
May 2016, https://www.guttmacher.org/fact-sheet/facts-abortion-africa.

10. Andrew Downie, "Abortions in Brazil, Though Illegal, Are Common," *Time*,
June 2, 2010, http://content.time.com/time/world/article/0,8599,1993205,00
.html.

11. Texas Policy Evaluation Project, "Texas Women's Experiences Attempting
Self-Induced Abortion in the Face of Dwindling Options," November 17,
2015, https://liberalarts.utexas.edu/txpep/_files/pdf/TxPEP-Research-Brief
-WomensExperiences.pdf.

12. See Tess Barker, "The New Reality: Women Charged for Murder After
Self-Inducing Abortions," *Broadly*, January 24, 2016, https://broadly.vice
.com/en_us/article/the-new-reality-women-charged-for-murder-after-self
-inducing-abortions. Also see Teresa A. Saultes, Diane Devita, and
Jason D. Heiner, "The Back Alley Revisited: Sepsis after Attempted
Self-Induced Abortion," *Western Journal of Emergency Medicine* 10,
no. 4 (2009): 278–80.

13. Paltrow, "*Roe v. Wade* and the New Jane Crow," 17–21. A 2010 case from
Utah involved a woman charged with illegal abortion after hiring a man to
beat her up in order to bring on a miscarriage.

14. Matt Flegenheimer and Maggie Haberman, "Donald Trump, Abortion
Foe, Eyes 'Punishment' for Women, Then Recants," *New York Times*,
March 30, 2016, https://www.nytimes.com/2016/03/31/us/politics
/donald-trump-abortion.html; Tara Culp-Ressler, "Abortion Bans Are
Putting Women Behind Bars," *ThinkProgress*, March 9, 2015, https://
thinkprogress.org/abortion-bans-are-putting-women-behind-bars
-119b8fba1c70.

15. Rachel Lu, "Why Pro-Lifers Don't Support Punishing Women for Abortion," *Federalist*, April 5, 2016, http://thefederalist.com/2016/04/05/why
-pro-lifers-dont-support-punishing-women-for-abortion/.

16. Flegenheimer and Haberman, "Donald Trump, Abortion Foe." The day after Donald Trump's remarks, the *New York Times* reported on the outpouring of condemnation by pro-life advocates throughout the country. The article quoted Jeanne Mancini, the president of the March for Life Education Fund, as saying that efforts to punish individual women would be "completely out of touch with the pro-life movement" and "no pro-lifer would ever want to punish a woman who has chosen abortion"; Bruce Haynes, a Republican strategist, as stating he could not recall "'any credible corner of the movement' calling for criminal sanctions against women who sought abortions"; Governor John Kasich as declaring, "Of course women shouldn't be punished"; and Senator Ted Cruz as stating, with reference to a woman who has an abortion, "Of course we shouldn't be talking about punishment."

17. Clarke Forsythe, "Why the States Did Not Prosecute Women for Abortion Before *Roe v. Wade*," Americans United for Life, April 23, 2010, http://www.aul.org/2010/04/why-the-states-did-not-prosecute-women -for-abortion-before-roe-v-wade/.

18. Reagan, *When Abortion Was a Crime.*

19. Ibid., 114, 164.

20. Leslie Reagan, "Victim or Accomplice? Crime, Medical Malpractice, and the Construction of the Aborting Women in American Case Law, 1860s–1970," *Columbia Journal of Gender and Law* 10 (2001): 311, 332. "Although state laws provided for the prosecution of women who had abortions, late-nineteenth-century state prosecutors went after the abortionists. Juries were reluctant, however, to convict people accused of performing abortions. As a result, prosecutors increasingly focused on prosecuting abortionists whose practice had resulted in the death or severe injury of a woman patient. This emphasis did not change until around 1940 (332).

21. Samuel W. Buell, "Criminal Abortion Revisited," *New York University Law Review* 66 (1991): 1774, 1785.

22. Suzanne M. Alford, "Is Self-Abortion a Fundamental Right?," *Duke Law Journal* 52 (2003): 1011, 1022. New York, Laws of 1869, Chap. 631, entitled "An act relating to the procurement of abortions, and other like offences": Every woman who shall solicit of any person any medicine, drug, or substance or thing whatever, and shall take the same, or shall submit to any operation, or other means whatever, with intent thereby to procure a miscarriage, shall be deemed guilty of a misdemeanor, and shall, upon conviction, be punished by imprisonment in the county jail, not less than

three months nor more than one year, or by a fine not exceeding one thousand dollars, or by both such fine and imprisonment.

23. Louisiana, Mississippi, and North and South Dakota have laws in place that would automatically make abortion illegal if *Roe v. Wade* were to be overturned. Pete Williams, "Abortion Could Be Outlawed in 33 States if *Roe v. Wade* Overturned: Report," *NBC News*, January 23, 2017, http://www.nbcnews.com/news/us-news/report-abortion-could-be-outlawed-33 -states-if-roe-v-n710816.

24. See *Commonwealth v. Weible*, 45 Pa. Super. 207 (1911). Also see Crissman v. State, 93 Tex. Crim. 15, 245 S.W. 438 (Tex. Crim. App. 1922).

25. Carmen Hein de Campos, "Mass Prosecution for Abortion: Violation of the Reproductive Rights of Women in Mato Grosso do Sul, Brazil," AWID Women's Rights, 2016, https://www.oursplatform.org/resource /mass-prosecution-abortion-violation-reproductive-rights-women-mato -grosso-sul-brazil/.

26. "Abortion Prosecutions on the Rise in Many Mexican States," *Mexico Gulf Reporter*, August 6, 2012, http://mexicogulfreporter.blogspot.com /2012/08/abortion-prosecutions-on-rise-in-many.html.

27. Center for Reproductive Rights and the Agrupación Ciudadana, *Marginalized, Persecuted, and Imprisoned: The Effects of El Salvador's Total Criminalization of Abortion* (New York: 2014, https://www.reproductive rights.org/sites/crr.civicactions.net/files/documents/El-Salvador -CriminalizationOfAbortion-Report.pdf.

28. Hadley Arkes, "One Untrue Thing: Life after Roe," National Review Symposium, August 1, 2007, http://www.nationalreview.com/article /221742/one-untrue-thing-nro-symposium.

29. Lynn Paltrow and Jeanne Flavin, "Arrests of and Forced Interventions on Pregnant Women in the United States, 1973–2005: Implications for Women's Legal Status and Public Health," *Journal of Health Politics, Policy and Law* 38, no. 2 (2013): 299–343, http://jhppl.dukejournals.org /content/38/2/299.refs.

30. L. M. Paltrow, "*Roe v. Wade* and the New Jane Crow: Reproductive Rights in the Age of Mass Incarceration," *American Journal of Public Health* 103, no. 1 (2013): 17–21, doi:10.2105/AJPH.2012.301104.

31. Ibid.

32. Five states have laws explicitly criminalizing self-abortion. The other states use alternative theories to bring charges against women. For example, thirty-nine states make it illegal for anyone other than a medical provider to perform the procedure. Although some states explicitly exempt

women from prosecution under state abortion laws, others are silent. As such, whether under self-abortion statutes or under laws restricting abortion to medical providers, women can be and have been charged with illegal abortion.

33. Sally Koh, "Indiana's Other Outrageous Law," *CNN*, March 31, 2015, http://www.cnn.com/2015/03/31/opinions/kohn-indiana-anti-abortion-law/. Prosecutors claimed that Patel ordered abortion-inducing drugs online and tried to terminate her pregnancy, but a toxicology report failed to find evidence of any drugs in her system. She received a thirty-year-sentence on the felony neglect charge, ten of which were suspended. A six-year sentence for feticide was to be served concurrently. Emily Bazelon, "Purvi Patel Could Be Just the Beginning," *New York Times*, April 1, 2015, https://www.nytimes.com/2015/04/01/magazine/purvi-patel-could-be-just-the-beginning.html.

34. Calvin Freiburger, "Death, Lies, And Relativism in the Purvi Patel Feticide Conviction," *Live Action News*, April 3, 2015, http://liveactionnews.org/death-lies-relativism-purvi-patel-feticide-conviction/.

35. Ibid.

36. Ibid. "The 33-year-old Patel is 'an educated woman of considerable means,' and 'if [she] wished to terminate [her] pregnancy safely and legally, [she] could have done so.' Instead, she repeatedly rejected a friend's insistence that she see a doctor, simply because she didn't want her traditional Hindu parents to know she'd had sex with a married co-worker. She didn't get a doctor to do it, but killed her son herself. Her son who was viable." See also, Texas Right to Life staff, "What Really Happened to Purvi Patel's Baby Boy?," *Texas Right to Life News*, April 9, 2015, https://www.texasrighttolife.com/what-really-happened-to-purvi-patel-s-baby-boy/. "Now, the liberal media's spin on the story goes something like this: Purvi Patel suffered a miscarriage and was thrown in jail for something completely out of her control because Pro-Life feticide laws are *that* outrageous. Cue the evidence-spinning and abortion lobby pandemonium."

37. Associated Press, "Indiana Court Tosses Purvi Patel's 2015 Feticide Conviction," *NBC News*, July 22, 2016, http://www.nbcnews.com/news/asian-america/indiana-court-tosses-purvi-patel-s-2015-feticide-conviction-n615026.

38. Paltrow and Flavin, "Arrests of and Forced Interventions on Pregnant Women," 309.

39. Ibid., 309–10.

40. Ibid., 311.
41. Ibid., 311.
42. Tara Culp-Ressler, "This Woman Says She Had a Miscarriage. Now She Could Face 70 Years in Prison," *ThinkProgress*, March 30, 2015, https://thinkprogress.org/this-woman-says-she-had-a-miscarriage-now-she-could-face-70-years-in-prison-c62d73ba32e1. "According to a study conducted by NAPW reviewing the prosecutions of women in relation to their pregnancies between 1973 and 2005, low-income women and women of color are disproportionately arrested under feticide laws. Black women are significantly more likely to be reported to authorities by hospital staff under suspicion that they harmed their unborn children."
43. "Twelve Facts About the Abortion Ban in El Salvador," *Amnesty International Report*, September 25, 2014, https://www.amnesty.org/en/latest/news/2014/09/twelve-facts-about-abortion-ban-el-salvador/. El Salvador has the highest rate of teenage pregnancy in Latin America. According to the National Family Health Survey, more than one-fifth (23 percent) of all teenagers aged between fifteen and nineteen in El Salvador have been pregnant at least once. Nearly half of them were under eighteen and didn't intend to get pregnant.
44. Ibid. Suicide accounts for 57 percent of the deaths of pregnant females aged ten to nineteen in El Salvador, though it is likely many more cases have gone unreported.
45. Moloney, "Rape, Abortion Ban Drives Pregnant Teens to Suicide."
46. Sunstein, "On the Expressive Function of Law," 2021, 2031.

Conclusion: Parting Thoughts on Leaving Behind the Abortion War

1. George Orwell. "Looking Back on the Spanish War" (1943), reprinted in *A Collection of Essays* (New York: Harcourt, 1946), 193–94.

INDEX

abortion: ban on, in Chile (*see* Chile); ban on, in El Salvador (*see* El Salvador); debate on (*see* abortion debate); doctrine of double-effect and, 32, 149*n*29; fetal status as a separate human being and, 31; impact of bans on the abortion rate, 44, 63; impact of bans on the birth rate, 63–64; laws against (*see* abortion laws); legal battles in the 1990s, 4; misinformation about oral contraceptives, 83–84; moral boundaries expressed in abortion bans, 41; potential medical consequences of a surgical abortion, 44–45; public choice theory and opposition to, 92–93; rates of maternal mortality from, 8, 124, 146n8; reasons women choose, 1–2; relevance of abortion's legal status for vulnerable women, 4–5, 6–7, 11; state-mandated misinformation about, 145–46n5; symbolic laws and, 41–42, 141–42; in the US (*see* United States); women's consideration of the laws concerning (*see* abortion-minded women)
Abortion and the Politics of Motherhood (Luker), 71
abortion debate: common ground in, 141–42; emotions embedded on both sides of, 139–40; fetal status as a separate human being and, 31; fundamental rights for women and, 36; moral boundaries expressed in

abortion bans, 3, 41, 81, 83–84, 85; pro-life versus antiabortion, 103; symbolic importance of abortion laws, 41–42, 141
abortion drugs, 8, 45–46, 124, 125, 151n8
abortion laws: anti-abortion activists' vision for, 79; in Chile (*see* Chile); constitutionality of states' anti-abortion laws, 114, 120, 122, 158–59*n*11; correlation between abortion rates and, 44, 114–15; doctors' compliance with (*see* doctors and abortion detection); in El Salvador (*see* El Salvador); impact on poor women, 66, 75, 78–79, 113, 115–16, 117, 123, 156*n*57; intent of, 113, 116–17; moral justification derived from, 137; questioning if the laws matter, 12; against self-abortion, 128, 131, 162–63*nn*22–23, 163*n*32; symbolic importance of, 41–42, 141; in the US (*see* United States)
abortion-minded women: constitutionality of states' anti-abortion laws, 114, 120, 122, 158–59*n*11; cost factor of motherhood, 97–98, 106, 107, 109–11; crisis pregnancy centers and, 99 (*see also* Birth Choice); de facto fertility policy in the US, 109–11; family caps on welfare recipients, 110–11; impact of abortion laws on poor women, 66, 75, 78–79, 113, 115–16, 117, 123, 156*n*57; impact of public policy

PRAISE FOR *Dream College*

"Dr. Ezeze has written one of the most comprehensive college guides I have read in my 30+ years as a college admissions professional. Using the wisdom and knowledge acquired over his impressive career, he has taken what can be a daunting process and broken it down into manageable and achievable pieces. This is a must-read not only for the parents of high school students but for those parents with children in middle school as well. *Dream College* is a valuable addition to the home reference library."

Sharon M. Alston, Executive Director for Enrollment Management,
American University

"*Dream College* is one of the most comprehensive guides to the college admissions process presently on the market. It goes so much further than other guides because Dr. Ezeze shares information about admission practices that he has gained by having personal and up-front conversations with admissions professionals at colleges across the country. The information in this book will be invaluable to students and parents as they begin the quest to not just college but to their 'Dream College.'"

Norma Paige, Guidance Counselor, Scotch Plains Fanwood High School

"*Dream College* is unmatched in the quality of its information, scope, and timeliness. I have known Dr. Ezeze for about two decades, and he really knows the college admissions business through and through—from research to application to making college dreams come true. This is a comprehensive and useful resource for all readers. This is a great book!"

Audrey T. Hill, Transfer Counselor/Professor,
Montgomery College, Maryland

"As a college student, I lament that I could not have Dr. Ezeze's book in my hands a few years ago. The emphasis on early planning would have eliminated misguided decisions. The chapters on college athletics and financial aid would have been indispensable during my college selection process. Fortunately, Dr. Ezeze also provides valuable information about what to expect while in college, which has been invaluable."

Erik Torenberg, University of Michigan, Class of 2012

"As a student I see *Dream College* as offering many routes to a single destination. Its comprehensive nature makes this book a must-read for high school students, college students, parents, and even counselors alike."

Nnamdi Obodo, University of Virginia, Class of 2012

Dream COLLEGE

How to Help
Your Child Get
into the
Top Schools

Kpakpundu Ezeze, Ed.D.

Dream College: How to Help Your Child Get into the Top Schools

By Kpakpundu Ezeze

Published by SuperCollege, LLC
3286 Oak Court
Belmont, CA 94002
www.supercollege.com

Credits: Cover: Kris Taft Miller
Layout: The Roberts Group, www.editorialservice.com

Trademarks: All brand names, product names and services used in this book are trademarks, registered trademarks, or tradenames of their respective holders. Super-College is not associated with any college, university, product, or vendor.

Disclaimers: The author and publisher have used their best efforts in preparing this book. It is sold with the understanding that the author and publisher are not rendering legal or other professional advice. The author and publisher cannot be held responsible for any loss incurred as a result of specific decisions made by the reader. The author and publisher make no representations or warranties with respect to the accuracy or completeness of the contents of the book and specifically disclaim any implied warranties or merchantability or fitness for a particular purpose. The accuracy and completeness of the information provided herein and the opinions stated herein are not guaranteed or warranted to produce any particular results. The author and publisher specifically disclaim any responsibility for any liability, loss or risk, personal or otherwise, which is incurred as a consequence, directly or indirectly, from the use and application of any of the contents of this book.

ISBN13: 9781932662481

Manufactured in the United States of America

10 9 8 7 6 5 4 3 2 1

Cataloging-in-Publication Data

Library of Congress Cataloging-in-Publication Data

Ezeze, Kpakpundu.
  Dream college : how to help your child get into the top schools / Kpakpundu Ezeze.
    p. cm.
  ISBN 978-1-932662-48-1 (alk. paper)
  1. Universities and colleges--United States--Admission. 2. College choice--United States. I. Title.
  LB2351.2.E94 2010
  378.1'610973--dc22
                        2010028027

DEDICATION

I dedicate this book to my sister Michelle Rose Hairston.

ACKNOWLEDGEMENTS

A CONFLUENCE OF PROFESSIONAL EXPERIENCES laid this project's foundation. The origins of this guide span three decades of service in secondary and higher education. In various capacities, I had the honor of learning from caring mentors at Lexington, Wellesley, and Washington-Lee High Schools, respectively. I expanded my experience as an educator in my service as an administrator with the Upward Bound Programs at Boston College, Worcester State College, and Howard University. At Wellesley College I held the position of Head of House-Academic Advisor, and at the University of Pennsylvania I was an Assistant Dean and a Residential Dean in the College of Arts and Sciences; in these two positions I was fortunate to interface with undergraduates on a daily basis. In many ways how I think about education in general, and urban secondary education in particular, has been informed by those many discussions among students, faculty, and administrators. In 1989, I launched my own educational consulting firm, Future Quest, Inc., offering guidance to primarily first-generation college-bound youth, who otherwise could not afford to pay for private consulting services but had the greatest need. The company has been in existence for twenty years and has assisted thousands of students with the educational planning and college placement process. Of particular interest has not simply been getting admitted to one's top-choice college, but also the importance of thriving academically and socially once in college and graduating on time. This book tries to catalog the insights I acquired through working with students and education industry professionals in the aim to benefit future generations of college-bound youth and their families.

A number of individuals have imparted invaluable advice and support during the course of this project. For their genuine friendship, fellowship, and direction on many aspects of this assignment, I am especially grateful to Sharon M. Alston, Donna Atkinson, Kevin Carlsten, Carol Cromer, DD Eisenberg, Audrey T. Hill, Andrea Hines, Steve Hines, Vera Faulkner, Michael Ferby, Bernadine Francis, Joyce Hemmons, Rebecca Lamb, Marie Lindsay, Norma Paige, Joe Steele, Glenn Tunstull and Reggie Van Lee. The insight of colleagues and valuable perspective of former clients speak in the interview contributions that frame each chapter. To my copy editor, Stephanie Harzewski, I extend special thanks for her exacting eye, advice, and encouragement.

I am also indebted to countless former students, without whom this project could not have been possible. I wish to thank all of my students for their energy and vitality. That youthful spirit has enabled me to feel young, when the reality is I am in the winter of my life. Among those many students from whom I have learned and hopefully I have inspired, some stand out among the many—Tanique Adell, Chancellor Agard, Tyler Brooks, Christian Calloway, Derric Daniels, Jasmine Drake, Helena Edwards, Nicole Falls, Neferteneken Francis, Sarah Greenberg, Christina Harastock, Patrick Jefferson, Aaron Jenkins, Constance Lindsay, Nnamdi Obodo, Allen Pinkney, Justin Silvey, Jasmine Smith, Erik Torenberg, Frank White, Jr., and Joshua Williams.

To my sister, Patricia Ann Holland, who passed in 1975, I give a special acknowledgment for her unconditional love and support throughout our childhood and young adult years. In many ways, her untimely death inspired me to make contributions to the field of education; in certain positions I aimed to contribute to the lives of those who were less fortunate, a trait which she admired most in my character. Through my work in general with young people, and this project in particular, her love of life and the values for which she stood live on bittersweetly. Over the decades, students' development and hope for the future have continuously affirmed life in the face of challenges. I would be honored if she finds this energy, which was very much a part of her own character, re-incarnated here.

And finally I want to thank any individuals whose names I have unintentionally omitted; I can only hope that they see their insights reflected through the course of this book.

PREFACE

MY FIRST INTRODUCTION TO DR. Ezeze was in 1998 when a mutual friend suggested I contact him about mentoring my budding career as an independent counselor.

I drove to DC to observe his weekly Tuesday evening vigil at the M.L. King Library where he volunteered to meet students who needed college advising, but who couldn't afford to pay for it. It was encouraging to witness these kids coming long after nightfall to wait their turn for a follow-up visit with Ezeze. Students would leave with a to-do list to accomplish before the next meeting and a noticeable sense of empowerment. There is something recognizably confident in the stride of a teenager who can envision the opportunities before them and carry out a plan with purpose to meet them. Ezeze helps students approach this pivotal time in their lives by presenting the tools they need to make good decisions and advises them within the framework of their accomplishments, their aspirations, and their potential. I have learned from him over the years that this is the ideal role a counselor plays for the college-bound student—to inform and guide, but also to encourage ownership on the part of the student. This piece is critical to their development, and the appropriate tone to set as they move into early adulthood.

For the parents who read this book, one that has been writing itself in Dr. Ezeze's experience these last 25 years, I can attest to the grace and skill Ezeze brings to his interaction with students and their families. Telling someone what they need to do is very different from assisting them in understanding their options and creating a plan of action. Through each stage of the selection process, long before applications are due, there is much to understand about how admissions will evaluate their applicants, and how students can fully leverage their experience in high school as they anticipate applying to college. And then, of course, there is the shopping to do for the right campus and decisions to be made in the larger context of academic and financial considerations at least. Completing applications can seem like the least complex step in the larger picture. The trick is to help the student move through these stages efficiently, setting goals and managing the path to meeting them, all while nurturing the student to be in charge of their future. The added benefit is better control of anxiety the student and their family feel in this exciting, but daunting step in a developing student's life. Dr. Ezeze doesn't promise manageable stress levels, but I know he delivers his expertise with the kind of composure that generates confidence, and this is worth so much in the tension-laden process we call college planning. Dr. Ezeze offers a smooth path toward the greatest rite of passage in a young person's life—the transition to college.

Parents, while you may get caught up in the worry over where your child might "get in," how to pay for it, or even how you might feel when your student leaves home, remember how important this stage is in your son or daughter's life. They'll go to college and get the education they need because you will work that out together. More importantly, they'll learn to become responsible adults while they're away. What better way to get them and yourself started than to make it possible for your student to begin this evolution by creating an atmosphere in which they are at the center of the process—front and center.

—Rebecca M. Lamb
Independent College Advisor

CONTENTS

INTRODUCTION

THE PATH TO AND THROUGH college is exciting, enriching, taxing and nerve-racking, but one of the greatest experiences of your teen's life! There are so many materials to prepare, so many options to consider, and so many new challenges to confront, yet, the challenges and the rewards do not end upon entering college. While getting your teen into college is accomplishing one milestone, surely, getting them through college is achieving another.

The importance of a college education to one's career opportunities need not require a long defense, yet, there are a number of alarming trends that are making many college hopefuls and their parents a bit anxious. For instance, gaining admissions into the college of one's choice continues to be increasingly competitive. Unfortunately, many high school counselors lack the time and resources to adequately address the needs of their ever-growing and complex constituency. In addition, the price tag of today's higher education continues to escalate. Even if one clears the first few hurdles of planning for, applying to and getting into college, has your teen chosen a place where they will be happy and productive?

As a former guidance counselor with fifteen years' experience and as an Independent College Advisor with twenty years' experience, I continue to recognize these trends and address them in *Dream College: How to Help Your Child Get into the Top Schools* in a clear and concise format for the parent who wants to be informed early. Because of the nature, intensity, and long duration of assisting teens plan for, apply to, and get through college, parents cannot simply be front and center, they have to stay front and center. By teaching parents what they need to know and do to get their teen into and through college, the guide aims to overcome the "guidance gap," the "financial fright," and the "competitive crunch." Furthermore, by knowing how to confront the key elements of educational planning and an effective college search, parents will be more equipped to help their teen choose a college where they are most likely to thrive. Few parents can afford to hire a private consultant to help them with the process, but most parents can afford to buy a book, or certainly access their public library. The point is, my experiences as a College Advisor have repeatedly proven that proper and timely guidance can give your teen a significant competitive advantage.

Dream College is divided into eight chapters plus appendices. Generally the chapters address three principal areas: planning for college throughout the high school years, applying for college in the senior year, and getting through the college years. While much of the information contained here addresses all students, independent of race, gender, or class, there are some specific chapters that speak to specific categories, for example, athletes, first-generation college bound, students with disabilities, and students of color. Each chapter has its own glossary and bibliography and opens and closes with a passage from either a former student or a parent. Through these retrospective voices the reader can learn from those who have gone before them and hopefully be able to relate to some of the experiences that have been revealed. If not, that is ok too, since everyone has a unique story. What is for everyone, of course, is understanding the how to and when of the college admissions process.

As a guide *Dream College* is designed to assist you and your teen through the many stages from planning for, to graduating from, college. While you might find it interesting to read from cover to cover, it can also work as a reference book; directing you to a particular section that addresses a specific question you have up front. In short, at the various stages, the guide is designed to supply you and your family with the information you need in a timely fashion.

Most important of all, however, is the continual re-evaluation of expectations. Planning for and experiencing a college education can generate an equally various set of pleasures, rewards, even frustrations. What is presented in *Dream College* is a comprehensive road map of those considerations that inform college planning and a student's choice of an institution, along with their staying power once that choice has been made. You as the parent play a key role at all stages, but as with most experiences, there must be clarity of purpose. What do you expect your teen to gain from the process? How engaged do you need to be in assisting him/her? What do you hope them to gain from their undergraduate education? What kind of individual do you want them to become? This will not be a static process, rather one that is constantly changing and evolving. I invite you to enjoy both the read and the process of helping your teen plan for, apply to, and soar.

CALENDAR
of College and Financial Aid Events

SEPTEMBER

Grade 9
- ❏ Outline high school courses to take for the next 4 years
- ❏ Sign up for extracurricular activities

Grade 10
- ❏ Sign up for extracurricular activities
- ❏ Sign up for the PSAT with Counselor (optional)

Grade 11
- ❏ Sign up for extracurricular activities
- ❏ Sign up for the PSAT
- ❏ Parents: See guidance counselor and make sure your child is in at least five academic classes and that they are on schedule for graduation

Grade 12
- ❏ Pre-register for Achievement Tests, SAT, or TOEFL
- ❏ Register for the SAT and ACT
- ❏ Go to Collegeboard.com and access the CSS Profile—you need to determine if any of the schools to which you are applying require that you complete that form
- ❏ Know each college's financial aid deadline
- ❏ Speak to teachers and counselors about recommendations. Give teachers the Teacher Evaluation Form. Give Counselor the Counselor Evaluation Form. Sometimes the form is called High School Evaluation Form, or Secondary School Report Form.
- ❏ Athletes: File your NCAA registration form

OCTOBER

Grade 10
- ❏ Take the PSAT (optional)

Grade 11
- ❏ Take the PSAT
- ❏ Attend College Fairs
- ❏ Apply for Discovery Card Scholarship (optional)

CALENDAR
of College and Financial Aid Events

Grade 12
- ❏ Start completing financial aid forms for private aid
- ❏ Start composing college essays
- ❏ Complete application and essay for Early Decision or Early Action

NOVEMBER

Grade 12
- ❏ Take 1 or 2 SAT Subject Tests. If you have already taken at least 3 SAT Subject Tests you may not need to take any more.
- ❏ Take SAT or ELPT/TOEFL
- ❏ Early Decision and Early Action applications due
- ❏ Continue filling out college applications
- ❏ Research Scholarships

DECEMBER

Grade 9
- ❏ Research Summer Enrichment Programs and/or jobs

Grade 10
- ❏ Research Summer Enrichment Programs and/or jobs

Grade 11
- ❏ Research Summer Enrichment Programs and/or jobs

Grade 12
- ❏ Take SAT and SAT Subject Tests
- ❏ Take ACT if applicable
- ❏ Check with teachers and counselors to make sure their recommendations are complete—they may need to be sent out by January 1
- ❏ Finish completing college applications

JANUARY

Grade 9
- ❏ Start applying for Summer Enrichment Programs and/or jobs

Grade 10
- ❏ Start applying for Summer Enrichment Programs and/or jobs

Grade 11
- ❏ Start applying for Summer Enrichment Programs and/or jobs

CALENDAR
of College and Financial Aid Events

Grade 12
- ❏ Mail out all college applications by January 1 if you have not previously done so
- ❏ Fill out FAFSA and CSS Profile and mail before February
- ❏ Parents: File taxes as soon as you can after you receive your W2 form(s)

FEBRUARY

Grade 11
- ❏ Start thinking about the college application process. Meet with Counselor to review academic and non-academic achievements and discuss financial aid

Grade 12
- ❏ Financial aid applications should be mailed off by February 15—you can still though research and apply to private scholarships

MARCH

Grade 9
- ❏ Schedule classes for following year

Grade 10
- ❏ Research SAT prep programs (optional)
- ❏ Schedule classes for following year

Grade 11
- ❏ Pre-register for the SAT, ACT, and TOEFL
- ❏ Develop list of colleges; check schools' SAT Subject Test requirements
- ❏ Schedule classes for following year

Grade 12
- ❏ Review your Student Aid Report (SAR)
- ❏ If you need to make changes on your FAFSA this is the time to do so via the SAR—you can do so electronically or via email

APRIL

Grade 9
- ❏ Register for the SAT if applicable

Grade 10
- ❏ Register for the SAT Subject Tests if applicable

CALENDAR
of College and Financial Aid Events

Grade 11
- ❏ Pre-register for the SAT Subject Tests; take 2 or 3; check college SAT Subject Test requirements
- ❏ Take the ACT
- ❏ Review graduation requirements

Grade 12
- ❏ You will be hearing from most colleges this month
- ❏ Send thank-you notes to people who wrote you recommendations
- ❏ Review financial aid packages
- ❏ May want to visit one or two colleges before making your final decision

MAY

Grade 9
- ❏ Pre-register for summer school or new/make-up work

Grade 10
- ❏ Pre-register for summer school or new/make-up work

Grade 11
- ❏ Take the SAT or ELPT
- ❏ Research scholarships

Grade 12
- ❏ Notify school of your choice by May 1

JUNE

Grade 9
- ❏ Start building your recommendations file; ask teachers for recommendations in the classes which you excelled
- ❏ Research scholarships
- ❏ Take SAT Subject Tests if applicable

Grade 10
- ❏ Take SAT Subject Tests
- ❏ Ask for recommendations
- ❏ Research scholarships

CALENDAR
of College and Financial Aid Events

Grade 11
- ❏ Take SAT Subject Tests
- ❏ Ask for recommendations
- ❏ College search
- ❏ Request applications from colleges

Grade 12
- ❏ Meeting with Counselor to discuss college retention issues

JULY/AUGUST

Grade 9
- ❏ Visit colleges: you don't need to have a formal visit

Grade 10
- ❏ Visit colleges: you don't need to have a formal visit

Grade 11
- ❏ College visits: call to schedule a formal visit
- ❏ Apply for private scholarships

Grade 12
- ❏ May need to register for Fall classes
- ❏ Attend Freshman Orientation

WHAT TO DO EARLY IN HIGH SCHOOL TO PREPARE FOR COLLEGE

It was not only important for me to say that education was important, I had to show them that it was important by my actions. Waiting until they were teens would be too late. I did not have much faith in the DC public schools, though in retrospect, I would have tried to get my daughters in private schools by applying for financial aid. However, I was able to come up with educational and cultural programs that augmented their public schooling. In elementary school they were introduced to classical music. I enrolled them in the DC Youth Orchestra where they learned how to play a musical instrument. Sometimes I would take them to museums and arboretums and they would keep a journal about their experiences. Each summer they were required to read several books and also took tennis lessons. A friend introduced me to a program called the SRA Reading Kit, which I used to help improve their reading skills. It had modules for other academic areas like math, writing, science, and history. These modules were grouped according to grade level, and I always kept my girls two grade levels ahead. By the time they took the SAT in eighth grade for a gifted and talented program at John Hopkins University, they had already been exposed to algebra and geometry.

During summer recess, they had to work on academics for four hours, and then afterwards, they were allowed to play for four hours. When it came to the school year, they knew I had a job and they had a job, and their job was to go to school and come home and study; my job was to go to work and come home and facilitate their studies. If the school did not give them enough homework, which was the case in earlier years, then they had to complete the homework I would assign. They were allowed to watch 30 minutes of TV a night, once they completed their homework, but it had to be age appropriate. When attending parent-teacher conferences, I would always take them along, because I wanted to make sure everyone was at the table and that we were all hearing the same message, whatever the message. In that way, there would be no miscommunication. I knew all of the teachers for all of my four daughters, and I knew how to reach them. For many years, I would sit at the dining room table with them at night until they completed their homework. One year, during my third child's senior year, I recall falling asleep at the table. Around 1 a.m. my daughters awoke me and said, "Ma, Go to sleep, we got this," and they had.

—**Bernadine Francis**
Washington, DC

EDUCATIONAL PLANNING

Your teen's experience over the next four years in high school will be filled with many rewards, both academically and socially. This chapter aims to equip you with the information as to how to position your teen to take full advantage of all the opportunities that await them. As planning early is crucial to your child's advantage, what follows is an overview of the seven areas that define educational planning. Each of the seven key planning areas—**courses, tests, extracurricular activities, community service, summer enrichment, recommendations, and early financial aid research**—are important to the college placement process.

COURSES

The courses your teen will take in high school and the grades he or she will receive in those courses are the most important and influential part of their college application. That having been said, your child should take on challenges, when the opportunity presents itself, and work hard and intelligently to get the best grades possible.

Below you will find two outlines for four-year high school courses of study. One is for the regular college-bound student and the second is for the accelerated college-bound student:

REGULAR COLLEGE BOUND

Grade Nine	Grade Ten
English I	English II
Algebra I	Geometry
World History	World Geography
Physical Science	Biology
Foreign Language I	Foreign Language II
Elective	Elective
Elective	Elective

Grade Eleven
English III
Algebra II/Trig.
US History
Chemistry
Foreign Language III
Elective
Elective

Grade Twelve
English IV
Pre-Calculus
US Government
Physics
Foreign Language IV
Elective
Elective

ACCELERATED COLLEGE BOUND

Grade Nine
Honors English I
Geometry
Biology
World History
Foreign Language II
Elective
Elective

Grade Ten
Honors English II
Algebra II Trig.
Chemistry
AP European History
Foreign Language III
Elective
Elective

Grade Eleven
AP English III
Pre-Calculus
Honors Physics
AP US History
AP Foreign Language
Elective
Elective

Grade Twelve
AP English IV
AP Calculus
AP Biology
AP US Government
AP Foreign Language
Elective
Elective

You already understand, but it is worth repeating, that in addition to the quality of your child's academic program, the grades that they receive in their courses are the most important part of their academic record when applying to college. Please note that colleges are most interested in the end-of-year grades, i.e. your child's final grades. This only applies to grades from sophomore through junior year. (See Appendix F for a sample high school transcript). In the senior year, the school counselor will also submit the first and second quarter grades. These are the grades, then, that will make up most of what is called the academic profile. The other piece of information that your child will need to complete that profile is the College Entrance Exam.

COLLEGE ENTRANCE EXAMS

Throughout your teen's high school career you will hear a great deal of discussion about standardized tests. Indeed, these tests are an important part of their college application, but the degree of their importance varies from school to school. In fact, there are some very competitive colleges that do not require entrance tests, while others make them optional. However, since most colleges still require some testing, your teen has to prepare for the exams.

Types of College Entrance Exams

A College Entrance Exam is a standardized test that most colleges require students to submit as part of their application. There are two standard tests with which you need to be familiar—the SAT and the ACT.

The **SAT** is a test of three and a half hours that measures aptitude in three areas: Critical Reading, Math, and Writing. The lower score for each sub-test is 200 and the highest is 800. Therefore, if your child had a perfect score it would be 2400.

The **ACT** is a series of subtests of three hours and twenty-five minutes that measures achievement levels in four basic areas: Reading, Math, Science, and Social Studies. Writing is an additional test that is optional, but I would advise that your child takes the Writing test as well. Since colleges want to have some standardized baseline data upon which to evaluate a student's writing abilities, it is advisable the students include the writing section of the ACT administration. Also, since most colleges will accept the ACT or the SAT, which has a non-optional writing section, it would give the ACT comparable weight to the SAT when judging an applicant.

Each of the four major sub-tests is graded on a 1-36 scale. There is also a Composite Score for all of the sub-tests ranging from 1-36. The Writing test is graded on a scale from 2-12. Therefore, a perfect score on the ACT would be a Composite Score of 36 and a Score of 12 on the Writing.

Most colleges today will accept the ACT or the SAT. If your child chooses to submit both they will take the higher of the two. In addition to the ACT and the SAT, some of the more selective colleges require two Subject Tests, sometimes referred to as the SAT Subject Tests.

The **SAT Subject Tests** are one-hour achievement test in one of several academic areas that measures your child's knowledge base in a particular subject, e.g. Spanish, Math Level I or Math Level II, US History or World History, Biology, or Chemistry. The lowest score is 200 and the highest is 800.

For students who speak English as a second language, it is advisable that they take the Test of English as a Foreign Language (TOEFL).

If your child takes Advanced Placement (AP) classes, they will also be expected to take the AP exam.

The **AP** Exam is a college-level exam, which measures a student's level of proficiency in the knowledge they have gained from their AP class. These exams are three hours, and they are administered at the high school. The score range for AP exams is 1-5, with 5 being the highest.

How Does My Teen Prepare for Standardized Tests?

There are several ways one can prepare for these tests. Educational Testing Service, the administrator of most of these exams, and American College Testing Program, the administrator of the ACT, have developed two exams that are designed to assist students in their preparation for the SAT and ACT, respectively.

The **Preliminary Scholastic Assessment Test (PSAT)** is the practice test for the SAT and, like the SAT, it comes with its own practice test booklet. So before taking the PSAT, a student can study on his or her own or in a small group. The PSAT is a three-hour exam that measures aptitude in Critical Reading, Math, and Writing. The score range for each sub-test is 20-80. The highest possible score, then, would be 240.

The **PLAN** is the practice test for the ACT and, like the PSAT the ACT, has its own practice test booklet.

Both the **SAT Subject Tests** and the **TOEFL** also have practice test booklets that your teen should review well in advance before taking the test.

Other options for your teen when preparing for these exams include the following:

- Take an SAT and or ACT preparation class at their high school. Many high schools offer them as an elective.

- Enroll in a private SAT and or ACT preparation class with a local educational consulting group. While these preparation classes can be costly, many of them will offer a reduced rate for families with low to modest incomes.

- Purchase practice test booklets and/or CDs at all major bookstores. These practice tests are much more comprehensive than the practice tests mentioned earlier.

When Should My Teen Take the Test?

That depends on the test and it also depends on your teen. However, most students would follow this schedule:

Test	Year in School	Date
PSAT	Ninth	October
PSAT	Tenth	October
PSAT	Eleventh*	October
SAT	Eleventh	May/June
SAT	Twelfth	Oct./Nov.
ACT	Eleventh	April
ACT	Twelfth	Oct./Nov.
SAT Subject Tests	Ninth	June
SAT Subject Tests	Tenth	June

SAT Subject Tests	Eleventh	June
SAT Subject Tests	Twelfth	December
TOEFL	Eleventh	May/June
TOEFL	Twelfth	Oct./Nov.
AP	Tenth-Twelfth**	May

Designed for juniors but many schools introduce the exam to freshmen and sophomores to give them a competitive advantage

** *The AP exams are administered at your teen's high school in May. If your child takes an AP course in the tenth grade, they would take the corresponding AP exam in May.*

When and How Often Should My Teen Take the Test?

How often your child takes the test is an individual decision. Most students take the SAT and ACT at least twice, some take these tests three times. It is to their advantage to take them more than once since they may do better with more experience and colleges today will take the best score. Note the table below.

Year in School	SAT	CR	Math	Writing
Grade Eleven	May	**550**	500	**510**
Grade Twelve	October	520	**560**	500

The scores that the colleges will record are CR 550, Math 560, Writing, 510. The colleges use the best scores from each section of the test, even if the scores are from different exam dates.

How Much Does It Cost for My Teen to Take the Test?

The SAT costs $47, the PSAT costs $13, and the SAT Subject Tests have a basic registration fee of $21. Foreign Language Subject Tests with the listening feature cost an additional $21, while all other Subject Tests cost $10. The ACT with Writing costs $48, and without Writing the cost is $33.

The TOEFL and the AP exams are the most expensive. TOEFL has a price tag of $170, and the AP has a basic fee of $87.

Please be advised that in most cases students who qualify can obtain a fee waiver that would pay for either the total or partial cost for all the aforementioned exams. The college advisor or guidance counselor will inform students how this process works.

How Are These Exams Used?

With the exception of the PSAT, these exams are used for admissions purposes. Please be aware that while most colleges require at least the ACT or the SAT, some do not. For example, there are some very competitive schools out there that do not require college entrance exams as part of their application process.

For those that do, you should think of it this way—your child's ACT and/or SAT score is only one part of their application and he or she may be interested in a college whose average combined SAT score is 1800 but their combined score is 1500. Does that mean your child will not be admitted to that school? Not necessarily. The good news is that there are many other aspects of the college application and any one of those pieces or a combination of such could render the decision in your child's favor. In short, these exams give the admissions office just one indication of how successful your child might be in their particular college from an academic perspective, but remember, it is just one indicator and in all cases it is not the most important. Again, the courses a student takes in high school and the grades they receive in those courses are the best indicators of how successful they will be in college.

Remember this rule when your child applies to college: They are more likely to get into a selective school with high grades in solid academic classes and low to average SAT scores, than with poor grades in solid academic classes with a high SAT or ACT score. Why? Admissions officers read high scores and low grades as a student who is not working up to their potential, where they read a student with high grades and a low test score as someone who may not test well on standardized tests, but who works hard. Who would you want on your team—someone who is lazy or someone who works hard?

The SAT Subject Tests are required by many selective colleges, but not all of them. They are used to determine a student's academic strengths in a particular subject area and, with a high enough score, they could be placed out of a college-level class that would satisfy one of the required courses in college.

The AP test, unlike the ACT, SAT, and SAT Subject Tests, is not used for college admissions, but can certainly help your child gain admission to a college since the AP test indicates that they took on challenging courses in high school. Generally if your child scores 4 or 5 on an AP exam he or she can not only place out of certain lower-level college classes, but they can also receive college credit. Whether or not your child should always accept the credit and move up to a higher-level class depends on the course and on your teen. The college advisor or guidance counselor at your child's high school is the best person to advise them or they can wait until enrolling in college and consult their academic dean.

Finally, the TOEFL is a test that admissions officers use to determine a student's proficiency in reading, writing and speaking English. It is important to note that at most colleges this score would be used with the Math score from the SAT to determine if your child is admissible. So it is advisable that your teen takes the TOEFL if they speak English as a second language.

How Is the PSAT Used?

While the PSAT is not used for college admissions purposes, it is, however, important to know who uses it and how.

- Students use it to prepare for the SAT

- The National Merit Scholarship Program uses it to determine if a student is eligible to receive a scholarship

- Colleges use the scores as a recruitment tool. In other words, once the colleges receive your child's scores they will start sending materials in hopes that your child will at least consider applying to their school. Their goal is to get your teen to apply and ultimately enrolled, if admitted.

Up until this point the guide has focused a great deal on what college admissions officers call the quantitative side of your teen's academic record, i.e. courses, grades, and tests. However, while it is important part of whom your teen is, there is more to a student than numbers. For example, often students make a contribution to their local community in a number of ways; a way that they do is getting involved with extracurricular activities.

EXTRACURRICULAR ACTIVITIES

An extracurricular activity is anything that takes place outside of a formal classroom setting. No matter how much time your teen spends on their studies, they certainly should have a life outside the classroom. They should not be afraid to experience some of the wonderful activities their school and community offer. If their school does not offer an activity in which they have an interest, they should ask the principal if they can initiate a new club. In this way they created an opportunity for him/her as well as others, and have shown leadership skills.

Colleges are interested in creating a diverse student population whose individual backgrounds and interests vary. Participation in extracurricular activities is an excellent way to show a college that your teen is more than just a one-dimensional person. They also help them develop teamwork and leadership skills. Best of all they are fun and rewarding.

How Colleges See Your Teen's Involvement in Activities

Extracurricular activities cannot compensate for poor grades or low test scores, but they can render your child a more attractive candidate especially when compared with a student who has similar grades and test scores. However, a student should not let these activities become more important than their school studies.

Bottom line: your teen should get involved, stay involved, and have fun. Extracurricular activities are a good way to augment their academic life in high school. It will also give admissions officers another indication of your teen as a total human being and the activities may even suggest how they might contribute to their college.

COMMUNITY SERVICE

Getting involved with a community service site is another way students can distinguish themselves in the college application process and they can start this activity early in their high school career.

Some high schools require that students participate in a community service activity as part of their graduation requirement. There are also some scholarships available to students who have been involved in community service.

Whether or not your teen's high school requires community service, it may be to their advantage to participate in these programs when applying to college and when applying for scholarships. In addition to the support your teen will be giving to a community organization, they will also feel the personal reward of helping their fellow citizens.

SUMMER ENRICHMENT

There are a number of summer opportunities in which your teen can become involved throughout their years in high school. Whether they are between their freshmen and sophomore or junior and senior year, there is a summer program out there for them.

Some of these programs are expensive, but some are free. Those that have a price tag attached to them often offer financial assistance to students who qualify. For example, SummerMath at Mount Holyoke College offers partial scholarships to female students who want to improve their math skills in a three-week summer program for rising tenth, eleventh, or twelfth graders.

The Lead Program, for students of color interested in business, is free and is offered at several universities across the country within their business schools. Students attend the program at the end of their junior year in high school.

The Annenberg Scholars Program at University of Southern California for rising juniors is a program the spans two summers. Students attend the program at the end of their sophomore and junior years in high school. For those who qualify, it comes with a $5,000 scholarship for each summer. Students take two college classes each year.

A final example of a summer enrichment program is called the MS^2 (MS Squared) Program. This program is housed at Phillips Academy in Andover, Massachusetts and is free. It is for students of color, mostly first-generation college bound, who have an interest in math and science. Students receive a full scholarship, which pays for their participation in the program for three summers.

Participating in summer enrichment programs and summer school is another way for your teen to enhance their college application. Taking summer school classes can be another way for them to advance into more challenging classes at their high school. Enrollment in a summer program at a college can also give them a taste of college life while still in high school. Internships and work experience during summers can also be considered a plus for the college applicant. In some cases your teen may want to turn their community service project into an internship.

Like extracurricular activities, a summer enrichment program embellishes a student's college application, but will not necessarily offset a poor academic record.

RECOMMENDATIONS

A recommendation is a written letter that describes in detail a student's academic performance and/or character for an admissions officer. From the very start of high school, your teen should begin thinking about how he or she wants the recommendation to read. Whether they realize it or not, they have control over how people view them and by extension what a teacher and or counselor will be able to say about them in the recommendation.

One can assume that because your teen is a well-mannered student that the teacher and counselor will present them in a favorable light but that does not necessarily make for a compelling recommendation. There are a lot of nice people in the world but simply knowing that doesn't tell us a great deal. That means your teen has to be more deliberate about letting people at their school know about who they are.

For example, your teen may have overcome a challenge or they may have had a unique experience that changed their life. Your teen can choose to participate in class, show leadership, and support other classmates. In other words, they should give the teacher and counselor something substantial to work with so that they can write more than just, "Rafael is a great kid." They need to show that Rafael is a great kid, with supporting examples, and only Rafael can give them the information to do so.

Although recommendations are not given the same weight as grades and test scores, they can inform a student's application by explaining something irregular in their application. This is why a student should give their teacher and counselor every opportunity to know who they are in and out of class. The more they are familiar with your teen as a total person, the better they will be able to write an accurate and compelling recommendation.

If all things are equal between two applicants, but your teen's recommendations are stronger, then your teen has the greater chance of being admitted. Remember also, that your teen most likely will need a recommendation before they apply to college if they intend to participate in a summer program, job, or internship. Quite often they will be required to submit a recommendation for these opportunities.

EARLY FINANCIAL AID RESEARCH

One of the basic keys to effective financial aid research is to start early. You want your teen to have the option of attending the college of his or her choice, regardless of cost. In order to do this, it is important that they begin researching financial aid opportunities earlier, rather than later, in high school.

Take for example, Devin. He wanted to apply for a city newspaper scholarship. In order to be eligible for the scholarship, he would need to satisfy three qualifications: have a 3.0 Grade-Point Average (GPA), be a resident of that city, and would have to deliver the newspaper for two years in high school. If he had waited until he was a senior to research this particular scholarship, it would have been too late. Fortunately, he conducted his research in his freshman year so he was perfectly aware of what he needed to do throughout high school to satisfy the qualifications of this scholarship and others as well.

There are many resources to start exploring financial aid options. One set of options available to your child can be found in the local libraries. Some libraries even have an entire section devoted to planning for college and financial aid.

Bookstores are another great resource and they have a wealth of information on financial aid in general and scholarships specifically.

The college advisor or guidance counselor is also a great resource. They will routinely receive information about scholarship opportunities. While most of them are for seniors, not all are. For example, Discover Card has a scholarship for juniors (http://www.discoverfinancial.com/community/scholarship.shtml).

The Internet is another resource (Appendix H) that lists detailed information on scholarships. Your teen can find information about scholarships for which they might qualify on a state and federal level.

Other resources available may be at your place of employment, church, and other civic/social organizations in the community.

Chapter 7 contains a comprehensive section on financial aid, but for right now all you need to know is that there are two major classifications of financial aid, **Need-based** and **Merit-based**. Need-based is dependent on your income, while merit-based is, for the most part, independent of your income. Merit-based aid is money your teen can apply for because of a particular talent. It is key to research merit-based scholarships early rather than late in high school to know what to do to qualify for them before the senior year.

Chapter 1 has led you through seven key areas of educational planning. By effectively planning your teen's high school years they will be better prepared to take the next steps toward college. As you read on, it will become even clearer how these early steps can impact your teen's future.

Now we're ready to approach the college application process in earnest starting with the college search.

● ● ● ●

Both David and Dana were introduced to the concept of college while they were in elementary school. I always told them that it was important for them to do well in elementary school and that would determine what types of classes they could take in middle school, also that they needed to do well in middle school to be able to take advanced classes in high school, and that they had to do well in high school in order to get into a good college. By the time they were in middle school, they knew the speech; it was ingrained in their mind.

Although the kids were in a good school system I still felt compelled to get involved and stay involved so I was always at the guidance office when it came time to choosing David and Dana's courses. This process started in elementary school where they took the most advanced math class in sixth grade; this then determined the math course they took in middle school, and then in high school. I encouraged them to have four years of one language—Spanish—and four years of science including Biology, Chemistry and Physics, in addition to other required academic subjects. I also encouraged them to take Advanced Placement (AP) classes and International Baccalaureate (IB) classes in subjects of interest to them or in subjects that would help them with college courses, such as (IB) English. It was relatively easy to encourage them since they were inclined to take these courses anyway and the sequencing of classes they started earlier led to these advanced classes in high school.

—Donna Atkinson, Parent

GLOSSARY

ACT: American College Testing. The ACT is a college entrance exam consisting of four academic sub-tests, Math, Reading, Science, and Social Studies. Writing is an optional fifth test.

ACT Program: The American College Testing Program. A non-profit agency that designs and administers tests, including the ACT, for use within the college admissions process.

AP: Advanced Placement. A college-level class offered in high school is referred to as an AP course. Each course has a corresponding AP exam administered at your child's high school in May of each academic year.

CEEB: College Entrance Examination Board. The CEEB develops the policies and practices for many tests like the PSAT, SAT, SAT Subject Tests, and the AP. They also provide other services, for example a Fee Waiver Program for the SAT and the SAT Subject Tests.

CEEB Code: A six-digit code number assigned by the CEEB to each high school that your child will use when registering for certain tests. The college advisor or guidance counselor will have the CEEB Code.

College Bound: A high school student enrolled in a college preparatory course and who intends to apply for admission to college.

College Catalogue: A publication describing the academic programs with the associated courses for all of the college majors and minors offered at that particular college or university. This publication also discusses graduation requirements for each major and minor. Today catalogues also come in electronic versions.

College Fair: A program organized to allow you and your child to meet and talk with representatives from different colleges and universities. Your child can attend these fairs at any point during high school. They do not have to be a senior.

College View Books: Publications developed by individual colleges and universities to promote and present information about their respective institutions: campus settings, academic programs, student life, and related campus features.

College Visit: A visit to a college by students to observe firsthand the academics, student life, and related campus activities. You are encouraged to visit colleges with your child. There are many types of campus visits and the college advisor at your child's school will inform you of such at the appropriate time. Your child can visit colleges at any point during his or her high school years. They do not have to be a senior.

Class Rank: Your child's standing in his or her graduating class. Rank is based on grade-point average and is usually presented in numerical order. For example, a class of 200 students would be ranked from 1-200, with number 1 being the highest rank in the class.

ETS: Educational Testing Service. ETS is a non-profit organization that develops and administers the test for the College Board, e.g. they are the administrators of the PSAT, SAT, SAT Subject Tests, and the AP. They also provide additional services such as a Fee Waiver Program for the PSAT and TOEFL exams.

GPA: Grade-Point Average. An average of your child's academic achievement as measured by grades. Computed by adding the number of quality points assigned to each grade and then dividing the number of courses into the sum of the quality points. Typically students are assigned 4.0 quality points for an A, 3.0 for a B, 2.0 for a C, and 1.0 for a D.

GPA/Weighted: GPAs that provide extra-quality points for more advanced classes. For example, in some high schools an AP class may assign a 2.0 quality point for a grade of A.

GPA/Unweighted: GPAs that do not assign extra-weight for accelerated courses.

NACAC: The National Association for College Admissions Counseling is a professional organization of secondary school counselors, independent counselors, university admissions officers, and financial aid counselors who assist students with the transition from high school to higher education.

NCAA: The National Collegiate Athletic Association is an organization through which the nation's colleges and universities speak and act on athletic matters at the national level. The NCAA Clearinghouse reviews academic records of prospective Division I and Division II athletes.

PLAN: Preliminary American College Test. A standardized test offered to high school sophomores who are considering a college education. It is designed to familiarize your child with the ACT, taken later, and provide an assessment of their career interests and study skills.

PSAT/NMSQT: The Preliminary Scholastic Assessment Test/National Merit Scholarship Qualifying Test is a practice test designed to prepare your child for the SAT. It is also used in the awarding of merit scholarships for qualifying students. Colleges do not use PSAT scores as part of admissions criteria.

SAT: Scholastic Assessment Test. A test used widely by college and university admissions offices. The test has three sections, Critical Reading, Math, and Writing.

SAT Subject Tests: Scholastic Assessment Test Subject Tests. A one-hour standardized achievement test in a specific subject area, required by some colleges. Some colleges will ask for three, while others will require two.

TOEFL: Test of English as a Foreign Language. A test given by the Educational Testing Service to determine a child's English proficiency in speaking, reading, writing, and listening. Students who speak English as a second language are encouraged to take this exam.

REFERENCES

Educational Planning

The College Handbook. The College Board. www.collegeboard.com

College Keys: Getting In, Doing Well and Avoiding the Four Big Mistakes. Roger W. McIntire. Summit Crossroads Press.

College Planning for Gifted Students. Sandra L. Beryer. Prufrock Press; 3rd edition.

The Gap-Year Advantage: Helping Your Child Benefit from Time Off Before or During College. Karl Haigler and Rae Nelson. St. Martin's Griffin.

Studying for Success: Tips to Help Build Effective Study Habits. Channing Bete Company. South Deerfield, MA. (800) 628-7733.

Summer Opportunities for Kids and Teenagers. Peterson's Guide. www.petersons.com

Summer on Campus: College Experiences for High School Students. Shirely Levine. www.collegboard.com

CHAPTER II

THE COLLEGE APPLICATION PROCESS

The college application process can be a stressful and daunting process for most college-bound students and parents. However, it is a process that if entered with the right temperament and preparation, will help set the tone for the rest of your academic career. If you are planning to start the process the first day of your senior year, you are too late and will exhaust yourself trying to catch up. Begin your junior year establishing strong academic credentials and strengthening your SAT, SAT Subject Test, ACT, AP, and IB scores. Although most colleges are leaning towards a test optional policy, many are still using the scores to determine scholarship opportunities.

Research summer enrichment opportunities, such as on campus academic or talent specific programs, internships, or job placements. Establish a strong rapport with your college/guidance counselor and secure a copy of your unofficial transcript at the end of your junior year to verify its accuracy. Use your summer wisely. Keep your recommenders and counselor updated with your summer activities and provide them with materials for your letters of recommendation. Visit many colleges both near and far, and request information through their mailing lists. Browse through previous application packets and begin drafts of your college essays. When you return for your senior year, you should be prepared to share with your counselor 5-10 colleges that you are interested in attending, drafts of your essays, and the names of all your recommenders.

Take advantage of colleges visiting your high school during the fall and attend college fairs in your area. Think nationally and out of the box when investigating your college choices. Look at schools that have a strong alumni network, that are looking to enhance a skill-set you may possess, that have affiliated graduate or professional schools, and those that can assist generously with financial aid. Do not be afraid to investigate themed schools, such as Historically Black College or Universities, single gendered, religious institutions, or Ivy League schools. Pay attention to deadlines and details. Your application can be overlooked if you submit materials late or ignore guidelines for submission. If you are convinced that your personality and abilities are best articulated in person, then it is imperative that you establish relationships with admission representatives.

Parents, you can assist your child by filing your income taxes and meeting other financial requests before the established deadlines. However, allow your son or daughter to take onus of his or her process. Help him or her through the process, but do not take over the process for your child. Listen to your child; do not force them into a major, a college, or a program because you think it is best for your son or daughter. Allow your child to explore what he or she would like. This is a decision that he or she will have to live with for potentially four years; your child will have to adjust and mature at whatever college he or she chooses, not you. If you follow these guidelines, you will be an effective consumer and successfully cross the path into the college of your teen's choice.

—Sanjay Mitchell,
Independent counselor and retired guidance counselor

SECTION I
THE COLLEGE SEARCH

HOW DOES YOUR TEEN FIND the right school? They want a place where they will be happy and productive. They want a place where they can grow and develop a more profound sense of identity. And remember they will be spending four years there. Also, with price tags running up to $200,000 for four years at a private school and over $100,000 at many public colleges, your teen should spend time to take the college selection process seriously.

With over 3,000 colleges and universities in the United States, your teen has a wide variety of schools from which to choose. They can use the *College Handbook*, which they will find in their college advisor's office or at the library, to select some schools worth exploring. Other resources include their counselor, teachers, family, friends, websites, college catalogues, and general college guidebooks.

When your teen starts the college search there are two questions they should ask. The first is: What do I want in a college? Clearly identifying their needs is an important part of the process in finding a school that's right for them. The second question is: What qualities can I bring to a college? An honest evaluation of their strengths and weaknesses is important to finding a college that is a good "fit"; after all, they want a college where they have a realistic chance of getting in and then fitting in once they are there.

CHOOSING A COLLEGE

What Does Your Teen Want in a School?

In answering this question, your teen should think about who they are and what they need. They should not assume that their best friend's choice will be a good fit for them. The below list of considerations will help your teen select a college that will well match their needs, wants, and potential contributions:

- A school that offers their major
- One that is near or far from home
- One that is in a particular geographical region of the country
- A school that is a particular setting, e.g. suburban
- Cost of school
- Size of student enrollment
- Size of average class
- Student/faculty ratio
- On- and off-campus housing options
- Greek life
- Athletics
- Public vs. private schools
- Diverse students and faculty
- Predominantly white colleges
- Historically black colleges
- Women's colleges
- All-male schools
- Religious affiliated schools
- Schools offering services for students who have learning disabilities
- Schools that don't require the SAT nor the ACT
- Study-abroad programs

WHAT QUALITIES AND STRENGTHS DOES YOUR TEEN BRING TO A COLLEGE?

After your teen thinks about what they want in a college, they should think about what they can offer the college. In evaluating themselves, they should not be shy; their competition won't be. On the other hand, your teen should not overestimate their accomplishments. If they have attended one meeting of the Chess Club, it's not a good idea to list it as one of their extracurricular activities on their application. Before answering the below list of questions, it is highly recommended that students go to Appendix A and devote at least an hour completing the Student Self-Evaluation. After this exercise they will be able to respond to the below questions more objectively:

- Are they a good, average, or below average student?
- How do they compare with other students in their class?
- What are their GPA and Class Rank?
- How good are their writing, reading, and math skills?
- What are their strongest and weakest subjects in school?
- Which subjects do they enjoy most and least?
- Have they taken challenging courses in high school?
- Have they taken any college admissions tests?
- If so, how do their scores compare with those of admitted students to the colleges in which they have an interest?
- Do they enjoy learning for the sake of learning or do they see it as a means to a career?
- Do they learn best in small classes where they can engage more often in classroom discussion?
- Do they learn best on their own or do they enjoy working in groups?
- What clubs, sports, committees, or cultural groups do they participate in actively?
- Have they ever held an office, obtained other leadership positions, or received an award or prize?
- What activities, hobbies, or other interests have been important to them either in or out of school?

- What do they want to do right after high school?

- What are their career and professional goals?

After your teen has explored what they want from a college and what they can bring to one, they can now decide which colleges they want to research. The goal is for them to come up with 8-10 schools ranging from Safe Schools to Reach Schools. Once they have identified the schools and have the applications in hand, they are ready to approach the college application process in earnest.

COLLEGE FAIRS

One efficient way to get an introduction to a college is through a College Fair. College Fairs take place throughout the country at some point during the academic year, though usually they will come to or near your community in the fall or spring. Some of the fairs are sponsored by major organizations like the National Association of College Admissions Counseling, and local churches, schools, sororities, and fraternities may sponsor other College Fairs.

It is also important to note that often when there is a College Fair in your area, the admissions representative may also visit your teen's school and, if this is the case, your teen may want to meet with the admissions representative, particularly if they are from a college in which your teen has an interest. In short, the tips that are recommended for the College Fair also apply in that scenario.

- Attend a College Fair at least twice in your high school career, in the spring of your junior year and in the fall of your senior year.

- As a junior you can use this opportunity to conduct some exploratory research and may even decide to visit a few of the schools during the summer that are represented at the fair.

- As a senior you can use it to establish a contact or another contact assuming that you have already visited the school. It may also give you a last option to add a few more schools to your list.

- Be prepared. Find out ahead what schools will be represented and have your questions ready. In the hour that you may be at the fair you will probably only have time to speak with five or six schools so you have to manage your time wisely. At the fair there will be other people competing with you for the attention of the college spokesperson so you have to be prepared and be succinct.

- Think of this as an interview—the only difference is you will be asking most of the questions.

- Bring an unofficial copy of your transcript, SAT and ACT scores along with a copy of your résumé. If you have the opportunity, ask the admissions officers to glance at your records. In that way, they are more able to give you some indication of your chances of being admitted.

- When speaking with the college representative, don't become distracted by your peers around you. Stay focused and maintain good eye contact.

- Ask if they offer fee waivers.

- If you are a junior, ask if the college offers any summer enrichment programs and, if so, ask if they free. If not, find out if you can apply for financial aid.

- Whether a junior or senior, ask if the college has any visitation programs for students of color. Often schools will pay for your visit, if you have the right grades.

- Before leaving, ask each admissions officer for a business card and follow up with an email or card thanking each one for his or her time.

CAMPUS VISITS

While College Fairs offer an affordable and time-efficient forum to glean an initial impression about a college, nothing compares to a campus visit for a more thorough assessment. There are several ways students can visit a campus, and they do not have to wait until they are seniors. In fact, it is advisable that they don't wait that long. Most students begin visiting colleges in earnest in their junior year. Spring of the junior year is ideal, though the summer preceding your teen's senior year is another option, though not the ideal if the regular students are not on campus. There may even be times when your teen is invited to visit a campus with all expenses paid. Under these circumstances, the school is clearly interested in the student and that is why they are willing to invest dollars in either getting them to apply or getting them to attend after they have been admitted.

Visiting colleges is a must, but it can also be expensive. This is where involvement in an after-school college access program or summer program can help you. Many of these programs have a budget to take students on college tours. One can also find this feature at some of the summer programs. Also, some high schools and church communities will sponsor college tours for students. Typically students will pay a nominal fee for church-sponsored tours, while if they are sponsored through the schools they usually are free. As a parent, you will also find that if your teen has performed well throughout high school, some colleges will invite your teen for an all-expense paid visit, and here again this is where being an asset works in their favor.

You do not need to feel compelled to visit every college that your teen visits, but you must visit the college they ultimately choose to attend. It will be hard enough to let them go emotionally when you are familiar with where they are going, but it will be much more difficult to let them go if you don't know where they are going. Moreover, you want to be there for them when they leave home, and knowing where they are, what the environment looks like, as well as something about the resources and support systems at the college will increase your comfort level and provide you with greater confidence to help your child navigate their college years.

Regardless of when or how your teen visits, here are some tips for campus visits:

Plan Ahead

- Call in advance to schedule an appointment. You may not always need a formal appointment, but you will not know until you inquire.

- Sign up for a tour and information session.

- Ask if you can visit classes.

- Schedule meetings with coaches, if applicable.

- Leave your name and address, so you can be added to the school's mailing list.

Tour

- Take an official tour, then take your own tour. Spend at least two to three hours on each campus.

- Evaluate the resources and physical plant.

- Assess the cleanliness, comfort, noise level, privacy, and safety of campus housing.

- Eat a meal on campus.

- Speak to campus security and obtain statistics on crime.

- Assess if it is easy for you to gain access into the dorms. If you can get in without ID so can others.

- Pick up a college newspaper.

- Evaluate computer facilities.

- Go to the student center and speak to students randomly when touring on your own.

- Visit the athletic center.

- Make sure you visit the library and science labs.

Special Interest Areas

- If you are planning on participating in sports you should speak to the coach and a few student athletes.

- Students interested in visual arts should visit the art facilities. You may want to meet with one of the art professors and at some point you need to determine if you need a portfolio.

- Students interested in performing arts need to visit the performing arts studios and concert halls. Find out whether or not you need an audition.

- Students who have a learning disability need to inquire if there are specific labs and services to assist students with their needs.

Talk to Students

Ask the tour guide questions, but more importantly ask questions of other students as well, such as all or some of the following:

- Why did you decide to attend this school?

- What do you like about the school?

- What do you dislike about it?

- How demanding is the workload?

- How would you describe the social life?

- How would you evaluate the quality of the relationships with the surrounding community?

Observe Students

- Try to get a sense if students have positive attitudes, are happy, and in general appear to enjoy their school.

- If diversity is important, find out how diverse the school is.

- If intellectual inquiry is important to you inside and outside of the classroom, listen to what students talk about as you visit the library, student center, cafeteria, etc.

- Some campuses are very friendly and others are not. You need to assess what is important to you.

- Do students seem to have lots of energy?

Reflect

- Immediately after you visit, write down your impressions for future reference. Remember every college has its imperfections.

- What was distinctive about the college?

- Were its students the kind of people you would like to get to know?

- Is this an environment where you would feel happy and intellectually challenged for the next four years?

- Trust your instincts.

SECTION II
YOUR TEEN'S APPLICATION

WELCOME TO THE COLLEGE APPLICATION process. Your teen will realize that this process requires a great deal of organization and attention to detail. To assist them with this endeavor, this guide includes, besides the four-year Calendar of Calendar of College and Financial Aid Events that follows the book's Introduction, a **College Application Process Checklist** that will help them stay on track and hopefully prevent them from missing any deadlines (Appendix E). When your teen thinks of deadlines, they should think beating the deadlines not just simply meeting them. In that way they will be certain that their paperwork is correctly submitted, professionally presented, and finally, is in on time.

The first step in making sure that your teen understands this next stage is to be certain that they are familiar with the terminology that is associated with the application process. There's a glossary of all the terms they need to understand this process at the end of this chapter.

WHAT, WHO, AND WHEN FOR REGULAR ADMISSION

Upon receipt of each of your teen's applications, it is important that they read them carefully. They need to know what is in the application, who is responsible for each section, and when each is due. In other words, they need to be able to answer the above questions for each application. While some of what they will need to do will be consistent across schools, for example, all schools will require a high school transcript, some information is specific to a particular school. The bottom line: make sure your teen knows what is required of each.

THE APPLICATION

There are many types of applications to which your teen has access. Most schools today give students the option of using the traditional paper version, but would prefer that they apply online using the electronic one. Approximately 300 schools use what is called the Common Application, which also has an electronic version, and allows students to apply to several schools by completing one application. With this application your teen has to pay close attention to the supplements that some colleges use to gather additional information that is not on the Common Application itself.

Whether the Common Application, regular paper version or electronic, most have several sections with which your teen needs to be familiar. Each section needs to go to a particular person, and it is your teen's responsibility to make sure they receive their forms and that they are mailed to the colleges by the due date. In some cases they will collect all the information and have it sent out under one mailing, but in most cases, they will mail their section of the application and counselors and teachers will mail out theirs separately.

Student's Section of the Application: This is the section where your teen is asked to provide information about themselves and their family. It will also ask them to list their classes, test scores, extracurricular interests, summer experiences, and awards. College applications tend to also ask if they have decided on a major. If your teen has not, they can check "undeclared."

Essays are also a common part of an application. They can be short answer essays or they can be one- or two-page essays based on an assigned topic. Other times your teen may be asked to write a personal statement and be allowed to choose their own topic.

School Report Form or Secondary School Report Form: This form is completed by your teen's school counselor and is sent to the colleges with their high school profile—a document which outlines the demographics of their school, its academic programs, grading scale, average SAT and ACT scores, and any special features of your teen's school. Also in this mailing the counselor would include a recommendation that he or she has written for your teen along with their high school transcript and test scores. It is important to note here that many colleges will want the test scores sent directly from the testing agencies, either from Educational

Testing Service if students took the SAT or from American College Testing Program if they took the ACT.

The Secondary School Report Form will ask for other kinds of information, e.g. first-quarter grades, the classes one is taking the first half of their senior year and a list of those they will take the second half (assuming they change), their SAT and ACT scores, class rank, and GPA. These forms usually include a checklist of qualities ranking students from average to above average to outstanding. Some of those qualities include: respected by faculty, respected by peers, creativity, sensitivity to others, a sense of humor, and more.

If the college has not provided a return envelope, your teen should provide one for your counselor. Make sure they include the deadline when the form and supporting documents are due and make sure they address the envelope and provide a stamp unless otherwise instructed.

Mid-Year School Report Form: This form is similar to the School Report Form and also goes to the counselor. The difference is it is mailed to the college during the mid-year after the second-quarter grades are available. Here colleges want to make sure that seniors are still in good academic standing or in some cases, whether or not their grades might have improved since the first quarter. Usually, a recommendation would not accompany this form.

Teacher Report Form: Like the counselor, the teacher is asked to evaluate students but his/her recommendation is based on classroom performance and thus colleges are looking for an academic recommendation from teachers, while from counselors they are expecting a character recommendation. Make sure that your teen pays attention to that distinction. Many colleges will ask for two academic recommendations from teachers and one character reference from a school counselor or perhaps from someone in the community. Like the previously mentioned forms, the Teacher Report Form also has a checklist, ranking the student in several areas similar to those mentioned earlier. If your teen needs to do so, provide a stamped, addressed envelope for the teacher. Here again, students should make sure the teachers know when the recommendations are due.

Transcript Release Form: Applications that do not require recommendations from your teen's counselor or teacher will include what is called a Transcript Release Form that they would give to their counselor. The counselor completes and signs the form, attaches your teen's transcript and test scores and sends them to the college either in an envelope provided by the college or, if not the college, then by the student.

Application Fees and Fee Waivers: While your teen may be able to have their application fee waived, most require an application fee. They should make sure they mail their fee, particularly if your teen is sending their applications electronically. Schools will generally accept checks or money orders.

If your teen qualifies they can receive at least four application Fee Waivers, a service sponsored by The College Board. However, please note they cannot receive the application fee waivers unless they have used one of the SAT Fee Waivers within the same academic year that they are requesting the application fees. Students should speak to their counselor to find out if they qualify for the Fee Waiver Program.

THE PROCESS

By now you should have a detailed understanding of what your teen can expect to find once they receive their applications. It is time for them to organize their paperwork and develop a schedule to address all that they need to do to deliver their applications to the various colleges on time. Below I have outlined a step-by-step process. There are several ways to organize this process and your teen may elect to develop their own system. That's okay—just make sure that they do not take this exercise for granted.

Step One: August

Write colleges to request an application and other relevant information. Students may do so electronically, if they choose. (See Appendix C for a sample materials request letter.)

Step Two: August–September

Read each application to determine what is expected of them. Students should pay close attention to deadline dates. Lastly, have your teen record each of their schools on their College Application Checklist (Appendix E). And make sure they do not forget to register for the SAT and ACT. If applicable, they should also register for the SAT Subject Tests and the TOEFL.

Step Three: September

Go online and access the College Board Website (www.collegeboard. com). Once they are there, have them go to College Scholarship Service and find the CSS Profile. They need to know if the colleges to which they are applying require the CSS Profile. While they will not be completing the actual financial aid form until January, they can register for the service in the fall.

Step Four: September

Set up a file and label it with the name of each college. If they are applying to ten schools they should have ten folders. Whatever information they have that pertains to a school, have them file it in the appropriate folder.

Step Five: September–October

Give the School Report Form to their counselor and the Teacher Report Forms to their teachers. Make sure they write on the form when the recommendations are due. In most cases, they will be sending the recommendations to the school directly. In some cases, their counselor will instruct them to bring the application and supporting documents to school and the counselor will send out everything from the office.

Step Six: September–October

Where required, contact schools to set up either an on-campus or alumni interview. At the end of this timeline, you will find a section with a series of "Sample Questions and Tips" that students should review before their interviews. If possible, they should interview with their least favorite school first and save their favorite one for last.

Step Seven: October

Students should begin filling out applications. They should not wait until the last minute. A last-minute application looks like a last-minute application and here is where your teen has to pay attention to the way he or she is represented. See "Tips on Filling Out the Application" later in this chapter.

Step Eight: October–November

Review all of the essay questions for each application. They may have ten applications, but only need to write four essays. If this is their scenario, then they could have less work, unless they have one of those very abstract essay topics. Once your teen understands the scope of the work, they can begin developing their first drafts. Your teen should allow at least two months to complete all of the essays. They should plan on writing three to four drafts for each essay. Make sure they have someone, preferably their English teacher, review their essays. See "Tips on the Essay" later in this chapter.

Step Nine: October–November

It is now time for your teen to contact colleges to schedule visits. In some cases, they may have already visited colleges and decided to apply to some of those schools because they had a great visit. In other cases, they may not have visited a campus, but may decide to do so at a later time. In a few instances, they may wait to visit after they have been admitted. Keep in mind some colleges may have special visitation programs, and students certainly want to take advantage of them. What is important is that, if your teen can, visit the school before they decide to enroll. See "Tips on Visiting Colleges" later in this chapter.

Step Ten: October–November

Attend at least one College Fair in the fall of their senior year. Most of the fairs will take place either in October or November. See "Tips on the College Fair" later in this chapter.

Step Eleven: November–December

Speak with their teachers and counselors to make sure they have completed their recommendations. Also, make sure their Counselor has your teen's most recent transcript ready to be mailed off with his/her recommendation. Remember it is their responsibility to follow up with the people from whom they are requesting information.

Step Twelve: December

Review all of their applications and essays. Before mailing them, they should make copies of everything and keep copies for their files, just in case the college loses their paperwork. It does not happen often, but when it does, having copies will save both time and stress.

Step Thirteen: December–January

Mail off all applications before January 1. Before they leave for Christmas vacation, make sure they pick up the Free Application for Federal Student Aid (FAFSA) from their counselor, or if they choose, they can access the form on line at www.fafsa.ed.gov. Your teen's applications are in and now and they can focus on applying for financial aid and private scholarships.

Tips and Sample Questions

To help students further navigate the process I have included a series of tips that they will find helpful as they are completing their application, writing their essays, and preparing for the interview.

TIPS FOR YOUR APPLICATION

The college application will consist of three major areas: academic, personal, and supporting documents. Earlier you read about what those supporting documents are. Your teen will not have any control over what a counselor or teacher writes on an evaluation form, but they do have control over their own presentation in the application. Here are some tips for your teen to consider so that they can present an application that will make them stand out, that is, for the right reasons.

- Pay attention to details of the application. Be sure to answer questions succinctly and directly without overcompensation.

- Be sure to answer all questions. If a question does not apply to you, you can use the acronym N/A.

- Maintain consistency in format. When citing dates either use September-June, 2010 or 9-6-2010. Choose one form, but don't mix them.

- Maintain parallelism in sentence structure and tense usage, where appropriate.

- Try to account for consistency. If French is your intended major or you love swimming, your application should reflect your interest.

- Augment your application with additional information, where appropriate.

- You may want or need to attach a résumé. (See Appendix G for a sample.)

- If you are using a paper version, copy the application and develop a draft for review by a parent, counselor, or teacher. After you receive the feedback, you are ready to fill the actual application.

- If you are applying online make sure someone reviews your application before you send it through.

- Even if there is not space for it, don't leave out a part of yourself which you consider to be integral. Here is where a résumé could work.

- To maintain continuity of thought, only work on one application at a time.

- Make a schedule for yourself so you won't be rushed to comply with the application deadline.

- Don't wait until the last minute. A last-minute application looks like a last-minute application.

THE ESSAY

The purpose of the essay is to allow your teen to present a dimension that reaches beyond grades, recommendations, and test scores. It also allows an insight into who that student is and what is important to them. Finally, it demonstrates their abilities for insight, awareness, honesty, and self-evaluation. Here are some tips to think about before starting their essay. I have also provided an example of an outline for the student's review. Various sample essays appear at the end of the essay section ("Essays That Work") for the reader's review.

TIPS FOR WRITING THE COLLEGE ESSAY

Dos

- Think small: write about something with which you are familiar and has been significant in your own life

- Reveal yourself in the writing. Come across as a genuine and valuable person. The best way to do that is to allow your writing to reflect who you are.

- Choose words carefully. If a simple word will convey the message, use a simple word. However, don't settle for the little word if the big one will convey what you really mean.

- Be modest. You don't want to sound like you are tooting your own horn. Instead, tell your story simply and in a way that portrays your feelings, perceptions, values, commitments, and interests.

- All winning essays bear in mind the creative writing adage "Show, don't tell."

  Telling

  "I love basketball. I play basketball some days alone after basketball practice. It is a good team sport and I hope to continue playing this sport once in college."

  Showing

  "We enter the game at the end of the second quarter. My favorite team is down by two points. If my cousin had picked me up when he was supposed to, we would have been on time for the game. We hurry to find our seats through the excitement of the half-time event. Before we know it we are here, with popcorn in one hand and a coke in the other. A guy to the left of me says, 'third quarter's about to begin. Georgetown enters from the right, St. Johns from the left; they are down by two points.'"

  You can see how showing is more captivating than telling!

- Perform a grammar and mechanics check. Review each sentence and eliminate unnecessary words or phrases. Check punctuation, spelling, capitalization, hyphenations, etc.

- Ask someone to read your draft essays. If that person can't understand it, neither will the admissions officer.

Don'ts

- Don't use big words to impress your reader. "In my early teens my grandfather tragically died" is better than, "in my early teens my grandfather tragically perished."

- Avoid clichés. Don't say, "What I have learned is to strike while the iron is hot." Better to write, "I learned to take advantage of opportunities when they present themselves."

- Don't use a flowery, pretentious style. Don't say, "I visited your school and was impressed by the beauty of the campus, all of the excellent facilities and the welcoming students and faculty." Better to write, "When visiting Swarthmore, I was impressed by the diversity of the students and faculty."

- Don't ramble; get to the point. Don't say, "I really love my job and more-over, enjoy going to work every day. It has really had a positive impact on my life." Better to write, "I love my job because I get to work with kids that have disabilities. This experience inspired me to give back to my community."

- Avoid abstractions and unsupported generalizations. "Everyone who owns a house must pay a mortgage," is better than "Everyone who owns a house has a lot of money."

- Do not patronize schools.

TIPS ON OUTLINING YOUR ESSAY

Choosing a Topic

- Colleges will either give you one or let you choose your own.

- Narrow the topic and be as specific as possible.

- Don't write about basketball because it's too broad.

- Do write about an experience you had at a particular basketball game. That narrows the topic and will help you focus the essay.

Preparing to Write

- Organize your thoughts.

- Develop a framework for your essay.

You may decide to write about a game you lost and what you learned from that experience. What your audience will read is a story that you have shared through your voice about that game and what it means to you.

Or, you can write about a game you attended and why that particular game resonates with you.

In both cases you also need to decide whether you want your story to be linear (start at the beginning go to the middle and move to the end) or whether you want it to be anti-linear.

You can have a dialogue between two people.

You can open or close your essay with a poem; there are numerous ex-amples. Whether you are telling a story about a game in which you played or one that you attended, you need to be very deliberate about how you are going to format your essay.

Writing the Essay

- Your first draft does not have to be the perfect essay; in fact, it probably won't be so don't put pressure on yourself.

- Write your first draft. Tell your story. Don't think about it; just get your ideas on paper. Then put it aside for one or two days.

- Your second draft is where you begin to focus on style, grammar, tone, and spelling.

- At this stage share the essay with your English teacher and/or a counselor. If you have a friend that writes well, you might share it with him/her.

Take full advantage of this opportunity to let this writing define you beyond your GPA and ACT/SAT scores. The final product should be your voice and not sound like your teacher. You don't have to be a genius to write a good essay. The key ingredients are time and sweat. Take the time to think thoroughly about your subject. A good essay is achieved through attention to detail and successive drafts.

ESSAYS THAT WORK (SAMPLE COLLEGE ESSAYS)

These unabridged student essays represent college admission essays that exceed simply a prose version of a résumé and instead reveal a sense of person not otherwise obvious from the application. They are peer models intended to inspire, not intimidate, your teen.

CHRISTIAN C., UNIVERSITY OF MARYLAND, COLLEGE PARK

The detention center at my old high school is located in the basement, hidden behind a nondescript wall and a stack of milk crates. It's an old classroom, like any classroom, filled with chairs and desks, and even a clean chalkboard. The room is stained in black marker, and the clock has read 2:43 for a year now. You can hear the security transceiver of the guard outside, *students are fighting again,* there's a teacher here somewhere. The room is always full, with the same brown faces; we keep forgetting the same rules. You can see the word "slavery" carved into the ceiling above us.

I began attending Wilson midway through my junior year; I was miserable at my former school, a private institution located in the Maryland suburbs. I had a lot of friends there, probably most would talk highly of me, but I was tired of constantly being reminded that I was one of the few blacks. When I first started attending the school in the 6th grade, I was one of two blacks in my grade, people would call us "one-and-a-half" when we hung out (I am half black). Someone used the "N" word to the other kid's face, but most of it was never intentionally racist, more of a running joke. Most of them were my friends, but they couldn't understand how hurtful their words were. By my junior year I was tired of the joke and I decided to leave.

The first day I attended Wilson, my basketball shoes were stolen from my locker. I was lost for the entire first month, most of the time spent trying to adjust to the new atmosphere. I was shocked by the metal detectors, the force of security guards and the graffiti on the walls; who could believe that I had wanted to come there. It is a large inner city school, with kids from every part of the city, which resulted in a lot of conflict between students from different neighborhoods. To the students, Wilson was a place to see your friends, not to receive an education. Hard work and success in the classroom was looked down upon there; people would ridicule those who cared about grades. The teachers had given up long ago, most of them sat at the front of their rooms, talking to themselves. Everyone was holding each other down, and I fell into that mentality in my desire to assimilate, but I was happy.

In January of my senior year, I saw a student stabbed to death at the bus-stop in front of my school; I realized then that I was a slave, not held down in physical chains, but rather bonded by a cultural psychology. My classes weren't filled with black people; my friends were off skipping school and playing basketball. They used to laugh at me, tell me I didn't have to go to class, try and convince me to skip. Most of the time I would go with them, and inevitably end up in that same basement classroom, end up in "slavery." Every time I saw the same faces and they were always black. No one ever saw "white" at Wilson, but when they saw "black" succeed, their "brothers" would grab hold of them.

It's been half a year since we graduated; my friends are still playing basketball, but I don't really know them. People say that I've changed, they tell their friends that I'm "faking," that I don't want to do anything. "Come and chill," they ask me. No, I'm tired of doing nothing. "He's different," they say. No, I'm just tired of being held down. I saw that same detention room last week, but it didn't bother me anymore because I am no longer a slave. Some are still down there, hidden away from everybody. It's always 2:43.

ANONYMOUS

"I don't know where the valve is, Howard," yelled Dom from the garage in the Sunoco service station.

"Well, you better find it or order another, 'cause she's comin' in this afternoon to pick up the car," replies Howard, the station's owner.

I work in this gas station two blocks from my house. I pump gas. I wash windshields and I check oil. I do all the odd jobs that the mechanics don't have time for. This job is dirty, the office smells, and the mechanics can't articulate a single sentence without cursing.

It's the greatest job in the world.

Now, my family is pretty well off financially, and realistically I don't have to work. I choose to work at the gas station because it gives me a sense of responsibility and the extra cash doesn't hurt. I have had other part-time jobs that, to put it mildly, I was indifferent toward. Compared to other jobs, though, the Sunoco has been a different, more meaningful experience for me.

First, let me introduce the cast of characters. There's the station owner Howard, who hired me. Everyone in the community knows Howard; every little lady with a car problem has unending faith in him to remedy all their automotive ills. Not only is he a fair and understanding boss, but he is also a friend to his employees.

There's Dominic the mechanic. Dom and I went to the same high school and Dom started working at the station when he was my age. He's now 23 years old, a husband and a father of two and he works at the station seven days a week. On the side, Dom manages to find time to volunteer as a fire fighter and paramedic.

Old Sam, 73 years old, works with me every Saturday morning. Sam has the art of the full service gasoline pump refined and perfected, from squeegee to tire gauge. He sits while chain smoking and sipping Budweiser each Saturday, and is very curious about what plans I have for my future. "Doctor like your father. None of this accountant, lawyer stuff," he commands every week. Between customers Sam hunches over sheets of handwritten numbers trying to decipher the mysterious code of the Lottery. Sometimes he wins a "Pick Four" or a "Big Three." Usually he does not.   None of these men went to college nor do they ever regret living the blue-collar life of the gas station. They are honest, extremely hard working and all have families to support, and most of all, they are happy. I believe they are happy because they are real, and they know they are real because every aspect of their lives confirms the truth of their existence through tangible, real situations. The satisfying sense of production and accomplishment after finishing a job completely, the bellowing laughter that fills the station following a crude joke, the wrenching pain in your back at the end of the day that fades away the moment your children run into your arms; I have witnessed all these things in these men. These essential pieces of life, these real, indispensable elements of existence, tell them in full stereo that they are real every day of their lives.

What I have learned working at the Sunoco? I have learned that looking a man in the eyes and having a firm handshake tell more in a first impression than any number of words. I have learned that the word "poor" is not a synonym for "unhappy." I have learned the value of a warm jacket and baseboard heat in the bathroom on a rainy November morning is greater than gold. I have seen the men that truly are the components that combine as a nation to create the American spirit is something that I should strive for, whether I end up as a mechanic, repairing carburetors and intake valves, or a surgeon replacing arteries and aortic valves.

EBONEE S., NORTH CAROLINA A&T STATE UNIVERSITY

As I sit here pondering on what to say, my mind travels back to the time when a friend asked me, "If you could describe yourself as any shape what would you be and why?" I can recall being completely stomped and I did not answer her question, but now as I sit here contemplating on my life and all that I have done, it finally hits me; a circle. A circle is what best describes me.

Many may wonder why I chose a circle, well one reason is because circles are round and I am a well-rounded person. I can remember my very first day of high school. As I walked the halls to class and soaked in my surroundings, I began to wonder where is my place in the graduating class. Then I immediately began answering my own question through hard work and determination in all that I did. In my quest to find my place, I found myself spending countless nights in front of the computer putting the finishing touches on an English paper. Every once in a while, I was calling up a friend to get help on challenging assignments. I found myself in tutoring and in ACT preparation classes to help me strive for perfection in order to be more like a perfect circle. I began dedicating my time to singing in the Glee Club and participating in an organization called Role Models, coaching, teaching, and guiding my peers. I had earned a spot on the Honor Roll for three years. I received recognition from organizations such as, the U.S.A. Achievement Academy and Who's Who Among American Students. I found myself on the National Honor Society at school and on an all-expenses paid trip to Washington DC to participate, as well as, represent my school in a program called Close Up. Most importantly, I realized that my place in the graduating class was in the Top Ten.

Another great factor about circles is that they have insides and outsides. The most important factor inside my circle is my family. Many students have it all academically, possess some of the best leadership skills and volunteer for every good cause outside of home, but they lack family values. Being with family and loved ones is what completes my circle. There is nothing like having a strong support system in my corner to help guide me along the way as I build the outside of my circle through academics, volunteering, clubs, and organizations.

Circles are also shapes that come in a variety of sizes. They can start out small, but end up big. The great thing about them is that there is always room for expansion.

That is how I have lived my high school experience. I started off small by taking honors classes. Then I expanded by taking AP classes and venturing outside of school to participate in programs such as Saturday Scholars and College Summit.

Though I have accomplished a great deal in my life, like a circle, I think of myself as a never-ending cycle. I have made my mark in elementary school as graduating valedictorian, found my place in high school as one of the top students and now I am ready to advance onto the next level. I am ready to make college apart of my never-ending cycle and explore a bigger piece of the world and take on new challenges to add to the inside and outside of my circle.

PABLO V., GEORGE WASHINGTON UNIVERSITY

As I descended from the plane and handed the soldier my passport, I realized things were different here. Sure, the soldier above the airport terminal pointing a rifle at us was a bit out of the ordinary, but there was something in the atmosphere that told me as said in the *Wizard of Oz,* "That I wasn't in Kansas anymore." We had touched down in Havana, Cuba, at about 5:30 p.m. on a dark day in late July of 1998. We went for two reasons, to meet my family and to bring them much needed supplies. While in Cuba, I discovered something else, something that was known to me only from history books and dinner table discussions at my family's house. This was the element that has been separating families, eliminating progress, and dismantling relations for forty years. What I found on the beautiful, yet decaying island were the effects of Communism.

The drive was long from Havana to my mother's childhood home of Santa Clara, a smaller and more tight-knit community in central Cuba. It was exciting to finally meet the aunts, uncles, and cousins I had never seen before. This was a special joy for us because, even though we'd never met, it felt like we had always known each other. I learned that even though the politics of Cuba have kept us apart, because of the unity our family is strong we found a way to finally come together.

My family, like most Cubans on the island, lives a very tough life. Although we send them clothes and canned goods from time to time, the Communist system frustrates even that progress. For example, the Cuban government limits the amount of food, medicine, and clothing that can be sent to the island. Also, the people have to exchange the Cuban currency (which has no national value) for American dollars so they can get by. This made me realize how many countless things I take for granted and how God has blessed me with all that I have. This experience has caused me to reflect on the fact that my mother left the island, and, as a result, I was born into freedom.

Cuba's current situation exists mainly because there is a lack of exposure to foreign influence. Communism thrives on this and keeps people brainwashed into thinking they live on constant alert. For example, people are very distrustful of others and everyone is under suspicion. While the revolution has brought security in the sense that the people feel safe from outsiders, it has also brought internal insecurity within the island because the inhabitants have become distrustful of each other. I learned by observing the Cubans in their daily routine, that where democracy and justice do not exist, there is no peace, only survival.

My experiences in Cuba have taught me many things, especially about the evils and abuse of Communism because it leaves people hungry—hungry for food as well as knowledge. I learned about my cultural roots and the true importance of family. The trip has made me a more gracious and generous person. I recognized the privileged of living in a democratic society and the importance of being free to express ideas and to really grow as a human being.

This event has sparked an interest in me to pursue a major in International Politics. I believe one of the most important issues facing our nation today is achieving strong and lasting relations with other countries and global peacekeeping. I want to play an active role in promoting peace and goodwill in the world.

ANONYMOUS

Walking through the hallways of the emergency room, I could visualize the struggles that each of the women and girls experienced trying to overcome their experiences of abuse. Each of the shirts hung represented one story, one person who now has a voice. As I walked further down the hallway I became even more disheartened. Looking at the shirts that the girls and I made in the Girls Club, my heart began to ache because these voices now had faces. Faces of young girls with bursting personalities, bright smiles and dark secrets behind their beautiful brown eyes. Secrets that haunted some of them for the rest of their lives. My thoughts became heavier as I walked further down the hall. There was a familiarity in the voice I heard. It was that of my own. I too had a bright smile and a dark secret hidden behind my brown eyes. I too was witness to the abuse in my home. And I too kept the silence.

Confusion was the most memorable feeling of my childhood. Nights of unrest and endless crying for fear that I would not wake up with my mother by my side. Yet although there were never bruises, my father's words were like poison that seemed to slowly kill my mother. And although he never directed it towards me, I always felt as if I was a child in my mother's womb. However, unlike some, my story was like that of a fairy tale. My mother grew stronger and no longer could his words weaken her. Their distance stopped the arguments, stopped the worry and we became the family that I always dreamed.

Yet the wounds were there and instead of treating them, I allowed them to remind me of the battle and my position on the front line. And as soldiers have flashbacks that haunt their very existence, so did I. Speaking nothing of it, I disguised my pain with my bursting personality, bright smile and brown eyes, until the secret turned from a memory that was being pushed further into the back of my mind to a reality that I had to face.

The Clothesline Project and the Girls' Club forced me to speak; forced my voice to be heard. Its message—"Although you don't hit her doesn't mean it's not abuse. And just because you don't direct it to me doesn't mean I don't feel it too"—is not only a means to help others break the silence, but also became a way to help myself and to heal my own wounds. Therefore allowing me to be another girl with a bursting personality, bright smile and beautiful brown eyes.

TYLER B., STANFORD UNIVERSITY

A Punitive Forgiveness

"TWC is saying that a storm is coming. I want you boys back at home by at least 5:00 so you don't get drenched." Dad has a way of saying things when there is a problem. He uses mediums like "bad storm" or "something isn't working" to communicate how he feels about a workday, stories on the news, and other happenings in Chicago that loomed omnisciently over its citizens. Dad is a person who is influenced by his environment, which is why he has to look deeper into cities for their inner beauty. In effect, every time we see the stories, the litter, and the "people," we frown upon it. I look to the sky often for hope, but now even clouds—the various shapes and shades of them that made me a carefree kid—do not make my world better like they once did. And one day in early May, the sky showed that it, too, was just as unhappy.

"If you feel that it will start to pour down, give me a call. I'll be in the area." l was taking the No. 87 down to Indiana Street when the tinted windows of the bus began fading gray to black. People continued to talk is if it had been a normal day in Chicago, but my eyes would not leave the glass. In front of my face, phantasmagoric and they were rapidly picking up speed. Then a woman in a long blouse hit the STOP button on one of the standing poles and the bus driver found the nearest sign to let her off, unaware of the fact that, outside, leaves rustled madly on their trees. In an instant, the bus's flimsy door flew open and her purse flew from her hands onto a weakening branch. My phone then rang.

"Tyler, where are you now? They're saying that strong gusts'll be going eastward—are you are close to 87th street?" I told him that I was nearing my stop and was going to be walking, so he told me to stay put. The bus rocked towards the concrete where the woman had left to chase her purse and the people fell silent. The kids stopped cursing, the adults dropped their books, and the driver sat immobilized. The bus rocked numerous times until a metallic whine came from the bottom of the bus, seeming to be the effect of all of the bus's weight shifting to one side. "Everyone move to the left half of the bus! If we don't, it'll fall over!" yelled a panicking passenger. Chaos ensued shortly after, but in due time everyone had conformed. I sat my bags firmly between the window and the head of the seat, grabbed hold of something, and closed my eyes, praying that no glass is broken or the bus is flipped upside down.

"Push! Push!" yelled our bus's leader. My phone rang several times, but I didn't reach for it, fearing that if I focused my attention elsewhere, I or everyone else would be hurt. The gusts pushed and we pushed. It seemed almost as if nature and man were having a showdown on a spring afternoon. However, we were not without assistance with this could-be-dire situation; sirens and loud voices were traveling in a direction towards us; spinning chopper and flashing camera sounds followed. We were being rescued at the same time we were becoming a story for tomorrow's news. My phone rang all throughout the save. I finally became able to answer it as the bus let off its distressed passengers. Exiting, I caught a glimpse of the broadcasting and interviewing, by-standing and gossiping, sobbing arid speechlessness. I then came to and Dad stood right there, taking me into his arms and letting his bold heartbeat soothe the throbbing pain of my head that rested on it.

"Are you ok?...Where's your stuff?...When did they hit?..." Dad asked many questions that came spontaneously and outran my answers. He and the rest of my family were worried sick. Flipping channels, talking furiously and loudly about the "what-ifs," and running up the phone lines, they jumbled their outrage and concern. I, however, quietly sat in the center of all of the noisy conversation when my attention shifted particularly to something else. For some strange reason, the sky had gone from an ominous black to a fluorescent white instantly. It held silently for a moment, and, suddenly, the silence was broken by sounds of pounding rainfall. Staring through the window, an illuminated feeling was transmitted to my spirit as I saw the rain that once fell from darkened skies now fall even harder from a glowing blanket sky. I heard a reporter say at some point, "things always come without precedence, so all you can do is do what you can and keep hope alive." It was funny to hear that, because, at the same time, nature said the exact same thing and all Chicagoans heard it speak.

TYLER B., STANFORD UNIVERSITY

Standing ten feet away from him, dad and I folded our arms and gave a keen beam of interest from our eyes while he gave speech. Dad was aware of the thousands of adult hecklers that verbally attacked the man like a dissatisfied mob, but what was particularly more interesting in my father's eyes was his manner of keeping control. Bill Cosby is not the kind of person that a normal citizen can regularly converse with, all due to the fact that he carries himself as a father, grandfather, and role model for rising teens and young adults. It did not surprise us that he would travel America to be Chicago's guest speaker for a "Men Only meeting" at the McCormick place on a Wednesday where all of us were in mid-week and attentively listening. And in it being a "Men Only" event, it did not surprise me that an epiphany about the definition of a man would be sparked through the wise words of men as sharp as Bill Cosby. I looked at my tie, my dad, and, finally, my year-old K-Swiss pairs at my feet because all of them were implying the detailed road I would walk—years from now—as an adult and as a man.

I remember wishing, years ago, that I could have big feet like Spyro the Dragon or Crash Bandicoot, as they were Sony Playstation®'s mascots for heroes. And though those fond figures recently faded to championed protagonists like Schindler, I retained the strong belief that a man could be defined by what he does—his profession. And then it hit me: if it called my name, I would venture off for various episodes of virtue, but the greatest of men master their fields and are then honored for that. My father will become Chicago's greatest construction worker and contractor and that will be so because he works non-stop for twelve hours.

In the respect of doing, thus, a man is a "man of action," though that is decided by the direction of the action. Statistics show that 50% of Chicagoan boys (as well as those all around the country) will not even graduate, which, in my eyes, eliminates 90% of the horizon. I've had my eyes set on MIT for the longest, mostly for the John Nash and Einstein-est of reasons, but the "other half" has spent most time within the American gutters, I have had a shifted focus in which the reality associated with the filthiest of conditions overwhelms my fantasies of fusing spirit and technology for the better of the people. Sadly, though, I hardly know what some people want besides a break.

Then, man becomes defined by however much he can become a blessing for someone else; some males have defied the rules of adolescent boys and have assimilated into the culture of expression or expressive language. Half of me is headed in that direction while the other half is headed in a direction of research and deep thought (of which many black males have never even heard spoken of for more than two seconds). Others will believe that the only way of blessing is through entertainment, like sacrificing morals as a celebrity or focusing all energy on physical activity. The last of us will believe that the only way to help is through reputation, usually equating to suicide or conducting and following through with the activities of a criminal. In those extremes, I feel like I'll either have to shape into one name on a page; help one person, or help everyone.

But that would be filling about six-and-a-half billion shoes when all I have is thirteen. Michael Jackson created number-ones for the gist of his life, traveled worldwide, and, because of allegations, almost brought an end to his career (as well as sanity). Bob Marley and Jimi Hendrix were gods of music and avid members of the 1960s and 1970s revolutions but died before they could even live to tell about it. I am choosing not to live the tragic life of an artist or genius, but I will require much resistance, boldness, and stamina if I want to achieve that notable kind of brilliance. My dad will keep telling me "you don't have to go through hell to get to heaven" and I will listen attentively, though I do not even know where the greatest of men have gone after life.

CONSTANCE L., DUKE UNIVERSITY

Summer, 1988. My cousins and I are swimming in a hotel pool in Spartanburg, South Carolina. My family is having a family reunion. We're splashing around in the pool, racing up and down. Uncle Walter, my grandmother's brother, is trying to teach us how to swim.

"Come on. You've got to cup your hand like this."

We all kind of follow the motion of his arm, but our attention span is short and so we go back to gallivanting in the blue green-chlorine water. Finally, we are all forced to get out of the pool by our parents after hours of fun. Everyone goes to their room to get ready for dinner. We all put our t-shirts on that say, "Clowney Family Reunion" on the front and have a large block-lettered "eighty-eight" on the back. The shirts are blue and come in all sizes, which reflect the vast array of age groups that have come to celebrate our family history.

After dinner, everyone goes back to someone's room that is adjoined to another room connected by a door. The children file into one room, the adults go into the other. The door is slightly cracked. My cousins and I are piled onto the double beds that are in the room. After about two hours of raucous laughter, my mother sticks her head in the door.

"Grandpa is dead."

My older cousins Tracey, Rochelle and Eddie began to cry. The younger ones looked sad, and started to cry, but didn't quite know why they should be upset. I just sat on the bed as my mother explained what happened. There were tears in her eyes.

"One minute, we were all talking and laughing and the next, he was just quiet with his head tilted to the side. Grandma called his name, but he didn't respond. Uncle Boobie and Uncle D tried to take him to the hospital, but by the time they got there he was gone."

By the time she finished the story, she was beginning to crumble and left the room. We sat there, not knowing what to do. I sat so confused. I knew that I should be upset, but I didn't quite know why. I had not really ever talked to Grandpa. The last years of his life, which confided with the beginning years of mine, he was in a wheelchair and suffered from diabetes.

● ● ●

We flew back home and the strain of the funeral proceedings was evident. My mother and her four siblings tried to comfort Grandma. Everyone who was at the family reunion came home with us to go to the funeral. A couple of days after the funeral, the excitement died down, Grandpa's obituary appeared in the *Washington Post*, "RENOWNED NIH RESEARCH CHEMIST DIES AT 72." When I read the obituary, I learned so much I didn't know about Grandpa. He served in the Army during World War II and was sent to Officer's school, which was highly unusual for a Black man during that time. Alter Grandpa's war service, he returned to college at Morehouse College in Atlanta, and was in the same class as Martin Luther King, Jr.

Grandpa went on to become a chemist at NIH (The National Institute of Health) where he was one of few people of color. Because he was Black, he was underpaid, and had to wait tables at a country club as a side job. He sent all five of his children to good schools. He worked hard to provide them with what they needed. Alter I learned these things about Grandpa I developed a whole new respect for him. Because of him, my mother was able to achieve all she has accomplished in life. Grandpa indirectly enabled me to live the quality of life that I have. Every day, when I drive to my prestigious private school, I pass the country club where Grandpa humbled himself to wait tables. Every day, I am reminded of his dedication and perseverance and I use his resolve to engender tenacity in myself.

NICOLE F., VANDERBILT UNIVERSITY

"Beep, beep, beep," sounds my alarm clock at 6:45 a.m. I want to go back to sleep, but then I remember that I have basketball practice at 7:45 a.m. "One week and two days until spring break," I say to myself over and over. Finally, when I'm ready to leave out for school, I realize that I have to pack my lunch, which will take another ten minutes.

At the end of the school day, when the dismissal bell rings, I watch all my classmates leave for home, but I cannot. "Oh, no, it's Monday, I have a student council meeting," I say disappointedly to my friend, Tsedal. Then when that's all over at 4:10 p.m., I go to my private tennis lesson with Coach Larry S. On the way, I stop at my house to pick tip an extra bottle of water, knowing that I'll be running after tennis ball for the next two hours. Of course, I grab fruit to eat in the car.

Finally, I return home to do my homework. "That will take about 3 1/2 to 4 hours including studying," I estimate. Once I finish that, the time is about l0:30 p.m., so I get ready for bed, knowing that I will have to repeat this process over again tomorrow.

Like most kids that attend school, I'm looking forward to not spring, but summer vacation. Currently, I'm overwhelmed with exams, quizzes, projects and book reports. It seems like every day there is something big that I have to do. Especially being an athlete, and scholar like a lot of my peers.

To solve this problem, I think it is necessary for everybody to use good time management. For example, not waiting until the night before to complete long-term assignments, which I find myself doing less frequently now. Students should just continue to work hard, and do well at school and other activities. Eventually, everything will pay off.

AARON J., WILLIAMS COLLEGE

He was a white guy, plain and simple. To me, that is what he was. He was just a white guy. I was not trying to be offensive, but when Pierantonios asked me what his race was I said that he was "white". I soon saw him change from a nice, friendly person to a run-for-cover Greek who looked as though he had been slapped in the face not once, not twice, but thrice. His face turned crimson red and his tone changed dramatically.

"Listen, Aaron," he said, trying to keep his composure. "The color of my skin is white. In that observation you are correct. But my race or ethnicity, or who I am, that is Greek. And I am proud of it. I am more than just a color. And to classify me as just a color does not do me justice. That does not describe my race either. Color is just a physical trait. Do you understand?"

I was caught completely off guard. By living and growing up in DC (Washington), I usually talked with people who were like me. Black. There were never any other races represented in conversations that I had. So, the thought of classifying another's race by color, and only color, was just common practice. I never gave it a second thought. When I saw Tony (short for Pierantonios) I automatically classified him as white. As that summer I spent at Camp Rising Sun with Tony progressed I learned many things, one being that he was Greek and that he was very proud of it too.

I began to see that classifying people into a minute category, especially one such as color being the sole determinant in one's race, was wrong. It was wrong of me and an injustice to whomever I classified. By doing this, I quickly shortened a person's identity so that it was "convenient" for me. In that one conversation, Tony helped me to change my entire outlook on people. I came to the realization that you cannot look at someone and determine who, or what, they are, whether Greek,

African-American, or any other race. I also understood that doing so was a disservice to that person.

I took this new outlook that I gained from Tony and our conversation back with me to DC. I took it to the family table. I took it to school and any other place where I could find someone to listen. This outlook developed as I returned to Camp Rising Sun for a second year. From it, I have gained a desire to participate in other programs where I am able to meet people of different ethnic backgrounds and engage them in conversation concerning issues such as race. Am I still learning about how people classify themselves? Yes I am. The difference is that I now see people and not just color.

NICOLE F., VANDERBILT UNIVERSITY

My interest in tennis grew slowly. I watched my older sister struggle to learn the game with little success and a lot of frustration. But some encouragement from my family and the thrill of making my junior high school team caused me to reach higher. At the age of twelve, I entered my first tennis tournament. The world of junior tournament tennis, as I soon realized, was no place for the uncommitted.

I lost in the first round of nearly every tournament that year. Most of my opponents had dedicated several years to the game and in dress and manner seemed so professional to me. I'll never forget my feeling of inadequacy when I was told by the director of a tournament in Lawrence, Long Island that the girl who just arrived carrying four rackets and wearing a FILA warm-up suit was ranked number 2 in the East and would be playing me. With my single racket under my arm and my school team jacket on my back, I began looking for a place to hide but the tournament rules were clear—no hiding allowed.

I lost to Grace K. that day (she now plays on the pro circuit) and thereafter to a lot of other Grace K.s and found that losing hurt and I didn't enjoy it one bit. At some time during that year, I was forced to make the first real adult choice of my life: either quit tournaments and enjoy the social side of tennis or devote the time and hard work necessary to become a competitive player. I had no idea that in choosing to go on I would benefit in ways far beyond the ability to hit a spin second serve.

At thirteen, I began working in every way I could, at least three hours a day, month after month, making personal sacrifices and constantly fighting frustration and disappointment. I was still losing to some of those same girls, but I was staying on the court a little longer and starting to learn from my mistakes. Often I thought of giving up, but I am not a quitter, and I guess, with each setback, I just became more determined to improve my game. I think the turning point was the Arthur Ashe Tournament in 1982 when I finally beat a "ranked" player. Looking back now at that moment of triumph, I realize that something far more significant happened. I was beginning to develop a new sense of self-worth and confidence that was spilling over into all my other activities. I also started feeling really good about myself. Not only did my grades improve, but I also began enjoying a broader range of people and activities. That is, I seemed to have the energy level to do pretty much everything I wanted.

My tennis skills continue to open doors of opportunity. I travel to tournaments out of state and in Europe and meet people with backgrounds very different from mine. Through these experiences and the tennis regimen of hard work and reward, I'm clearly more independent and mature than I would have been had I not chosen to be a serious player. My non-tennis playing friends often ask me whether the time and dedication I give to tennis is really worth it. My answer is an emphatic yes. I love the game, I love the prestige of being one of the best tennis players in the Eastern United States, and I love the emotional strengths that tennis has given me.

FRANK W., BATES COLLEGE

I had the wonderful opportunity to be a delegate representing the United States at the Children's International Summer Village (CISV) in Paris, France. CISV is an international exchange program that enables students to visit different countries to meet their contemporaries and learn about each other's culture. Although I felt a little nervous about being away from home and staying with a new family, I was at the same time excited and eager to meet new people and experience a different place. For me, Paris was new and mysterious and would help me gain a new perspective on life.

I lived with the best host family ever, but also learned that despite the beauty of the Eiffel Tower and the Louvre that not all places are as perfect as they seem. After being in Paris for two weeks, I went shopping with my fellow delegates, including my cousin Jasmin. A woman in the store was staring at us from a distance. She came closer and started yelling racist, belligerent words. She called us "dumb Americans" and then said "Ugly black people, get out of the store and leave France." We immediately ran out of the store and told our counselor. Our counselor and the store owner called the police as the woman ran down the street. We learned from the store owner that the woman was unstable.

My host family was saddened and so apologetic about the woman's words. Their caring feelings and concerns made me appreciate that all people are not alike and to not judge others because of the actions of a few. The hateful words of the sick woman taught me an important lesson, too. She made me realize that people may see me as a stereotype and not who I actually am. There's nothing I can do about that, except to make sure I do not stereotype others.

I am Frankie W., Jr. I am not a stereotype. I am a well-rounded student and person. I enjoy singing R&B and gospel music. I also love playing piano and I enjoy playing basketball and golf. I hate to admit that I like writing poetry and seeing my emotions on a piece of paper. I believe in dedication and hard work. I am a young man who intends to continue to study hard so that I can achieve my dream of becoming an anesthesiologist. Medicine will allow me to make a difference in people's lives.

The CISV international experience taught me to be open to new experiences and to learn from them. I now know that there is much to be learned from the "school of life" through experiences outside the classroom.

ANONYMOUS

Dancing Across Worlds

I'm in Washington, DC, in ninety-degree weather for my cousin Lauren's wedding. It's been a long day. I've gone through breakfast, pictures, the wedding, more pictures and now the reception. I'm sitting at a table with my brother and sister, overwhelmed with the feeling of embarrassment as we watch my dad perform his signature "running-man" dance. After what seems like an eternity, the music stops, and my dad, Mr. Saturday Night Fever, is forced to sit back down.

Two distinctly different looking men stand up and approach the microphone. One is the Rabbi and the other is Imam, which I learned earlier, is a Muslim cleric. The Imam begins speaking and after a few minutes he says something that grabs my attention. "I wish that *CNN* could be here, because Lauren and Nasser's love for one another sets an example which the world should follow."

My cousin Lauren grew up in Connecticut in an upper-middle class Jewish family. She attended private school, followed by an Ivy League education and law school. Her new husband Nasser, however, had a different background. As a child from war-torn Eritrea, his parents, in desperation, sent him to live in the United States. He spent his teenage years moving back and forth between foster families. Once he was old enough to live on his own, he worked long hours to support himself and eventually put himself through college. I first met Nasser when I was six years old and instantly became comfortable with him. Through the years he was always present whenever I visited Lauren, and he taught me many of the essentials in a young boy's life, like how to play pool and shoot a jump shot. Although Lauren and Nasser had been together for eleven years, our family seemed oddly surprised when Lauren announced they were getting married. The Imam finishes speaking and hands the microphone over to the Rabbi. "It is my pleasure to introduce two dances; the first will be the traditional Jewish "Hora," followed by the Eritrean "African Money Dance." The bride and groom ask that all those who wish to join, do so."

I look over to my dad. His eyes light up with excitement because he knows he's getting back on the dance floor. If only my entire family was that excited when they learned Lauren and Nasser were getting married. Although my parents have always taught me and my siblings to be accepting of all people, I was surprised to discover that some of my other relatives, particularly the older ones, were not so open minded. As I heard some of their negative comments, I realized that for the first time in my life, I felt ashamed of my family. These were people I had thought of as fair minded, people who had themselves experienced prejudice first hand. It struck me how much easier it is for people to talk about being tolerant in the abstract, than to actually live it, especially when it hits close to home.

As the dancing began, I realized how brave Lauren and Nasser were for following their hearts instead of society's norm. Their love and spirit seemed contagious, as I witnessed everyone in the room, black, white, Jewish, Muslin, the willing and the reluctant, move seamlessly from one traditional dance to the other. For at least a moment, it seemed that all the foolish barriers that divide people, simple melted away. What started out as just my cousin's wedding turned out to be one of the most powerful experiences of my life. If only the problems of the world could be solved by dancing "Hora" and "African Money Dance." *CNN* where are you?

CHRISTINA H., BOSTON COLLEGE

"Our flight's canceled! We have to hurry!" My older brother, Michael, told my younger brother, Matthew, and me as he began running through the airport.

Every year, our connecting flight home from camp is inevitably canceled. It was no different this time. After dealing with every manager and supervisor working that day, we were given the dreaded red and white striped pin, which noted our new status of "Unaccompanied Minors." We waited patiently for three hours before we were put on a flight going to New York City. None of us cared that we would be landing at a different airport; we would let our parents worry about that. We were sprinting fast as we could to the gate so we would be able to get home as soon as humanly possible.

As I walked to my seat, which was separated from my brothers, I saw a grown man sitting in the aisle seat of my row. "Hello," he said cheerfully enough, but he failed to stand up so that I could more easily get to my seat. I mumbled to myself about his lack of manners, as I climbed over him. Soon after I sat down, he introduced himself and we began talking. In an attempt to seem interested, I asked him what his occupation was. When he told me that he was a motivational speaker and a wheelchair racer, I was shocked. His words enraptured me; I truly was interested in the conversation then. My heart sank as he told me of the car accident that changed his life. The driver of the other car was drunk as he drove past the stop sign at over fifty miles per hour. He walked away from the accident with minor bruises, but his actions caused the paralysis of an innocent man. The man would never be able to walk again. I was disappointed in myself for judging his "poor manners," as we discussed the wheelchair races in which he had competed. We soon began talking about his experiences as a motivational speaker. He told me that he traveled often by plane to his various destinations around the country. I was stunned that he used an event that paralyzed him as a springboard to make himself more visible and mobile.

We were the last four people to get off the airplane when it landed in New York. My brothers and I walked around the waiting area, trying to find out parents. My new acquaintance stayed with us until they arrived. I reflected on the day during the two-hour drive home to Pennsylvania. I thought about how this man was trying to make the world better. I wanted to do my part, such as improve myself, for a start. But I hoped to help in more ways than being more patient or less judgmental.

As an active member in my school's SADD chapter, I also helped to start the club. When I was a sophomore, several of my friends and I worked tirelessly to get an active SADD group into our school. I had the man from the airplane on my mind constantly as the club was forming. I attended meetings and conferences outside of school to help the program run more efficiently. With each progression, I saw my hopes fulfilled. The thought of that man's accident kept me motivated.

In many ways—small and large—I have worked hard, trying to make life finer for those around me. I do not remember the man's name from the airplane, but I will always remember his message. I attempt every day to make the world a better place, just as he did from his wheelchair.

SARAH G., TUFTS UNIVERSITY

The End of Friends

It was Thursday night and I sat on the sofa crying with five of my closest friends. There were chips and dips and bottles of soda scattered on the table in front of us, all covered with crumpled tissues that we used to catch our tears. For us, this was it. We were saying goodbye to six people who had been there for us for the past ten years. It was the

Friends series finale, the last episode, and we all thought our lives would never be the same again.

Nothing could prepare me for the reality of the next day when I was forced to say goodbye again. This time it was two of my real friends and classmates who had died in a tragic car accident. Again, I gathered with my closest friends and this time we cried uncontrollably, devastated by our loss. Kevin sat in the front of me in math class, always with the best grade, and David sat behind me in homeroom, always walking in casually after the bell. I never dreamed their seats would be empty when I returned on Monday.

I think my dad said it best one night when he was trying to console me. "You and your friends are forced to grow up and face the harsh realities of life at a time when you're not ready, and there is nothing more difficult than that." It was true. The following week was the hardest of my life. It was filled with memorial services, wakes, funerals and receptions as we said goodbye. I spent that week hugging people I had never talked to, crying with my friends and being supported by a small community that has seen more than its share of tragedy.

The island of Martha's Vineyard is seen as a tourist attraction by the rest of the world. It lures the rich and famous who come to relax and experience a glimpse of what has become our daily lives. However, the Vineyard's beautiful scenery and cute little towns are not our island's greatest assets. It's the people that make this piece of land special. The year-round population is not fancy or wealthy. They are down-to-earth, hard-working people, some whose families have lived here for generations. Somehow, being set apart from the rest of the world makes us closer and more dependent on each other. I have seen this entire island come together to cheer and celebrate football championships, and I have also seen the amazing outpouring of love and support after tragedies. Though my community has rallied together through difficult times, I have never quite experienced the magnitude of warmth and caring in the island's hearts as I did in the days following my friends' deaths.

It wasn't until a week later that I thought about *Friends*, when the clock struck eight on Thursday and I remembered that the show I had been attached to for so long had ended the week before. For ten years, I had followed my weekly ritual, watching every single episode without fail, and now that it was over, it didn't matter. I thought about my life and how it had changed so drastically in just a few days. How foolish tears I cried over television characters had turned into real tears of loss and mourning. *Friends* would be a phase in my life, something that I loved but would soon forget. Not so with Kevin and David. They will always be with me. When I thought my life would never be the same after *Friends* ended, I had no idea how right I was.

TANIQUE A., RIDER COLLEGE

I walk up to the brown-haired lady at the desk. She sits there typing on her computer; she is most likely scheduling appointments. I wait, hoping she will look up and see me standing there and she does. "May I help you?" "Yes, Mr. O. is expecting me. My name is Tanique." "Oh yes, he will see you now, please go right in." I thank her and walk towards Mr. O.'s door. As I approach, I'm slightly nervous because I am afraid I will somehow embarrass myself as I sometimes do. I walk in confidently, truly believing everything will go smoothly. "Ah Tanique, come on in and sit down. How are you?" "I'm fine thank you. I'm here about my schedule, it has a few mistakes." "Oh yes, I remember. I'm afraid there are no mistakes. You cannot switch into Honors English or Honors Anatomy and Physiology because your Co-Op class interferes. You will have to drop Co-Op if you want those classes."

My heart skips a beat. I can't move or speak right away. I recover quickly so that he doesn't catch my pause, but my voice is shaky. I am now faced with an extremely tough decision, the hardest one I have ever faced. "There is no other way that I can have those classes and still keep Co-Op?" "No, I'm afraid not. It's up to you. Why don't you go home and think about it, talk it over with your mother, Then come see me tomorrow with your decision" "Ok, I will. Thank you." I say with a strain.

I walk around the rest of the day very upset, while my friends attempt to make me feel better. I just keep thinking this can't be happening. But it is, and it is really hard to focus on the classes with this heavy weight on my mind. But I force myself to because I will make the best out of the classes I have. When I arrive to English, my last period of the day, I am depressed. I think to myself, this is unfair. I don't need to be here, I'm better than this, I'm an honor student. Last year, with exception of math, all my classes were honors and I did really well in them, so how can I be here? I know why, but it's still hard to digest. I promised myself that even though I'm a senior, I would still work hard and take challenging classes. Not because I needed to, but because I wanted to. If I can't get honors English, then life goes on, and if I do, it's all the better. But for now, this is my English class; I sit up straight and turn my attention to the teacher. I won't slack just because I'm unhappy, that is not me.

Unfortunately, I could not get into the other honors classes without dropping my Co-Op. I put up a big effort, so did my mom, but we just had to accept the facts. I decided to keep Co-Op because I felt that it would be a great opportunity for me. This truly was one of the worst days of my life and most definitely my hardest decision. I was worried that not having those other honors classes would make me appear less competitive and therefore some colleges would not accept me. I don't regret my decision to keep Co-Op because it's something I really wanted to do and it turns out that I really enjoy Ms. M.'s English class. If a college does not feel that I have what it takes to be in their school because of my lower-level classes this year, then that is their decision. Hopefully the college will empathize with my experience of picking my senior schedule. Yes, I have taken challenging classes before and would have done this year had my schedule permitted. Not because it looks good on my transcript, but rather because I love learning and the intellectual challenge that comes with demanding courses.

CHANCELLOR A., COLUMBIA UNIVERSITY

I vividly recall being in the second grade and my mom going against the advice of the teachers at the French Immersion school I attended—not to attempt to teach the student to read English. Unfortunately, things did not turn out the way Mom had anticipated. Instead, whenever presented with an English book, I inevitably broke into tears no matter how simple the text and complained that reading English was "too hard." Mom quickly gave up. In the meantime, because I loved reading, I read every French book and age-appropriate French periodical I could put my hands on.

At some point during my fourth-grade year, I recall picking up an English book in a series by British author, Enid Blyton. It was entitled *Five on a Treasure Island.* The protagonist was a girl who called herself "George" despite the fact that her name was really "Georgina." The other three children were siblings and George's cousins. The fifth member of the group was Timmy, the mongrel. The book was the first in a series in which the four children always happened upon strange incidents, ended up having adventures and solving mysteries. George's family owned an island not far away from Kirrin, where George lived and the others visited. The children often spent lazy days and nights on Kirrin Island, swimming, having picnics, exploring dungeons, and sleeping in the old castle. In this particular book, the children happened upon treasure on an old shipwreck while staying on the island, encountered crooks that wanted to purchase the island in order to get the treasure, and were eventually able to prove the reason for the men's interest in the island.

Without realizing it, I approached reading this book just as I had any other until those instances when I came across words that I was unable to fathom. I must have used contextual clues because, in each instance, after some pondering, I was able to figure out what the words were and comprehend the text. The book took me more than twice the amount of time it typically took me to read a book that size; however, because of the author's fast-paced writing and ability to fuel the reader's imagination, I struggled through the book until I completed it.

Five on a Treasure Island made an impact on me because completing it was a major accomplishment as I had read a language that I had never been taught to read or write. Throughout the process, I was challenged to find clues to understand unknown words. In addition, I was forced to use my imagination as Blyton did not provide details about the scenery or develop the characters. On the other hand, she paced the story in such a manner that one was unable to put down the book. Thus, it was both challenging and stimulating. It is memorable to me, not only because I read it independently, but also because this and subsequent novels by Enid Blyton and other British authors helped me to understand my grandmother. I no longer felt that she used strange words and phrases such as "tap" (faucet), "I'll box your ears," or "there are apartments to let." I also realized that she did not have strange taste in food, e.g. sardine sandwiches, ginger beer, and tea with milk. Rather, I began to develop an appreciation for British English, culture, and writing style.

NNAMDI O., UNIVERSITY OF VIRGINIA

If your life story could be told with music what would it be? Would it be an upbeat rap song that everyone could dance to? Would it be a slow country ballad that brought an audience to tears? Would the lyrics follow the melody or would they be so profound that they carry their own weight?

First Movement

The music begins slowly. The melody only whispers because there is no one to hear.

Though bland, it somehow finds a way to capture your attention. You become intrigued by its sound. It tells the story of a stagnant young child who seems to not be going anywhere, but has his mind on everywhere else except where he is. Because of this tension, the music confuses you and, not surprisingly, it confuses him too. He plays on, hoping to one day be rid of this blandness. As the songs draws to a close his issue remains unresolved. He is still there, but only a little older. The world has only given him a room to stay the night, yet he wishes to one day own the entire house. He plays his last chord loudly and holds the keys until the sound is heard no more.

Second Movement

This movement is a bit different from the first: more cheerful and less melancholy.

The melody is syncopated, so much to the point that you feel the notes skip, hop, and jump. It seems this piece is a refined version of the first, taking its successes and making them standards and taking its failures and making them lessons. As the melody hops and skips you can tell this child is now a little less stagnant than before, yet he still seems discontent. He still yearns for more. The music gets faster as we feel him reaching–to the point where he has overstepped his boundaries. With a descending scale at the end of the song we learn he has fallen and quickly. It ends with his woes unnoticed.

Third Movement

It is fast, very fast. All blandness and stagnation are gone. He adores this pace, but struggles to keep afloat. The music is played swiftly not missing a note. It is what he has been waiting for. The chords roar and the melodies wail. He seems content. When the music is done he realizes that something is still missing.

I hope I have performed an adequate job illustrating what my life would be like in sonata form. My reason for transferring comes from my desire to find out what is missing. See, most people want to transfer schools to be more challenged academically or to move to a school closer to home or even for financial reasons. I would not be telling the truth if I said that any of these reasons haven't influenced my decision to transfer. These reasons alone tell only half the story. As I noted in the Third Movement, the pace is fast and that there was also something missing. There's a reason for that. There is a reason why my description of the Third Movement is shorter than the previous two. I truly enjoy having a fast-paced lifestyle and this pace has a purpose. I am in search of something, something that I have ultimately decided that my present institution cannot fulfill. This does beg the question as to why I think your school can help me find what I am looking for and my response is that my desire to apply to your school is no random act. I won't leave you in the dark. I probably should tell you what the reason is. What I'm looking for is merely a direction. It sounds simple, but to me it feels like I'm juggling the stars all at once. I want to do so many things in such little time. Life is all too short and my patience is even shorter. I feel as though your school can help me whittle my way down to reality. Apart from academic excellence and notable alumni, your school has the tools I need to learn more outside the classroom, which I value as highly as learning within the classroom. Movement, whether musically or literally, has been the story of my life. I thrive on it. Hopefully if I am granted the chance to attend your institution I can find a home.

THE INTERVIEW

In the Glossary there is a detailed definition of the word "interview." I wanted you to think more creatively about the word, so you would not assume that the only way to think about the interview was the traditional way. However, in this section, think about the more traditional, formal interview where your teen will be sitting face-to-face with either an alumnus or admissions officer who will be asking them questions.

Interviews are usually structured in three sections: icebreaking, information sharing, and closing:

Icebreaking: The first few minutes of the interview are usually devoted to such pleasantries as the weather, your trip to the campus, or comments about the campus tour. This time gives you an opportunity to calm down and relax. The key is to be yourself. Also, you are a consumer and as such you want to check out the people who are connected to the school, so if you think of it that way, you are also interviewing the admissions officer. If you can get yourself in that frame of mind you will feel more relaxed.

Information Sharing: Here is where the admissions officer addresses the serious questions of the interview. He or she expects you to do most of the talking. Your responses should be concise but not too concise. It is also important to avoid rambling. Most interviewers consider the interview a success if the interviewee has talked about 75 percent of the time.

You don't have to wait until the end of the interview to ask your question if it seems natural during information sharing. If you are talking about track and the admissions officer says casually that they had run the same event that you ran, when they were in high school, you take the spotlight off you and ask them about their experience with track. After they respond, you could lead into a statement about your desire to contribute to the track team in their college if admitted.

Closing: The interviewer will bring the interview to a close by asking you if you have any questions. It is a good idea to have two or three questions prepared. Also, during the information sharing section something might have prompted a question but for whatever reason you decided not to ask the question at that moment. You can use this time to ask the question if you choose. The bottom line is, you will be expected to have some questions and these questions should not be ones that you should already know from the information the college has sent you. For example, you might not ask a question about what the average SAT score is because you should know that. But you could ask, "If my SAT score is somewhat lower than the average compared to those admitted students, would that decrease my chances from being a serious applicant?"

The interview usually last about twenty to thirty minutes. If it goes over that time that is a good sign, if it only lasts ten minutes that is not a good sign. Regardless of the length of the interview, follow up with a thank-you note. (See Appendix D for a sample letter.)

One way to prepare for the interview is to simulate one with a friend, teacher or counselor. In preparation for that exercise, consider some typical questions that have been used during the interview process. A good strategy would be for students to write out their responses to these questions so if and when they are asked to respond to any of them, they would have already thought about some ideas to use in their responses.

Sample Questions

- What do you enjoy doing in your spare time and why?
- Have you faced any personal challenges in your life and how have you overcome them?
- What is your favorite book and why?
- What is your favorite movie and why?
- How do you enjoy spending your free time?
- If your friend were to describe you what would he/she say?
- What is your favorite subject in school and why?
- What is your least favorite subject in school and why?
- Who is your favorite teacher and why?
- What are three things you value most in life?
- What do you see yourself doing ten years from now?
- What kind of qualities do you look for in a friend?
- What do you feel about a female running for President?
- What do you feel about global warming? (A current event topic)
- What inspired you to choose your major?
- If you were rich and did not have to work, what would you do?
- Do you have any questions?

TIPS FOR YOUR TEEN: THE INTERVIEW

- Acquaint yourself with the school beforehand.
- Arrive a little early.
- Shake the Interviewer's hand firmly.

- Be sure to make eye contact.

- Be prepared to ask questions.

- Exhibit positive body language. Do not slouch, but try not to be stiff either. Think comfortable and you will look comfortable.

- Answer questions directly, but don't be afraid to elaborate.

- Be yourself.

- Be enthusiastic.

- Be honest.

- Do not interrupt the interviewer.

- Listen, take your time, and reflect. It is better to say something thoughtfully rather than impetuously.

- Remember, the interview is only an additional acquainting process, one meant to give a school information about you that cannot be seen on your written application. It is not an inquisition.

- Make note of your Interviewer's name and promptly write a thank-you note after you return home (Appendix D).

TIPS ABOUT INTERVIEW ATTIRE

Dress appropriately for the occasion. If your teen were going for a job interview he or she probably would not wear jeans and sneakers: they should regard the college interview the same way. For ladies, a skirt or slacks with a simple blouse is appropriate. Ladies need not wear heels; flats will do, but if one opts to wear heels I would recommend that they not be too high as one does not want to trip or have an accident. Gentlemen can wear dress slacks and a dress shirt. A tie and jacket would be welcomed but are not necessary. Loafers or dress shoes would be essential for gentlemen. Students need to and should want to make a good initial impression. The first image that an admissions counselor will see is how your teen is attired; let this image be positive or simply neutral, as you most likely do not want what your teen was wearing to be what the interviewer most remembers about the meeting.

SECTION III
SPECIAL CATEGORIES

WHEN PLANNING FOR AND APPLYING to college, there are a number of special categories of students that come to mind. This guide includes several such individual chapters, e.g. students with learning disabilities and the high school athlete. This section aims to address considerations for students involved in the visual and/or performing arts. It is important to note that all students follow, for the most part, the same procedures, but students who fall under "Special Categories" have additional tasks to which they must pay particular attention.

THE VISUAL AND PERFORMING ARTS STUDENT

There are two major types of students in this category. Some want to attend a regular university that offers the option to take courses in the visual and/or performing arts areas, while other students want to attend schools or conservatories that only offer visual or performing arts.

There are some cases where a student may elect to enroll in a conservatory at a university. The University of Indiana at Bloomington is a good example. It is a major university with many schools offering a number of majors. It also has the School of Music, which is one of the most competitive music conservatories in the country.

Whether or not your teen chooses one type of college setting over the other, they may be asked to present a portfolio in the case of the visual art student or a tape or video in the case of the performing arts students. Also, there are many colleges that require auditions for students who are interested in the performing arts.

Visual Arts Students

- When your teen researches his or her schools, find out if they require a portfolio.

- If they do, your teen should ask for guidelines on developing a portfolio.

- Your teen should ask their high school art teacher to help them; in many cases they are taking art classes at their school and may already have a portfolio.

- Your teen should attend the NACAC College Fair in their area for students interested in the visual arts. Information on these fairs is available at www.nacacnet.org.

- If they don't have a strong art program and don't feel they can adequately put together a portfolio, they can find good art programs that don't require portfolios as part of their admissions process.

- When they do require them, your teen will have to ask if they have what is called a Portfolio Review Day when they bring their portfolio to the college to be reviewed by professors from the art department who then make a recommendation to the admissions committee.

- While your teen will be expected to submit grades and test scores like all students, at schools that require the portfolio, a high rating on Portfolio Day may trump average grades and average scores. Of course, this will vary from school to school.

- Make sure your teen inquires about scholarship opportunities for visual arts students.

Performing Art Students

- When your teen researches their schools, they need to ask if tapes, videos and/or auditions are required.

- Your teen needs to schedule their audition dates and, like the college interview, if they have more than one audition try to schedule their first audition at their least favorite school and schedule their last audition at your favorite school.

- Your teen should ask their music or dance or theater teacher/private coach to assist them with this process. They might even ask a friend or family member to tape the audition so they can evaluate their performance.

- Your teen should attend the NACAC College Fair for students interested in the Performing Arts. Information on these fairs is available at www.nacacnet.org.

- If they don't have formal training in the performing arts, they may want to apply to a school that does not require an audition.

- For those students who will have an audition, keep in mind they will also have to submit grades and test scores, but an outstanding audition could offset average grades and average test scores.

- Make sure your teen inquires if the college has scholarships for performing arts students.

As you can see there is a lot of detail to which a student must pay close attention in what I call the mechanical process of applying to college. Throughout this process, parents must pay close attention to the student's level of engagement. After all, if he or she cannot handle what is expected of them at this stage, I would question whether they will be able to navigate the many responsibilities of college once enrolled. Give them guidance, support, encouragement, and within reason, some assistance, but in the final analysis, you want to be confident that they have done most of the work and not you.

● ● ● ●

We were very involved in all aspects of the college application process. Shayla applied to nine colleges. Due to the sheer volume of applications, she needed as much assistance as possible to keep up with all the deadlines and various requirements. Because of her major, she had to prepare for auditions as well as to create a CD portfolio for one university of original music productions. This submission required some level of studio recording, mixing, etc. Shayla had twice the amount of work to do through the process because she had to submit a general college application, which included essays, plus complete applications for the School of Music that had its own set of requirements.

Shayla was blessed with the opportunity, initiated by an independent counselor that my wife and I hired, to participate in a summer enrichment program at Carnegie-Mellon University during the summer proceeding her senior year which prepared her for the vocal auditions required for some the colleges. At Carnegie-Mellon, Shayla was exposed to singing classical music, which she needed to audition at several colleges. During her senior year she took voice training in preparation for all the vocal auditions. Even though Shayla's interest was not in vocal or instrumental performance, the Audio/Sound Engineering major falls under the School of Music for the majority of colleges and thus she had to show that she was competent in music.

—Steve and Andrea Hines

GLOSSARY

Alumni Interview: An off-campus interview with an alumnus from the college who usually lives in your teen's city or town.

Application Fee Waivers: An Application Fee Waiver is a service provided by the College Board for eligible students. Under this program, students will receive four college application fee waivers. Your teen should see their school counselor to determine if they are eligible.

College Search: A list of colleges to which a student will apply based on a number of characteristics informed by his/her interests.

Common Application: Allows students to apply to several schools by completing one application. Your teen should check with each college to determine if additional essays and materials are required.

Early Action: EA. The application is due by November 1 with a notification date of December, usually before Christmas. EA is not binding, so, if admitted, your teen does not have to attend.

Early Decision: ED. The application is generally due by November 1 with a notification date in December, usually before Christmas. ED is binding, thus if your teen is admitted to the college, he/she is required to attend.

Essay: The College Essay, sometimes referred to as the Personal Statement, is a written document that your teen will submit to the college, which provides them some sense of who they are beyond their class rank, GPA and test scores.

Deferred Admission: This term refers to the scenario in which Admissions decides to postpone judging a candidate's application for re-evaluation with the Regular Admissions pool.

Deferred Admission Student: A student is admitted, but decides to defer enrollment for one year.

GED: A General Education Development test that measures a student's proficiency in reading, literature, social studies, science and math. Students who pass the test receive a general high school equivalency diploma.

High School Profile: A form that describes the demographics, programs of study, and unique features of a particular high school. This profile is used by college admissions officers so that they can understand an applicant within the context of his/her school setting.

Interview: An interview is any contact a student has with a college representative. Whether your teen is visiting a college for a formal interview or speaking to an admissions officer at a College Fair, or simply speaking with a college representative who is visiting their high school, they should view all of these experiences as an interview.

Notification Deadline: Notification deadline is the date that students have to inform the colleges of their decision to attend. The standard notification deadline date is May 1.

Open Admission: A policy that allows all students to be admitted as long as they have graduated from high school or have earned a GED.

Online Application: The process by which a student can submit his/her application. Today most colleges would prefer that your teen submit their application electronically.

Recommendation: A narrative written by a teacher and/or counselor required by many colleges. Most selective colleges require academic recommendations from two teachers and one character recommendation from the school counselor.

Rolling Admission: The process by which an institution reviews applications as they are received and offers decisions to students as applications are reviewed, usually within three to four weeks.

Regular Admission: Applications are generally due by January 1 or February 1, with students notified by April 1.

Reach School: A very competitive school to which the student has a small chance of being admitted.

Safe School: A school to which a student will definitely be admitted.

School Report: The School Report, sometimes called Secondary School Report Form, is the part of the college application that students give to their college advisor or guidance counselor. This is a recommendation form that is also used to provide academic information about the student. Usually the counselor will send the transcript and the School Report to the colleges in the same mailing.

Teacher Report: A form that is part of many college applications that is given to a teacher so that he/she can provide an academic assessment of a particular student. Often this form is accompanied by a recommendation.

Wait List: A list of students not initially accepted at an institution who may be admitted at a later date, usually in June.

REFERENCES

The College Application Process

Barron's Compact Guide to College. Barron's Educational Series College Division. Barron's Educational Series.

Book of Majors. The College Board. www.collegeboard.com

Campus Visits and College Interviews. Zola Dincin Schneider. The College Board. www.collegboard.com

College Admissions Face to Face. Ann. S. Utterback. Transemantics.

The College Admissions Mystique. Bill Mayher. Farrar, Strauss, and Giroux.

Colleges that Change Lives: 40 Schools that Will Change the Way You Think about College. Loren Pope. Sourcebooks, Inc.

The College Finder: Choosing the School That's Right for You! Steve Antonoff. Wintergreen Orchard House.

The College Handbook. The College Board. www.collegeboard.com

The Fiske Guide to Colleges. Edward B. Fiske. Sourcebooks. www.fiskeguide.com

The Gatekeepers: Inside the Admissions Process of a Premier College. Jacques Steinberg. Penguin.

Get into Any College: Secrets of Harvard Students. Gen Tanabe and Kelly Tanabe. SuperCollege. www.supercollege.com

Insider's Guide to the College. Yale Daily News. St. Martin's Griffin.

Rugg's: Recommendations on the Colleges. Frederick E. Ruggs. Rugg's Recommendations. www.thegrid.net/frugg

Your College Application. Scott Gelband, Catherine Kubale, Eric Schorr. The College Board. www.collegeboard.com

Writing a Winning College Application Essay. Wilma Davidson and Susan McCloskey. Peterson's. www.petersons.com

CHAPTER III

FOR STUDENTS WITH DISABILITIES

My English Teaching Fellow returned my first paper to me with a C- and I was anxious to get his feedback. I had never received a grade lower than B throughout my high school years, but now I was in college and things would be different. Before I could speak, the tutor surprised me by apologizing. I was taken off guard and I thought to myself, why is he apologizing, maybe the paper deserves a higher grade and now he is going to tell me he made a mistake. I was wrong—he was not apologizing because of the grade; he was apologizing because he felt bad for having to upset me because of my physical disability. In a word, he felt sorry for me and he did not want to cause me any pain. I was able to assert myself and inform him that I did not want nor need sympathy. What I needed was to learn how to write and I thanked him for taking the time to give me the detailed feedback. It was the first time in my life I had been told that my academic skills in writing needed much improvement. In many ways having this frank and honest discussion with my tutor made me feel more human, and served me well throughout my college years.

—Joshua Williams

STUDENTS WITH DISABILITIES ARE SOMETIMES thought to be extraordinary for their accomplishments, or they are characterized as fragile and helpless. While their disabilities may present more challenges for them than the average person, they are no less human, and as such should be treated with respect. At the same time, they should be expected to achieve to the best of their abilities like any other human being. In Joshua's case, he did improve his writing. His major in Journalism and subsequent job in that profession are a testament to his abilities.

Whether you are or are not a parent with a disability yourself, you know the challenges your child who has one can face. Unfortunately for students with disabilities, they live in a culture that is designed for and by those who do not have disabilities. The good news, however, is individuals with disabilities are protected by laws, and many of those laws are designed to inform a student's education in positive ways. The purpose of this chapter is to briefly discuss how families can use these laws to support their kids as they are planning for, applying to, and getting through college. Like all parents, they tend to advocate for their students during the pre-college years but once they are in college it is expected that they will begin to advocate for themselves. For the student with a disability, being able to become more independent in college is imperative since it can be a marker of his success as an independent person in life. Preparing for and choosing the right college is essential in this journey for the student with disabilities.

DEFINING DISABILITY

According to the American Disabilities Act (1990), a civil rights law that prohibits discrimination against people with disabilities, a disabled person is defined as an individual with a physical or mental impairment that limits one of more of the major life activities: performing basic personal care, walking, seeing, hearing, learning, and working. Some of these disabilities are more apparent than others, particularly those of a physical nature like muscular dystrophy, and some are less apparent like dyscalculia, which is defined as difficulty with calculations or the rapid processing of math facts. Whether your teen has a visible or invisible disability, current assessments of their strengths and weaknesses are imperative. To make this diagnosis, a school psychologist will provide a battery of tests at no expense to you. Many of these tests will include at least the Woodcock Johnson III and the WAIS-III–The Wechsler Adult Intelligence Scale (WAIS) intelligence quotient (IQ) tests are the primary clinical instruments used to measure adult and adolescent intelligence. The Wechsler Intelligence Scale, 4th edition (WISC-IV) is used for students from ages 6-16. To consider and assess both emotional and neuropsychological factors, more projective measurements are necessary, for example, the Thematic Apperception Test (TAT) and or the Rorschach for older teens and adults. For younger teens, the Roberts Apperception Scale, 2nd edition is commonly used. Finally, the Tell Me A Story is a projective measurement for African and Hispanic American students up to age 16. The results of these tests will indicate if your teen has a learning disability, what the nature of it is, and what, if any, services, and/or special accommodations are needed in the classroom setting. This document is generally referred to as an IEP, Individualized Educational Plan, and should be updated and sent to colleges at the appropriate time.

For those with physical disabilities like hearing, or more obvious physical impairments like blindness, other issues are paramount. You and your teen will have to evaluate the infrastructure and make sure that it is designed to accommodate your teen's physical impairment. For example, is the terrain hilly or flat? Are campus buildings user-friendly for students with mobility-related disabilities? Are public bathrooms wheelchair-accessible? Is the campus shuttle accessible to students with disabilities throughout the regularly scheduled class and meal times?

Part of your teen's IEP that is sent to the college should address the unique academic as well as the physical needs of your teen.

THE HIGH SCHOOL YEARS

CLASSES

Like all students, those who have a disability who are college bound need to think about laying a foundation to reach that goal. That means, with the appropriate support services, they should be expected to take college preparatory courses and when possible stretch themselves by taking some of the Advance Placement and/or honor classes as well. Some students who have a learning disability will have an IEP, which will inform what classroom accommodations are needed. Students with physical disabilities may be attending schools for the blind, or other examples are students who are limited to wheelchairs, but who may attend regular school. Independent of what category your teen is in they should make the most of high school and know that they too can go to and succeed in college.

TESTING

All students will be expected to take either the SAT or the ACT, but some students who have a learning disability will be able to take these exams under standard conditions while others may not. Students who require accommodations for the SAT and ACT must request these accommodations from either Educational Testing Service (ETS) in Princeton, New Jersey, or from American College Testing (ACT) in Iowa City, Iowa. Speak to your child's guidance counselor early in the school year to make sure the paperwork is processed on time. It usually takes four weeks before the regular registration deadline to process the paperwork and parents will need a copy of the student's IEP, which in most cases should also be in the guidance office at your teen's school.

In addition to the standardized college entrance testing, parents should also be aware that their teens may qualify for special accommodations in their classes at school as well. For example, they may need extended time on tests and exams, or they may need to be moved to a room that is very quiet with no distractions so they can focus. They may be allowed to use a computer for an essay test to help them organize their thoughts and handle issues around spelling; or, they may need a teacher to re-explain written instructions. It is up to you to advocate for your teen since the teacher may not always know they qualify for these services.

EXTRACURRICULAR ACTIVITIES

Encourage your teen to get involved with in- and out-of-school activities. They may be able to participate in sports and clubs with students in general and/or they may want to join a club for students who have disabilities. Some students who have physical challenges elect the latter, though there is no reason why a student who is confined to wheelchair cannot join the chess club at his school if that is his interest. Similarly, there is no excuse for a blind student being discouraged from attending her high school's football game. Hopefully with family and community support these students too can benefit from what life outside class in high school can offer.

APPLYING TO COLLEGE

As you and your family begin the research for college, keep in mind that you want the college to know about you and you want to learn something about the college. While you are learning about the college keep in mind three basic requirements: the admissions requirements for each school; the general graduation requirements for the particular college; and if you have decided on a major, the graduation requirements for your particular major. These are central questions that should be answered before your teen decides if a school is right for them. For example, your teen may not have the qualifications to get into a school of his choice or a school that he thought would be good for him or the school may not offer his major. But, once they have found some schools that meet their basic requirements and whose requirements they meet, they are ready to advance to the next level.

When applying to college if your teen's disability is not obvious they will have to self-disclose. Self-disclosing will not work against them. In fact, it can help them ultimately by guaranteeing that they have chosen a place that is right for them. While searching for a college can be filled with an equal set of rewards and challenges for most, it is particularly challenging for students who have disabilities because they have so many more factors to consider when researching schools. They also have the added burden of struggling to become more independent, while still having to be dependent in ways that other students do not.

When sitting down with your teen and helping them assess their strengths, weaknesses, and needs try to let them come to the answers to those questions on their own. Let them take control over defining who they are and what they want and need. It is a good transition stage as they move away from letting you advocate for them and moving towards advocating for themselves.

Make sure that your family has an up-to-date Psycho-Educational Test with the most current IEP. You will need to submit this document to colleges when you apply. Also, before conducing your college search, advise your teen to read the test reports and the IEP. In most cases the jargon will be easy to understand and interpret. Hopefully, this will not be the first time your student has had an opportunity to discuss the results of these tests with you and the school counselor.

One of the best resource guides for students with learning disabilities is *The K&W Guide to Colleges for Students with Learning Disabilities*, by Marybeth Kravets and Imy Wax (Random House). This does not mean that your teen should not reference other guides mentioned in this book, but for the student who has a learning disability this one is a must. Please know that there are hundreds of schools in the country that have wonderful services and programs on their campuses to assist your teen with their journey to become independent and well educated. It is your responsibility, along with your teen, to do your homework and find that right school. Knowing your teen and what his needs are is the first step, and by now you have already achieved that first one and you are ready to search the web, read through the guidebooks, make some phone calls, and eventually get on the road and visit some of the schools. And while I value the knowledge one can gain from talking with friends, reading, and surfing the Internet, there is nothing like a face-to-face visit to a campus. In that way you can test out some of the services firsthand. While visiting, make certain that you visit the Office for Students with Disabilities and be honest about what your teen's strengths and weaknesses are. It would also be advisable to bring the IEP with you when you visit the school in case you have to reference it or in case an academic advisor or counselor requests to see it. These offices will vary in the kind of and quality of services they provide but most should offer support in academic advising, vocational counseling, personal counseling, diagnostic assessment, and remedial skill development to name a few.

In addition to the characteristics that shape many students' college search, students with disabilities sometimes have to consider other factors, for example, if the school offers a learning environment that will accommodate their learning style. Some students prefer small schools because the way they learn requires a smaller classroom setting, while others may not want to be as visible and may prefer a larger school. Still others who have a physical disability may want a campus that is more flat or at least one that has wheelchair accessibility within buildings and shuttle service to and from buildings. In a larger school navigating one-self across campus could consume too much energy and thus a smaller campus could be more appealing. Still other students prefer to live at home and commute to school. At home they have resources and know what they can expect while at college they will have to depend on the un-known and in some cases it may not work. On the other hand, staying at home could stifle growth and limit one's independence. Still for other students, distance learning is an option, but this too has its limitations since one does not have the opportunity to interact with fellow classmates and benefit from the undergraduate experience that living on campus offers. Your research and subsequent visits should help your teen narrow down their college search which should consist of at least nine or ten schools with at least three of which they definitely can get in, generally referred to as "safeties" or "safe schools."

FINANCIAL AID

In addition to applying for the Pell Grant and Federal Supplemental Educational Opportunity Grant, students should also check with their college to find out what scholarships are available for students with disabilities. The Nordstrom Corporation annually awards competitive scholarships to students with disabilities and the National Federation for the Blind offers scholarships for outstanding students. Of course, students with disabilities should be encouraged to compete for scholarships that are open to all students particularly those earmarked for students with competitive GPAs.

GETTING THROUGH COLLEGE

Hopefully your teen has chosen a school that will accommodate their needs and provide you as a parent with the comfort level so that you will not have to worry about your teen living independently and being his or her own advocate. You and your teen are aware of the support services at the college and you both are aware of how and when they should be accessed. Your teen is now on off to navigate this new landscape as an independent agent. Trust that you have provided the wisdom, knowledge, and common sense for exercising sound judgment. Know that you have taught your child how to stand up and be counted and to do so even under the worst of conditions, and do so in a dignified manner. While it was true for high school that successes or failures were a reflection of you as the parent, in college they are more a reflection of your teen. Let them make their mistakes—they are human and entitled to do so—but know that it is the end result that counts and in four years, armed with your emotional support and love, your teen will be okay.

● ● ● ●

My daughter had to defer entry into college for a year due to orthopedic complications from kidney disease. She took a year off in order to heal from double hip replacement surgery.

As a third-generation graduate from a historically black college, I was delighted by the prospect of Etienne becoming a fourth member to attend my alma mater. Her first semester went well, she was able to live in the dormitory, and she performed well academically. Then, at the end of the semester, she had a serious medical relapse and that is when the bottom fell out in terms of support services from the university. Although Etienne followed university protocol, registering as a medically compromised student, and provided all the documentation from our doctor, the university failed to meet her physical and educational needs. The list of egregious slights, incidents, and errors are too numerous to mention. We transferred to a predominantly white institution not far from our home, hoping that we would not have to face the same challenges experienced at the previous school. Unfortunately, basically the same scenario came to pass there as well. Each situation, though slightly different, had the same effect. It demoralized and depressed my daughter, and she eventually expressed a desire to quit school. My response to her was, I could lower the bar because of her circumstances, but I would extend the finish line.

I am proud to say that her spirit has not been broken entirely by these obstacles. She has enrolled in a local community college that is meeting all of her needs and doing so in a timely and professional manner. Two and four-year colleges should review the policies and practices from this community college on how to respond to students with physical disabilities.

Etienne eventually found out that a live donor was prepared to give her a kidney in the middle of second semester at the community college. Despite the fact that her recovery would take five to eight weeks, she did not withdraw from classes. With the help of positive support from her instructors, she is back in class and did not miss a beat.

I strongly recommend to parents that whether their child has a physical or a learning disability that they thoroughly evaluate the university's policies and practices and challenge the protocol if they feel it is not responding to the needs of their child. Take them to task if they fail to live up to their promises and transfer your student if you must. They already suffer enough confronting the medical and physical challenges.

—**Carol Cromer**

RESOURCES AND REFERENCES

For Students with Disabilities

ABLEDATA, 8630 Fenton Street, Suite 930, Silver Spring, MD 20910
Phone: 1.800.227.0216
Website: www.abledata.com

ACT, P.O. Box 4028, Iowa City, IA 52243-4028
Phone: 319.337.1332
Website: www.act.org

American Association for the Advancement of Science, 1200 New York
Avenue, NW, Washington, DC 20005
Phone: 202.326.6630
Website: www.aaas.org

Association of Higher Education and Disability (AHEAD), P.O. Box
21192, Columbus, OH 43220
Phone: 614.488.4972
Website: www.ahead.org

Council for Exceptional Children, 1920 Association Drive,
Reston, VA 20191-1589
Phone: 703.620.3660
Website: www.cec.sped.org

Disability Rights Education and Defense Fund, 2212 6th Street,
Berkley, CA 94710
Phone: 510.841.8645
Website: www.dredf.org

Distance Education and Training Council, 1601 18th Street. NW,
Washington, DC 20009
Phone: 202.234.5100
Website: www.detc.org

Educational Testing Services, SAT-Special Services for Students with
Disabilities, P.O. Box 6226, Princeton, NJ 08541-6226
Phone: 609.771.7137
Website: www.ets.org

HEATH Resource Center, One Dupont Circle, Ste. 800, Washington,
DC 20202
Phone: 800.433.3243
Website: www.acuept.edu/programs/health/

College Confidence with ADD. Michael Sandler. Sourcebooks.

The K & W Guide to Colleges for Students with Learning Disabilities.
Marybeth Kravets and Imy F. Wax. Random House.

THE COLLEGE ATHLETE

I played quarterback at Woodson High School in Washington, DC, which has the reputation of producing some excellent athletes. I was an excellent student as well, because I was expected to be, and if I was not my family would not allow me to play football. Because I had good grades and was a strong athlete, I was a strong prospect for numerous college coaches; Fordham was one of them. My high school coach was very engaged in the process, by making sure that I complied with NCAA Clearinghouse Guidelines with respect to my high school roster, and he also made sure that I prepared for and took the SAT by my junior year in high school. By doing so when recruiters came he would have all my stats available as well as tapes to share with the college coaches. Once the college coaches saw my tapes and they were sufficiently impressed, then they would want to know my GPA and SAT score to see if I would make the cut. In the case of the Fordham coach, I did, and the Assistant Coach came to my home, and then the Head Coach came and eventually I was invited, along with one family member to visit the college with all expenses paid. Lots of guys have the talent but they do not have the stats. If I had one piece of advice for future high school athletes who want to play ball in a DI or DII program they should go online and access NCAA Clearinghouse Guidelines their first year of high school as well as have their parents send them to same football camps in the summer where they can test their athletic skills on a national circuit and also learn from college coaches what the academic expectations are in high school. Then they will know what they need to do and all that is left is to get busy.

—**Derric Daniels**
Fordham University graduate

STUDENTS AND PARENTS ALIKE SOMETIMES have an unrealistic sense of their teen's athletic ability. However, if your son or daughter has expressed an interest in participating in sports at the college level, you will need to stay front and center and be vigilant about the stages involved. This includes the planning, recruiting, and marketing process, as well as a thorough understanding of any signed agreements once your teen has committed to playing sports at a particular college.

Early on families need to develop an understanding of the athlete's responsibilities throughout high school as well as during the entire recruitment process. Parents must be familiar with the NCAA Initial Eligibility Rules and ensure that a successful academic experience is the overriding consideration for the college decision. After all, the probability of competing in athletics beyond the high school level is doubtful for most. The statistics below are not to discourage students but rather to illustrate this point. If however, after absorbing the statistics presented here, your teen is still committed to participating in sports at the college level, then this chapter is for you.

Men's Basketball

- 1 in 35 high school senior boys will go on to play basketball at the college level.
- Approximately 1 in 13,000 high school players will be drafted by an NBA team.

Women's Basketball

- 3.3 percent of high school players will go on to play in college.
- .02 percent of high school players will play professionally.

Football

- About 5.8 percent of all high school senior boys will go on to play in college
- .08 percent of all high school players will make and NFL roster.

Baseball

- Only 6.1 percent of high school players will play in college.

Men's Hockey

- Only 11 out 100 high school senior boys will play hockey in college.

Source: NCAA

The level of college athletics at which a student competes will depend on their talent and the commitment they are willing to make to that sport. As you read further in this chapter, remember tracking the educational planning and college placement process of an athlete is a team responsibility, that of the student, parent, school counselor, and coach.

What follows is an overview of the various stages with which families must be familiar as they guide their college-bound athlete toward fulfilling their goal of participating in sports at the college level.

HOW SPORTS ARE ORGANIZED AT THE COLLEGE LEVEL

If your teen is an athlete and they want to participate in a competitive sport program at the college level, there are several divisions. For those who choose to participate in sports but choose not to do so competitively, they can participate through intramural sports which can be just as much fun without the pressure.

NCAA Division I commonly referred to as "DI" is the highest level of intercollegiate athletics and includes many of the universities that you see competing on television. Colleges that field football teams and are further classified as Football Bowl Subdivision, formerly Division IA and Football Championship Subdivision, formerly Division IAA. The difference between these levels is the quality and depth of talented athletes and the philosophical and financial commitment a university makes to its athletic program. Whether a DI or DIAA athlete, all face an enormous time commitment; there is no off season. Athletes sometimes feel like playing their sport is a job and often feel pressured to perform.

NCAA Division II or "D2" includes small-sized schools with lesser-known athletic reputations. The teams usually feature a number of local or in-state student-athletes, with most paying for school with some combination of scholarship money, grants, student loans, and employment earnings. Even in "D2" programs students still face a substantial time commitment to the sport.

NCAA Division III or "D3" is the largest within the NCAA. However, "D3" athletes receive no financial aid related to their athletic ability. Emphasis here is on the participant rather than on the spectators. Generally, athletes compete because they love their sport. They are highly skilled and competitive, and in some cases they have as much talent as their peers at "DI" and "DII" programs, but the time commitment is not as huge as Divisions I and II. Some athletes at DIII schools maintain that while they love playing sports, playing at a DIII school also allows them the opportunity to have a more normal undergraduate experience.

Some colleges maintain concurrent memberships in two different divisions so, for example, a school may have and men's ice hockey team playing at the Division I level, and play at the Division III level in all other sports.

NCAA ELIGIBILITY RULES

Prospective student-athletes must meet established standards to practice, compete, and receive athletically related financial aid. In Divisions I and II, students must be certified by the NCAA Eligibility Center. In Division III, eligibility for admission, financial aid, practice, and competition is determined by institutional regulations.

Sometimes the rules for NCAA eligibility can change so it is important to make sure that one is clear that the rules that are informing the decisions students, parents, and coaches are the most current. Generally speaking, students must graduate from high school with a minimum number of core courses. They also must have minimum core course grade-point average, and finally they need a qualifying score on the SAT or ACT.

With respect to the grade-point average, it is important to emphasize that the grade-point average has to be calculated among the required core courses. Each high school has its own list of NCAA-approved core courses. Only courses that appear on this list can be used in calculating a student's core grade-point average. A student may have a an overall grade-point average of 2.8 out of 4.0, but when one deletes the non-core courses the grade-point average could go down and thus jeopardize the student's eligibility. If you want to find your high school's list, go to www.ncaaclearinghouse.net and select High School Administration. Then you would click on List of Approved Core Courses and follow the prompts. It is vital that your high school's list of approved core courses is current. Review your list at least once each year to avoid eligibility issues.

It is also important to note that when I am speaking of grade-point average and qualifying test scores, I am doing so for only eligibility with the NCAA specifically. This does not mean they have necessarily satisfied the requirements for a particular college. When students are doing their research they should contact the coach and/or admissions officer at the colleges in which they have an interest to determine what specific requirements are required for the college athletes. Requirements for college-bound athletes at some schools do vary from those required of the non-college bound athlete, but at other schools they are the same. This is particularly the case at many of the competitive colleges. See the GPA and Test Score Sliding Scale on the NCAA student website at www.ncaastudent.org.

ACADEMIC PLANNING IN HIGH SCHOOL
FOR THE COLLEGE-BOUND ATHLETE

Before discussing the specific core curriculum that a college-bound ath-lete would follow in high school, it is important to note that there are specific high school courses that the NCAA Eligibility Center will accept, for example, Spanish I, or Algebra I, if it is placed on the high school transcript with a grade and a credit, and it is on the high school's list of approved core courses.

If your teen is aspiring to participate in sports at a Division I college he or she must earn sixteen credits in the following core courses:

- 4 years of English;

- 3 years of math in Algebra I or higher;

- 2 years of natural science and one must be with a lab, for exam-ple, Biology;

- 1 year of an additional English, math, or science class;

- 2 years of social studies; and

- 4 years of additional courses in any area above or foreign lan-guage, non-doctrinal religion, or philosophy.

Prospective student-athletes must complete the core curriculum by the graduation date of his or her class based on entry into grade nine. If the prospective student-athlete graduates on time, one additional core course may be used for initial-eligibility purposes, may be completed at any high school, must be completed within one year of graduation, and can be used to improve the core-course grade-point average.

If your teen is aspiring to participate in sports at a Division II college he or she must earn fourteen credits in the following core courses:

- 3 years of English;

- 2 years of math in Algebra I or higher;

- 2 years of natural science and one must be a lab science, for ex-ample, Chemistry;

- 2 years of additional English, math, or science;

- 2 years of social studies; and

- 3 years additional courses in any area above, or foreign language, non-doctrinal religion, or philosophy.

Prospective student-athletes must complete the core curriculum before initial full-time collegiate enrollment.

The grade-point average and test requirements for Division I prospective student-athletes correspond to the sixteen-course rule and can be found on the enclosed Initial-Eligibility Index Sliding Scale. For Division II prospective student-athletes, there is a minimum core grade-point average of 2.0 and a minimum SAT score of 820 or an ACT sum score of 68. For Division II prospects there is no sliding scale.

Whether a DI or DII prospect, all tests must be taken on a national test date under standard test conditions unless you are a student who has been classified with a learning disability and has a documented (IEP) Individualized Educational Plan, which allows you to take the test administration under different conditions. In all cases, test must be reported directly to the NCAA Eligibility Center by the testing agency. Test scores on transcripts were deemed unacceptable as official documentation as of August 1, 2007.

WORKING WITH YOUR HIGH SCHOOL COUNSELOR AND COACH

If you are fortunate your teen attends a school where the high school counselor and coach are working in chorus to assist you and your teen in the planning and application process. While it is important that the staff at your teen's school work constructively on their behalf, they also are developing and sustaining relationships with appropriate professionals at the various colleges and universities nationwide. More specifically, the school counselor has a strong network across colleges with the various admissions counselors, and the coach has established a working relationship with several coaches at a number of colleges as well. In this way the counselor and coach can use their leverage to support you and your family.

Earlier on in this chapter I discussed the importance of families, counselors, and coaches working as a team, and I want to re-emphasize this here again since I judge this to be vitally important. Of course, this same principle applies to the non-student athlete as well, but since the focus in this chapter is on the prospective college athlete, I am addressing them as a specific group. That having been said, I would recommend that you as parents think about your counselor as a resource who can also work in chorus with the coach in the best interest of your teen in several ways.

Counselors and coaches first will know, or at least should know, the eligibility requirements. With this knowledge they will be in a better position to coach your teen appropriately. They can also work together in shaping a high school program that speaks to the requirements established by the NCAA Clearinghouse, and they will be able to do so in a timely manner so that by the time your teen is a junior or senior he or she is well on their way in satisfying these requirements. If for some reason they don't, there should be time in the junior and senior year to compensate for what they did not achieve in the earlier years of high school.

Not only should the counselor think about the courses, but they also should design a testing schedule that prepares the student for the SAT and the ACT earlier in high school by exposing the student to the PSAT and PLAN. By having exposure to these preparation tests, the students will be more able to negotiate the SAT and ACT. Of course, they should also be advised to take the SAT and ACT at least twice, thereby increasing their chances of achieving the desired score. Once students have accomplished the desired GPA and SAT or ACT score, they are able to position themselves more competitively for the college team of their choice.

Before a student can determine if they have the desired GPA, they will need guidance on how to calculate it, and here again is where the counselor can add some value. Parents should encourage counselors to sit with the student and family to discuss the GPA of the student at the end of each academic year. The student should be advised that it is imperative to start off with a strong GPA because if not they will be under pressure to bring up a low GPA throughout their high school years. Once the student knows how to calculate his or her GPA they can do so independently. A counselor will emphasize the importance of academic performance at every step of their high school career and ninth grade counts. Poor grades and test scores can result in future eligibility problems and decreased interest from college recruiters.

Parents who have students with learning disabilities should expect that their school counselor will understand the policy and practices specific to LD students. For example, they may work very closely with the Special Needs department, and the student may have been given an Independent Educational Plan. For example, the student may qualify for extended time on the SAT. If this were the case, the counselor would coach the family on how to register for the test under these circumstances. One thing to keep in mind if your teen fits this category is the timing factor. To register a student for the SAT who qualifies for specific accommodations one has to do so much earlier than those students who are registering for the SAT without special accommodations. For more on students who have learning disabilities please refer to Chapter 3.

All counselors will create an efficient system for processing clearinghouse applications including submission of the final transcript. Generally a counselor will arrange a meeting with the parent, student, and ideally the coach, if he or she can attend the meeting, to evaluate the past performance of the student and to make recommendations for the final years of high school. This assumes, of course, that this meeting is occurring at some point in the junior year, separately from an earlier meeting that should have taken place in the freshmen year and/or in the sophomore year.

Parents can also expect that the counselor will arrange a meeting about conducting a college search. Depending on the counselor caseload this meeting would be combined with the aforementioned one where after the counselor evaluates the student's past performance and makes recommendations, for example, for the senior year, and the counselor can then move to a discussion about the college search.

Too often the college-bound athlete approaches this process re-actively when in the ideal world all students should approach this process pro-actively. Athletes, on the other hand, are always being told what to do, as opposed to being encouraged to think for themselves, unless it is the quarterback who makes the decisions for the football team. But even in this example, his coach may be advising him.

That having been said, when choosing a school, ask the counselor to help the student identify colleges that fit his or her criteria, for example, size, location, campus setting, availability of academic programs, and, of course, level of athletic completion. A question that I would also recommend that families consider is, Would my teen still attend this college even if they were injured and could never again compete? If the answer is yes, then that sounds like the school would be a good match, but if the answer is no, the student might want to think about whether he or she should seriously consider the school, since there is no guarantee that an athlete will be able to play all four years.

Much of what has been said up to this point has placed much of the responsibility in the hands of the counselors, and, from my position, that is as it should be. Counselors work with a wide range of students, and as part of their caseload they will have some athletes assigned to them. However, earlier I spoke to the importance of team effort and thus it is incumbent on the counselor to reach out to the school's athletic department to identify potential college-bound students. The counselors and coaches could meet to develop a guide for the college-bound athlete that includes academic and athletic tasks for each year. As part of their program, athletes can invite knowledgeable objective college athletics representatives to speak to you, the parent, your teen, counselors, but most importantly, high school coaches. In some schools there is one counselor who works with all the athletes, but in most schools, one counselor has a more general caseload, and thus is working with the non-athlete as well as the athlete.

For all students, planning for and choosing a college is not a static process. One day a teen may be interested in playing sports at Duke, and two weeks later Duke could be off the radar and University of North Carolina is now being seriously considered. Whatever the process, the student's parents and coaches must stay involved. Remember, this is a team effort.

MARKETING YOUR TEEN

Earlier we spoke about the importance of team effort with respect to planning for college, but there are students who do not have a good working relationship with either their counselor or their coach. This is not to say that the student is a problem; in fact, he or she could be a very good student academically as well as a well-respected member of the school community but have the misfortune of having a counselor and/or coach who is inundated with multiple problems and tasks. In this case, some students may not receive the attention that they deserve and need. If your teen fits into this category, parents have to be more deliberate about marketing their teen.

When I think about marketing your teen, I am thinking about a three-step process: as parents you need to honestly assess your teen's academic and athletic abilities; identify appropriate colleges based on that assessment; and communicate with the college coaches.

In assessing your teen's athletic ability you have to be very objective and rely heavily on the coach. Whether or not the coach is directly involved, he or she should give your son or daughter and you an honest evaluation to prevent an inflated sense of what your child's athletic skill sets are.

If your child does not have good relationship with the counselor, he or she will have to identify colleges independently. The final list should be based primarily on the quality of the academic program, not just athletic interest. Once you and your student have developed the college list, he or she can begin reaching out to the coaches at these schools. It's important to:

- Identify the names of the head coaches

- Send an email to the coaches expressing interest in that college of interest

- Create an athletic resume that summarizes their academic and athletic accomplishments

- Promptly return a coach's request for information and always be truthful

- Be seen at summer camps, recruiting showcase events, travel teams, summer leagues, etc.

- If possible, earn the recommendation of the high school coach that the college recruiter may contact

- Families do not depend on coaches to make a tape: develop your own and make sufficient copies in the event that during the recruitment process a college may ask for one to be sent to the recruitment office.

THE RECRUITMENT PROCESS

If your teen has prepared for college both from an academic and athletic perspective he or she is going to a very marketable candidate, and when coaches begin their recruitment cycle your teen is going to stand out. College coaches evaluate recruits in three areas: athletic ability, academic achievement, and quality of character.

Early in the recruitment process college coaches have to identify prospective college athletes, and they can do so in several ways:

- Evaluations from high school and club coaches

- They see athletes play in varsity competition, sports camps, showcase events, summer leagues, and tournaments

- Newspaper clippings

- Recommendations from current student-athletes, alumni, or community leaders

- Reputable recruiting services

- Student-athletes marketing themselves and introducing themselves to the coach

Once the coach has been made aware of who is potentially a prospect he or she can now be more deliberate about reaching out to your teen. There are several ways that a college coach indicates their interest in a prospective college athlete:

- Letters that are sent directly to the home of the student

- Personal handwritten correspondence sent to the home

- Students may receive questionnaires, brochures, or media guides

- Talking with the high school, summer league, or club team coach

- Phone calls to home

- Watching games and/or practices at your teen's high school

- A school visit where the high school coach may show some tapes of your teen's performance on the field, court, etc.

- Home visit where he would speak with the teen and the family

- Invite the prospective student to visit campus for an official visit

Students and parents should be able to gauge the recruiter's level of interest by the quality and quantity of the contacts from the coaches. I would not be too aggressive if you find that the coach is not responding to your calls and or emails. He or she is probably not interested. But I also would not give up. If you qualify for admissions to the college, independent of your athletic abilities you will have the opportunity to make an appointment and visit the coach to discuss the possibility of being considered as a walk-on.

RECRUITING SCOUTING SERVICES

If you have the means to hire a professional recruiting scouting counselor, please know that like most counseling services, some are reputable and some are not. Since your teen is your most precious resource, I would recommend that you do your homework and gather as much information about the recruitment scouting service before you sign on. I certainly feel that asking for two or three references is in order. You also want to compare fees, as sometimes fees can be quite hefty for private consulting service. In addition to references, I would also suggest that you determine if the counselor is a member of professional organizations. For example, the Independent Educational Association sometimes has members who provide private educational consulting services for the college-bound athlete. A final thought is to contact the colleges in which your teen has an interest and inquire if any of the coaches are familiar with the recruiting scouting services. In the ideal world the counselors from the private company should be working jointly with your teen's school counselor, but in other cases families may hire a private counselor because they lack the confidence that the school counselor and/or school coach can adequately represent their teen. Since I have worked both as a school-based counselor and an independent counselor, I recognize that in both one can find reputable advocates for you and your teen.

CERTIFICATION AND NON-CERTIFICATION DECISIONS (DIVISION I)

By the end of the recruitment process you want to know that your teen is certified, which means that he or she has met all of the requirements, is able to practice with the team, compete, receive aid, and is eligible to do all of the above for four years.

If the student is designated as a non-qualifier, he or she has not met all of the requirements, e.g. lacks core courses, has not graduated, and does not meet sliding scale requirements. Since they do not satisfy the aforementioned, there cannot practice, may not compete, and may not receive financial aid.

CERTIFICATION DECISIONS AND NON-CERTIFICATION DECISIONS (DIVISION II)

Like in Division I, the "Qualifier" meets all requirements, may practice, compete, and receive aid for four seasons of competition. But unlike Division I, Division II has "Partial Qualifier" status as long as the student has graduated from high school, has satisfied the minimum test score requirement, and has a GPA of 2.0 on a 4.0 grading scale. If the student satisfies these requirements, they may practice and receive aid, and compete for four seasons.

The non-qualifier does not meet the requirements for the qualifier or partial qualifier because they lack the core courses, the GPA, and the test score requirement and has not graduated from high school. Therefore, they may not practice, compete, nor receive aid any of the four seasons of competition.

EARLY CERTIFICATION (DIVISION I)

When thinking about an athlete's certification status they may want to position themselves for Early Certification. This means they can certify as early as their junior year. The criteria for early certification requires that the athlete has a minimum combined SAT of 1000 or a minimum sum ACT score of 85 and a core-course GPA of 3.0 or higher on a 4.0 scale, in a minimum of 13 core courses upon completion of six semesters or the equivalent. The 13 core courses must include three core courses in English, two in math, two in natural or physical science, and six additional courses in any NCAA core area.

EARLY CERTIFICATION (DIVISION II)

An athlete for a DII program will need a minimum combined SAT score of 1000 or a minimum ACT score of 85 and a core-course GPA of 3.0 on a 4.0 scale, in a minimum of 12 core courses upon completion of six semesters or the equivalent. The 12 courses must include three core courses in English, two in math at the level of Algebra I or higher, two in natural science, including at least one laboratory course if offered at the high school, and five additional core courses in any NCAA core area.

IMPORTANT POINTS TO REMEMBER REGARDING SCHOLARSHIPS

All athletic scholarships awarded by NCAA institutions are limited to one year and are renewable annually. A four-year award does not exist in the athletic world. Athletic scholarships may be renewed annually for a maximum of five years within a six-year period of continuous college attendance. Athletics aid may also be canceled or reduced at the end of each year for any reason the coach deems necessary.

Finally, please note that athletic awards vary widely, ranging from full scholarships—including tuition, room, board, fees, and books—to very small scholarships and books only. Your Letter of Intent, which is your contract with the college athletic program, will spell out the details of your scholarship. Like any other contract, make sure you read and understand the contents before you and your teen sign.

● ● ● ●

The best recommendation for a parent who has an athlete applying to college is to make sure your son or daughter has a backup plan in case of injury, getting cut or simply losing interest in the sport. The backup should be a good, solid education. So few college athletes ever make it to the pros, so life after sports has to be addressed.

There are rewards and challenges of being a student athlete. The difficulty is not only the time and commitment entailed in most sports programs, but also the loss of being a part of the social fabric of a school.

The rewards are that from day one, an athlete has an instant group of friends/teammates and can avoid the inevitable awkwardness of being a freshman in a new setting having to make new friends.

And because there is little time for an athlete to find time to party between practices, games, and academic classes, he or she often has more focus and discipline, especially during the months the sport is being played. Often that structured environment transfers into better grades, especially if the sport has coaches that oversee study hours and tutors to make sure the athletes are not falling behind.

—DD Eisenberg

GLOSSARY

Blue Chip Athlete: A highly skilled, accomplished, visible athlete who is known to college coaches at a relatively early age. Most people in the school and community are familiar with this athlete.

Intramural: Sport programs developed within the confines of a particular college or university where students can compete with their fellow classmates.

NAIA: The National Association of Intercollegiate Athletics is the governing body for a group of smaller colleges.

NCAA: The National Collegiate Athletic Association is a governing board for most sports at the college level. Intramural sports do not fall under the aegis of the NCAA.

NJCAA: The National Junior College Athletic Association is the governing body of two-year college athletes. NCJAA members compete at the Division I, II or III level depending on the institution's commitment to athletics.

National Letter of Intent: The NLI is a voluntary program administered by the NCAA Eligibility Center. By signing the NLI, a student agrees to attend the institution for one academic year. In exchange, the academic institution must provide athletic financial aid for one academic year.

Official Visit: An official visit is any visit to a college campus by a student and his or her parents paid for by the college. The college may pay for the following expenses: roundtrip transportation; room and board; and reasonable entertainment expenses, including complimentary tickets to a home game.

For Division I students, before a college may invite a student on an official visit, the student will have to provide the college with a copy of his/her official high school transcript and SAT, ACT, or PLAN scores and register with the NCAA Eligibility Center.

Redshirting: In college sports a term referring to delaying a college athlete's participation in order to lengthen his or her eligibility.

Unofficial Visit: Any visit by a student and his parents to a college campus paid for by the student or by his parents. The only expense a student may receive from the college is two or three complimentary tickets to a home athletic game.

A student may make as many unofficial visits as he or she would like and may make those visits at any time. The only time a student cannot talk with a coach is during a dead period, which is a planned period, often in August, during which there is no involvement or contact by the school or coach with students in order to limit the time coaches can coach their athletes.

Verbal Commitment: A verbal commitment describes a college-bound athlete's commitment before he or she signs, or is able to sign, a National Letter of Intent.

A college-bound athlete may announce a verbal commitment at any time. While verbal commitments have become very popular for both athletes and coaches, this commitment is not binding on either the athlete or the school.

Only the National Letter of Intent, accompanied by a financial aid agreement, is binding by both parties.

Walk-on: A walk-on is a student who is not formally recruited by the school but who becomes an official team member. An outside party may have brought the student to the coach's attention; sometimes the athlete was of interest to the coach at the time of his or her candidacy for admission but not courted by the school because of budget limitations. While a walk-on may receive financial aid, the student is not supported by an athletic scholarship.

Yellow Chip Athlete: A skilled athlete who can continue their athletic careers beyond high school but is less visible to college recruiters. There are differing opinions on the college level at which the athlete can compete.

REFERENCES

The Sports Scholarships Insider's Guide. Dion Wheeler. Sourcebooks. 2nd ed.

The Student Athlete's Guide to Getting Recruited. Stewart Brown. SuperCollege.

ESPECIALLY FOR STUDENTS OF COLOR

While studying at Swarthmore I worked in the Music Library. I recall working on one occasion and listening to music at the library's circulation desk, which was a fairly common experience among student library workers. This particular day sticks out for me because I was asked to lower my music by the librarian. This would not have been an unreasonable request even though the volume of my music was relatively low. What the librarian said to me was shocking and disheartening. He added to his request for the lowering of my music that the student, the only student in the library at the time, a white woman, was entitled to study un-molested because she paid full tuition. Though it was never made clear whether or not she had paid full tuition, the insinuation was clear, I was a second-class citizen in the librarian's eyes. She was *entitled* to all that the college had to offer and I wasn't. According to him I was less worthy to reap its bounty by virtue of my presumed economic status and, as quiet as it was kept, my race. It was a sobering moment for me. I realized that for many at Swarthmore my presence was merely tolerated and not entirely welcomed. I'm grateful, however, that I had the tenacity to know that my self worth and right to be at Swarthmore was not predicated on my economic status or my race but simply on my ability and desire to learn and to develop myself holistically. So in response to the librarian's classism and racism and to all who felt that I was only at Swarthmore by quota and or government mandate, I simply graduated…along with the "legitimate" students.

—Allen Pinkney

WHILE THE COLLEGE ADMISSIONS PROCESS bestows rewards and obstacles for all students, it can be especially challenging for students of color who want to attend one of the nation's highly selective, predominantly white institutions of higher education, or one of a number of the country's increasingly competitive historically black colleges.

Although the decline in the popularity of affirmative action has undermined race-based scholarships at some public institutions, there are other colleges, particularly the private schools that are not dependent on state funding, and still provide scholarships for students of color. Do not let recent headlines frighten you. When researching schools ask about these scholarships, and keep in mind that if your teen is viewed as someone who can add value to a college community, schools will want them. That means when putting together the financial aid package they will offer you more grant money and fewer loans as an incentive to attend. The more selective schools often have a larger endowment and can consequently offer better financial aid packages. For this reason, it is important for your teen to perform well academically so that they can qualify for the institutions that are more selective and thus offer applicants greater funding.

AFFIRMATIVE ACTION AND YOU

While most students of color, especially today, rely on affirmative action-admissions decisions to gain acceptance into highly competitive white schools, many have benefited from race-based decisions. That option, however, can no longer be taken for granted because recent changes to affirmative action have forced colleges to rethink the way they handle race-based admissions and scholarships. For example, a court case involving the University of Maryland College Park and Daniel Poderesky (1990) became a litmus test for scholarships based on ethnicity. Poderesksy, who is of Hispanic and Jewish extraction, claimed ethnic minority status in applying for a scholarship earmarked for African Americans and was rejected for the scholarship on the grounds of racial ineligibility. He applied for the Benjamin Banneker Scholarship Program for African Americans, a program devised by university officials to attract minority students. Claiming that he was racially eligible, he initiated *Poderesky v. Kiwan* and eventually obtained a court ruling in his favor. The university took the case to the appellate level where it was denied. Some of these earmarked scholarships have been made available to all students, regardless of race, and a few schools that offer them have been told by their State Attorney General that they can no longer offer raced-based scholarships, even if the scholarship comes from a private source.

This change of heart toward affirmative action has already produced significant results. After a ban on affirmative action by the University of California, the law schools at University of California at Berkeley and at UCLA reported a drop in African-American applications of about 80 percent. These decisions have influenced admissions policies at the undergraduate level as well; as of the year 2000 at the University of California at Berkley, race was not used as a factor in admissions decisions. The much-publicized result was the number of African Americans accepted that year fell dramatically from the previous year's figure, and the number of Latino students also dropped.

THE MYSTERY OF ADMISSIONS COMMITTEES

These issues may or may not play a role in a college's decision to admit you. One thing you can count on, though, is that some admissions committees view students of color differently, this is particularly the case for those who are first-generation college bound. *Here we are taking into consideration race and class.* Your best source of advice on how to prepare your teen is their guidance counselor. If he or she has a reasonably good relationship with the admissions staff at your school, your teen may get an idea of what that school's admissions policies are for students of color. For example, if a student of color misses a deadline date and they really want and need your teen, they may make an exception. Similarly, if a white student, who is first in her family to attend college, misses the deadline, they may overlook that fact and consider her application. Here the assumption is that they need more females who are first-generation college bound to round off the entering class. Some schools will take students of color with a slightly lower than average SAT score if the student has an exceptional GPA and is willing to participate in a summer enrichment program at the college preceding his/her freshmen year. Others will look more seriously at leadership qualities and place less importance on the SAT or ACT score.

Whether your teen is a student of color from a privileged background or from an economically disadvantaged background, if they have problems with standardized tests, they are encouraged to take the most rigorous academic program their school can offer. And, once they have positioned themselves in those challenging classes, make sure they study four to five hours a night so they can obtain good grades. In that way they can leverage their academic record if their scores are average or below average. This advice is especially useful for students who are first in their families to attend college, and who, generally, attend economically poor schools. In schools where resources are low, students tend to score poorly on standardized testing. This is not to say that good test coaching cannot help them improve their scores, nor is it to imply that they are unintelligent. On the contrary, it is just simply to say that kids who score better on standardized testing tend to attend the more selective high schools that are in the more high-income areas, and thus they have a competitive advantage over poor students. Most colleges recognize this factor and try to make amends for it when reviewing these students' applications.

Students of color, especially those from economically under-resourced schools, can receive fee waivers for not only their SAT but also for applications from most colleges. This is not usually the case for historically black colleges. Most of them do not offer fee waivers. Also, many of the selective predominantly white colleges offer fly-in programs for students of color as part of their recruitment process. Here you will be offered an invitation to visit a college for usually two days, and your transportation, housing, and meals are paid.

Since your teen can never be certain how any particular admissions committee views students of color, it is imperative to make a strong case for admittance. This chapter will explain their options in detail and advise you on how to make the most of their educational opportunities.

SCHOLASTIC CHOICES AND PERFORMANCE IN HIGH SCHOOL

You have undoubtedly heard of high school athletes competing rigorously to receive the nod from certain college teams. That's just how competitive your teen must be during their high school academic career if they want to increase their chances of getting into the college of their choice. There are many variables in the admissions process, and your teen will not have full control over many of them—admissions policies and the quality of your school system; and even SAT and ACT scores have an element of chance. But your teen does have more control over their GPA, and they have a much better chance of getting into a selective college of their choice with a strong GPA and a low SAT score than someone who has low grades and high SAT scores. Now there are many exceptions to this rule. In fact, many state schools and second-tier schools would welcome a student with an above-average SAT score, even with low grades, because that high SAT score can bring up the average score for the incoming freshmen class and that particular institution. But while that may help the college, it will not necessarily be good for your teen when he is admitted and does not perform well because of poor study skills. At the end of the day, nothing can take the place of demanding classes and good grades.

Your teen is given four years of high school to take the appropriate classes. Encourage them to use those years to absorb English, math, science, history, and foreign languages. Don't just allow them to take the minimum academic requirements—they should go all out and stretch and challenge themselves. If you live in a community that does not offer challenging academic programs, not to worry. Your teen will not be penalized for what the school does not offer; they will be penalized for what not taking advantage of what the school does offer.

If your teen is fortunate to attend a school that offers Advanced Placement classes—college level classes offered in high school—then they should be strongly advised to take some of them throughout their high school years. Most teens take them in the junior and senior year but sometimes one can find students taking AP European History as sophomores. Your teen should not hesitate to take the challenging courses if you judge, based on your knowledge of his/her learning style, that they can handle the course.

Unfortunately, students of color are not often enrolled in the AP classes. In some schools, still today they are either not encouraged or expected to do so. In other cases they are encouraged to do so but they choose not to take advantage of the opportunity. This underutilization is most disheartening because it speaks to a larger societal issue. Historically, for example, we as people of color were denied access to certain opportunities, but today, when, we have access to these opportunities, we forgo them. It is important for you as parents to remind your teens about our history and let them know that an opportunity denied is no different than the opportunity forgone. At the end of the day one is still left behind and eventually losing the race.

For students of color who want to be enrolled in AP classes in school districts where they are either minimally offered or not offered at all, some school districts have formed partnerships with local colleges and universities. The more industrious students, who in many cases have exhausted all of the academic offerings at school, are being allowed to enroll in those local institutions of higher education where they will allow your teen to take college-level classes for credit. Make it your business as a parent to explore all of the available school and community-based academic programs that are available to accelerate your teen's intellectual growth. As always, I would recommend that you start with your teen's school counselor, but do not make one person your only resource. Ask people in your community, on your job, and in your church about academic enrichment programs. More often than not someone in your personal or professional circle can give you some information that will advantage your teen.

ACHIEVING COMPETITIVE SCORES ON THE SAT AND ACT

The courses your teen takes in high school and the grades they receive are far more important that a single SAT or ACT score. Now having said that, please know that standardized test scores are still part of the formula for gaining admittance for most colleges. A solid SAT score can tip the scales in your favor for getting into your number-one school of choice and/or obtaining a private scholarship. Preparation for taking the SAT should begin with the experience of preparing for and the taking of the PSAT.

While most students take the PSAT in their junior year, consider having your teen taking the test as early as their sophomore year. This is not uncommon at many schools. In fact, some students are exposed to the PSAT as early as their freshmen year. Here as a parent, you have to be careful, by making sure that your teen has the appropriate course content to handle the test subject matter. For example, while many students from affluent areas, and some from middle-class and lower-income communities, may have already taken Algebra 1 in the 8th grade, other students will not be taking Algebra 1 until the 9th grade. Students will be introduced to Algebra on the PSAT and can be discouraging if they have never seen this subject and turn them off indefinitely with respect to standardized testing. In all cases students will have been exposed to Algebra 1 by the 10th grade and, if not, certainly by the 11th, which is when all juniors are required to take the test.

Taking the test in the sophomore year increases your teen's chances of obtaining a higher score in their junior year, when the test really counts. High scorers are nominated as semi-finalists in the National Achievement Scholarship Program for Black Students, the National Hispanic Scholars Recognition Programs, and other programs that bestow distinction and financial assistance to all students who score well. In the senior year, students and their counselor will be asked to submit additional information and will find out if they were finalists at a later date in the senior year. Students of color are also eligible to compete for the general National Merit Scholarship for all students as well. In this category the score cut for consideration is higher.

DON'T FORGET ABOUT TEST PREP FOR YOUR TEEN

Students of color who attend school systems with limited resources are often not prepared for the PSAT and SAT, putting them at a disadvantage. If they are not aware of the existence of test preparation courses like Kaplan and The Princeton Review, to mention just two, they are at a second disadvantage. If they cannot afford the course, they are at a third disadvantage. If they don't know that can sometimes obtain scholarships to pay for the courses, they are yet at another disadvantage. And if they believe that they can't do well on the test, they are at the worst disadvantage of all.

Test prep courses are definitely helpful, and they are more accessible than you might think. I would invite you as a parent to call the test preparation centers in your community and ask about financial aid and other special programs. Your teen may qualify for a scholarship, or perhaps they may be able to take advantage of a prep course offered by an increasing number of community-based organizations that have partnered with national test prep centers like Kaplan and the Princeton Review.

Many students of color I have counseled report that the ACT is an easier test than the SAT. The ACT is more content based so it measures what a student knows in specific subject areas. While I have not witnessed any particular data that shows on average students of color who take the ACT score higher than they do on the SAT, my intuition suggests that students who score well on one tend to score well on the other, and students who have challenges with one standardized test, i.e. the SAT, will have challenges on the ACT. However, if the culture of your teen's communities is promoting the ACT as an easier test, when your teen takes the test, they probably would have less anxiety and perhaps more confidence, thereby increasing the chances of better performance.

Since most colleges today except scores from both exams, it is a good idea to recommend that your teen prepare for and take both. Presenting scores from two different tests gives the admissions counselors more information about you, allowing them to make more informed decisions. However, please note that your teen can determine what score they want to send, thus, if the ACT score is indeed higher, then they should only send the ACT.

PARENTS, BE CAREFUL NOT TO ACCEPT JUST ANY PREP COURSE

While I applaud test prep companies that are trying to bridge the gap between those parents who can afford to send their teens to schools with limited resources and those parents who cannot, I also caution parents to be aware of a crash or poor quality prep class. Too often what I see being offered to students of color from poor schools is a watered-down version of the SAT or ACT prep course, where they are most in need of a course that is more comprehensive and one that is tailored to their skill sets. This cannot happen in thirteen hours, for example. Now, it also requires a lot of work on the part of the student and their family. It also requires that one sets reasonable expectations given your teen's skill sets. For example, if your teen has a 280 on his Critical Reading section of the SAT, it is unreasonable, in most cases, for one to expect his score to jump to 580. A more reasonable score increase might be 400. That will not get him into an Ivy League school necessarily, but with a solid GPA (3.5) and a combined SAT score of 1300 it will open a few more doors to some second- and third-tier schools.

STANDARDIZED TESTING AND STUDENTS OF COLOR

There is nothing new today about the perceptions that people in general have about standardized testing and students of color. Research has shown year after year that students of color tend not to score as high on standardized testing when compared to their white counterparts. These discussions started over thirty years ago and still exist today. Why is this?

To begin—I think the question needs to be addressed across class lines. Having worked with a variety of students across different classes, I have witnessed that my students who come from economically advantaged backgrounds score, on average, higher on the SAT than those from lower-income backgrounds. Whether I am working with an Italian from East Boston, or an Irish from South Boston, or a black from Washington, DC, when these students came from working-class families, they all tended to score below their peers who came from more affluent communities. In the case of my Italian students from East Boston, their counterpart may live in Lexington, Massachusetts, and attend the affluent high school in that community where on average SAT scores place their students above the 75th percentile; or, in the case of my Irish students, who lived in South Boston—South Boston looks quite different now than it looked then in the seventies, her counterpart could live in Wellesley, where the average SAT score for the Irish American in that community is higher than the average in Lexington. In DC, students, whether black or white, attending the exam schools like Benjamin Bannekar High School or one of the privates like the National Cathedral School always score higher on their SAT exams compared to students from lower-income families who attend one of several local public and or charter schools. The charter schools nationwide report that they are making progress in increasing the scores of poor students, but I believe, with very few exceptions, the empirical evidence is inconclusive.

As an educator, what concerns me is not the obvious discrepancy in scores, but the perceptions that people have about students who receive low scores on these test, and more importantly, the perceptions that students hold of themselves when they receive low scores. Why? Because those perceptions impact their self-esteem, which often contributes to lower academic performance.

For the parent of color who comes from an economically advantaged background, I urge you to encourage your teen to read more and take advantage of all the resources that they have so that they can increase their scores. Many students of color who are second- and third-generation college bound already have good scores but could do better. I have worked with them and some have received near to perfect scores but, in general, they have not received the scores that I would have expected them to achieve, given the relatively economically privileged backgrounds from which they come.

For the parents of color who come from economically disadvantaged backgrounds, know that your teen can get into college with low SAT scores. Some schools do not require them realizing that students from high-income communities are advantage in this area, and they want to even the playing field. However, as mentioned earlier, there are programs to help your teen improve their scores, within reason. Earlier I spoke to what others were doing to help you, your teen, and your family. What I want to address here is what you can do for your teen and, by extension, what they can do for themselves.

WHAT YOU CAN DO

Students who do well on the SAT READ everything all the time. Of course they watch TV and play video games, after all they are teens, and we expect them to do that. But TV, computers, video games, and texting have to be limited. Your teen needs to read every day. Now that does not mean they have to read a book a day, but they could be expected to read one or two articles in the newspaper. They could read a magazine article. Of course, if they are fortunate enough to have homework where they are being required to read, that necessitates that they sit quietly and use their brain reading for at least two hours in the evening. Should they finish their homework, or if they do not have homework, you should require that they complete your homework. This works well with younger students, since if the expectation of reading, if not established early in their lives, is more challenging to incorporate at later stages.

You should also take your teen to museums and art galleries. Through these experiences they can absorb a great amount of information and vocabulary. You can introduce them to new words, a great exercise for pre-teens. And your most powerful tool is they should see you reading something every day. Books, newspapers, and magazines should be in the house, in the living room, bedrooms, and bathrooms. If your teen sees you reading they are more likely to read. You can't expect them to read if you are not reading.

If you cannot find an SAT prep class, or you cannot afford to purchase one of the SAT prep books or online programs, you do have access to the practice test booklets that your teen can obtain from his guidance counselor. Those are wonderful resources, if utilized. I encourage your teen to use the test prep booklet and do so at least fifteen minutes a day. In that way they are becoming familiar with the test structure, and they are becoming familiar with the test items that will appear on the actual test. But you have to be deliberate about encouraging all of the above or else you will not experience long-term rewards.

FEE WAIVERS

Students of color who attend under-resourced schools, like all economically disadvantaged students, are entitled to receive not only test fee waivers, but also college application fee waivers. To find out more detailed information about these services ask your teen's school counselor to contact the College Board in New York City at 212.713.8000 or 212.520.8570.

EXTRACURRICULAR ACTIVITIES AND COMMUNITY INVOLVEMENT

It is probably fair to say that your teen will have a good chance of being admitted to the college of their choice if they can convince the college that they have the skill sets to handle the academic work and that they would be an asset to their college community. What would make them an asset?

First, they must earn good grades and make the time to prepare for and take the appropriate college entrance tests. Then they must add another dimension to their application by demonstrating that they are well-rounded as individuals. They can do that by taking advantage of the extra-curricular activities, community service projects, and summer opportunities.

Most high schools offer a number of extra-curricular activities. If your teen's school doesn't have a club that addresses an interest of theirs, they can create one. They should broaden their horizons by exploring the various clubs and teams at their school. Outside of the classroom there are many organizations designed to help students of color prepare for college, while at the same time providing them with the opportunities for internships, tutoring, mentoring, and summer enrichment experiences. Through your church, community organizations, and schools, students can find a wealth of information to help them chart their path as they prepare for college.

As your teen begins to explore and identify these various programs that might be a good fit for them, ask them to sometimes think outside of the box, step outside their comfort zone, and try something new. You may also want your teen to defy the stereotype. It is not uncommon to find students of color, particularly males, participating in basketball and football, but how often do you hear about black or Latino students participating in golf, soccer, or skiing? Think strategically when pursing your interest. Creating a unique profile for your teen as a person of color will capture the attention of the admissions committee.

SPORTS

If your teen is talented in sports encourage them to go ahead and participate—but don't forget to advise them to develop other extracurricular interests outside of sports, since an injury can end their career abruptly and permanently. Also remember that students of color are often expected to play sports but not expected to cultivate other interests and you want them to stand out.

If your teen is thinking about participating in sports at the college level, please make sure the family does their homework. Take a look at the academic support programs that are available for your teen at the particular colleges that are interested in your teen, and that hopefully he too is interested in. More specifically, as a parent, you should be looking at the graduation rates, especially those of students of color. If the school offers special programs for athletes, speak to athletes of color to assess the quality of those services.

PART-TIME JOBS

Students of color from poor families, like all students from similar backgrounds, work part time during high school and throughout college to makes ends meet. Some are afraid of taking out loans so they work to reduce them. While working is a respectful endeavor and serves as an extra-curricular activity, it can also be a deterrent. Working long hours can impact one's GPA both in high school and in college since it takes away from study time. Students who do not have to work either in high school or in college have a great advantage over those that do. What I would recommend that you encourage your teen to do is count the dollars and not the pennies. By working 15 hours a week at McDonalds throughout high school a student cannot earn enough money to pay for one year's education at most schools. However, if they focus on their studies they could earn a full scholarship worth $200,000 over a four-year period. This would free them up from having to work during college and thus increase their chances of doing well academically as well. Remember to encourage your teen to count the dollars and not the pennies.

THE APPLICATION PROCESS/FINDING SCHOLARSHIPS

For many people reading this book, their teen will be average, and they should know that generally high-income families tend to pay more for their teen's education and families with modest means or low income will qualify for financial aid. Our higher educational system tries to make it possible for all to attend college if they so wish.

Still, like all students, students of color need to be proactive when it comes to searching for scholarships. *The Black Student's Guide to Scholarships, Revised Edition,* by Barry Beckham, is a good resource. The Hispanic Scholarship Fund (HSF) is the nation's leading Hispanic scholarship organization; see http://www.hsf.net. Students of color primarily interested in one of the historically black colleges may be eligible for merit-based scholarships. Many historically black colleges, by way of attracting the best and the brightest students of color from predominantly white institutions, are offering merit-based scholarships to students who earn high scores on the SAT and ACT. One of these schools, Howard University, even offers scholarships to National Merit Finalists. Many predominantly white colleges still offer some scholarships earmarked for students of color. Some of the best-known scholarships of this type are the Ralph Bunche Scholarship given to an African, Asian, Hispanic, or Native American student at Colby College; the Walter N. Ridley Scholarships to support African-American students at University of Virginia (UVA); the John B. Ervin Scholars Programs for African-American Students at Washington University; and the Presidential Diversity Scholarships for all students of color at Saint Lawrence University.

Keep in mind as a student of color you have some leverage at predominantly white schools if the institutions are deliberately trying to increase their diversity across race. Thus, if you are fortunate enough to receive scholarships but that scholarship is not quite covering the cost and you and your family desire more funds, you can call the financial aid office at that college and try to negotiate your financial aid package. You might be surprised. If they really want you and if they really need you because of what you can bring to the class because of your racial diversity, they may be willing to offer you a better financial aid package. If you don't ask, you know what the answer will be.

PRIVATE SCHOLARSHIPS AND YOUR FINANCIAL AID PACKAGE

Many students receive monies from both the college and from private sources outside of the college. If you are a student who has done your homework, you have identified many of these private sources, submitted applications to those for which you were eligible and if you were one of the lucky ones, you received a few of them.

Let's say that your full year's cost of attending college is $45,000 at a private institution and at that school you have received the following financial aid package:

Pell Grant	$3,000
SEOG	$1,000
Institutional Grant	$25,000
Stafford Loan	$2,000
Perkins Loan	$4,000
Work Study	$1,000
Parent Contribution	$9,000
Total	**$45,000**

You received a $5,000 dollar scholarship from the Coca Cola Foundation and you received an additional scholarship of $3,000 from your local church. In most cases, these private monies will be sent directly to the school and some colleges will say that you no longer need a $25,000 dollar grant from them since you have $8,000 in private scholarships. As a consumer of education, you are not trying to make the college rich, but you are trying to reduce your out-of-pocket cost for your education. So, what you want to do is use those funds to either offset the parent contribution or the student loan. Can you do this? Well, it depends. Some schools will let you use the funds to your advantage while others schools will not. You may also be willing to negotiate with the college whereby they may allow you to use a percentage of the funds to reduce your loan and they will take a percentage to reduce your scholarship. Here again, if they see you as an asset as a student of color in adding diversity to their campus, you may have some leverage.

THE ADMISSIONS ESSAY

In Chapter 2 you were provided with some useful hints on writing an essay that will set you apart from others. (Examples of successful college essays appear in the chapter, several of which directly address race.) The issue for some students of color is the choice of topic: some feel obligated to write about a race-related subject, while others do not. If you feel that your experiences as a person of color has contributed to your personal development in some unique way, and that such a topic will make for a compelling essay, then by all means write about a race-based topic. For example, one of my recent students, who is bi-racial, discussed the challenges he faced in growing up with a white mother and black father. He went to a predominantly white independent school where he and his best friend who is black were the only persons of color in the class. The white students dubbed them "one-and-a-half" because one of the students was black and he was half black. That was how their peers greeted them throughout their high school years. My client spoke to pain he endured while in high school and it has taken him some years to come to terms with his racial identity. His essay was at once honest, compelling, and quite human, and it worked.

On the other hand, I have been associated with summer enrichment programs where staff who have encouraged students to write about a racial issue and in my mind that was and is not appropriate. It is your story: you decide what part of it you want to share and how you want to share it.

Finally, if the college gives you a choice to write or not to write an essay, it is your best interest to go ahead and write an essay. It has been said that many males of color do not like to write. That may be a stereotype, as I know many who love to write. But also, I have noticed that some students of color particularly in many of the urban schools for which I consult do not apply for scholarships or apply to a certain college because they are required to write an essay. If you have a choice or if it is recommended, write the essay. If there are two applicants with similar GPAs and you write an essay that arrests the attention of the admissions committee you are in and the other applicant is not. This is an opportunity for you to tell your story—don't forego that opportunity.

THE APPLICATION, CHECKING THE BOX

Most school applications offer you the opportunity to identify the ethnic or racial category to which you belong. Whether or not you should place a check mark in the appropriate category is a personal choice. However, if you are uncertain as to whether you can be considered a student of color from the college's point of view, as in the case where one parent is black and the other is white, you should let the admissions officer know that you are a person of color. If the school is committed to diversity, and most schools are, this could increase your chances of being admitted.

There are some black, Hispanic, and bi-racial students who have protested and refuse to check the box. In my opinion this is not a useful strategy since one should not take offence to someone asking you to check a box identifying your ethnic or racial identification. On the other hand, once you are enrolled in college, if you find that the institutions and its environs want to put you in a box, in terms of what they expect from you, then that could be a problem since it limits who you are and may not be compatible with how you view yourself. Also, be careful about not limiting yourself. I have known some students who put themselves in a box and that too can often limit the nature and the quality of their undergraduate experience.

CHOOSING THE RIGHT COLLEGE FOR YOU

Many students of color are the first in their families to attend college, while many other families have established a legacy at various institutions. Whether you fall into one of those categories or exist someplace in between, the college selection process can be intimidating, but it does not have to be.

A logical place to begin your research in finding the right college is the student guides to colleges, available at bookstores, libraries and your counselor's office. Encourage your teen not to be limited either to the guides specifically aimed at students of color or to the general guides since the ones targeted at students of color can be useful. View-books and CDs showcasing colleges can be another good resource, and you as a parent as well as your teen might be attentive to how students of color are positioned in these visuals. Are they only seen on the athletic field, or do they appear to be integrated throughout, both in photos emphasizing academics as well as the social aspect? Sometimes you may see only one or two students of color in a sea of white students, and if you feel comfortable being the lone minority then, it might be a consideration, if the school offers an academic program and other characteristics in which you have an interest. Only you can define what diversity means to you and how much diversity you need, if any. Remember, this is one of the most important decisions of your life, and you need to equip yourself with as much information as possible.

THE CAMPUS VISIT: SEEING IS BELIEVING

After your teen has perused the college guides and picked several schools that they think offer what they are looking for, I would suggest that the family schedule on-campus visits. Don't despair if you feel that the travel expenses are prohibitive. Many colleges have visitation programs earmarked for families with limited financial means. Some colleges schedule visits to their campus for prospective students before the application process, while others invite prospective students upon acceptance. Students should contact the admissions office of the schools in which they have an interest to find out about these visitation programs. If they don't have one, they may put you in touch with one of their students of color from your area, or even your school who can serve as a resource and may even invite you as their guest for a visit. Another option for students is to contact the alumni association and ask for names of individuals that live in your community. These contacts can also serve as helpful resources for you and your teen.

Campus visits are extremely important especially when there is a stark contrast between your home surroundings and the college setting. Consider the following scenarios:

- Is your teen a black student from white upscale suburban neighborhood, attending a predominantly white public high school and planning on attending a historically black college in an urban area?

- Are they a Hispanic student from the South Bronx, attending a predominantly white boarding school in New England, and considering a competitive Midwestern university on the south side of Chicago in an upper-middle-class black neighborhood?

● Is the student a black student from an urban black East Coast community, attending a predominantly black high school, considering a predominantly white college in a suburban community on the West Coast?

Do you think your teen can identify with any of the aforementioned students? If not, it might be a good exercise for you and them to sit and think about how they would identify themselves in relationship to the types of colleges they are considering. There are a host of questions on which students and their families need to reflect. For example, as a student of color at a white university, would you be prepared to have your intellectual competency challenged inappropriately? Or, are you willing to be expected not to know much about Physics but be expected to know everything about African-American history? Is it important for you to see yourself reflected in the faculty, administration, and student body? Some students report that they will feel comfortable with ten percent minority students, while others are indifferent and feel they can be successful independent of the numbers of minorities. Others want more representation of students of color and a diverse faculty. What would make your teen feel comfortable?

With respect to the curriculum, is it important to you to see the intellectual voices of people of color represented across the curriculum, or is it sufficient for you to have them represented only within the African Studies or Latino Studies Department? At institutions where students of color feel more comfortable, the contributions of people of color are taught throughout many disciplines and certain colleges require some of these contributions as required courses.

While your teen is visiting these campuses, they need to find out about the attrition rates for students in general. They should then ask what the attrition rate is for students of color. That will give them some indication of how comfortable students of color feel at that particular institution.

Statistics at all schools, black colleges and predominantly white ones, can be misleading. A predominantly white college could have a high retention rate for students of color, but that does not necessarily mean that the students are happy with that college. Dig deeper, because looks can be deceiving and some students will remain at an institution for the wrong reasons, a boyfriend or girlfriend wants them to stay, or a parent who is overly impressed with an Ivy League school may want their teen to stay because they want to say that their child graduated from an Ivy. This mismatch can be a problem especially if the student is unhappy. A four-year stint in an unpleasant environment could translate into other problems like alcoholism and drug abuse resulting from depression or feelings of powerlessness because of an overbearing parent. Make sure that you are not this kind of parent and let your teen make a point to engage students in conversation so they can learn more about the entirety of a student's experiences beyond statistics in a guide book. Also, seek out organizations like the school's black or Hispanic alumni association. Groups like these can make all the difference in how students of color feel about their campus life. Generally if a student has had a positive experience at his/her institution they are going to be active alumni. Students of color who are active in the alumni associations are a good marker for the quality of their undergraduate experience at their alma matter. If they had a good time, they will want to stay connected and contribute so that future generations of students will have the same, if not better, experience.

On-campus conversations should also include a discussion about the school's financial aid policies and procedures. Pay attention to the details of the financial aid process, and, this is important, make sure your family meets all of the deadlines. If the student's forms are completed correctly but sent late, your teen will be put at a disadvantage. If the forms are sent in on time are they are completed incorrectly, they will be returned to you for correction. Hence you lose time. The bottom line: financial aid is very time sensitive. The forms must be completed accurately, on time, the first time.

Many students of color and their families are reluctant to take out loans for their education. Don't be reluctant to encourage teen to finance their education with loans, because this is a major investment in their future. I would recommend that you opt for the subsidized loans, where the federal government pays for the interest while the student is in college. They will not have to begin repaying the loan until six months after they graduate. If a student decides to go to graduate school, they can defer the loan payments. If they are in the field of education and they choose to work in an economically disadvantaged community, they will be exempt from some, if not all, of the loan debt. In any case, students will have ten years to pay off their loan, and the average income of a college graduate will be sufficient enough to meet that obligation if they budget well.

If, as a parent, you are not pleased with the financial aid package awarded by the school, let them know and try to negotiate a better package. Remember, your family has a voice in this process. It is not bad etiquette to negotiate a better financial aid package for your family. If your teen is not satisfied with all of the arrangements of your package, go to the office with prepared to argue your position. You may also need to bring supporting documentation. But be willing to negotiate. You may not get all that you want but you may end up with something closer to what you desired. I cannot say this enough. If you don't ask, you know what the answer is going to be.

THE ADMISSIONS INTERVIEW

Students who present themselves with confidence and poise are most likely to succeed in interviews. Some students worry about being asked about their ethnicity or race in the admissions interview, but this should not be a cause of concern. Usually, they will not be asked such a question unless there is something unique about your background. For example, their father could be African American and their mother may be Japanese, and they may have lived the first seven years of their life in Japan. Moreover, you as their parent made certain that they were fluent in Japanese as well. If asked about their background, in this case, they should respond with confidence and let the admissions officer know that you are proud of your background and that the culmination of who they are has enabled them to identify with a broader range of people. If the interviewer does not raise the topic of your bi-racial status, your teen might consider doing so if it seems appropriate within the context of the conversation.

In general, though, issues of race and ethnicity would be more appropriate to discuss with other people on campus. Admissions officers are there to sell the school, so bringing up potentially uncomfortable issues whether they are black or white could be uncomfortable and might backfire. Students, faculty, and administrators of color would be a more likely to talk about these issues more candidly. Discussing race-based issues with white students can also provide you with an interesting perspective as well.

HISTORICALLY BLACK COLLEGES AND UNIVERSITIES (HBCUS)

The decision to attend a historically black college or university—these schools are often referred to as HBCUs—is highly personal. These schools are naturally very attractive for black students who want to experience their education with a community that reflects their heritage. They are sometimes very attractive for Hispanic students or bi-racial students who identify with black culture. And more and more I am finding that white students are attending black colleges on the undergraduate level. They have historically attended their professional schools, i.e. Schools of Medicine, Law, and Dentistry.

Even if your teen is sure that they can excel at a predominantly white college, they might be better served at an HBCU if they feel you do not have strong sense of their racial identity. Or they may have attended an all-white high school in a wealthy suburb and come from a family where you as the parent introduced them to knowledge to develop and enhance their racial identity, but the student may elect to go to a black college, simply because they wanted to experience something new. On the other hand, like the above example your teen also has a strong racial identity, but he attended a school in poor school with limited resources, thus his educational foundation is weak. In this case, an HBCU might be better choice, assuming the student wants to attend a four-year college, rather than a two-year community college. Since many historically black colleges have always had a mission to serve the under-served, their admissions standards are not as competitive as some white colleges and thus the student would have a better chance of admission. And because many market themselves as small and nurturing, the students could be better served academically.

If a student has problems with self-esteem and is not a strong student academically, an HBCU is definitely a good option. Here they can improve their academic skills and enhance their feelings of self worth and pride.

BLACK STUDENTS AT WHITE SCHOOLS: A BIT OF HISTORY

The black student on the white campus is a byproduct of the revolution that erupted in the 1960s. Prior to the sixties, on campuses like Penn, Bates, Cornell, MIT, and Dartmouth, one could see a few black faces but they tended to be superstars. Amherst took a few blacks from the most prestigious families in the country as did schools like Williams, Hamilton, Carleton, and Franklin Marshall and a few others saw to it that a black presence continued in earnest.

However, something historical happened on February in 1960. Four students from North Carolina A&T University in Greensboro staged their historical sit-in at the Woolworth's food counter. The outcome was the dismantling of the legal basis for discrimination in public accommodations. Their actions and those of Rosa Parks—she refused to sit at the back of a bus—in Montgomery stand as two decisive events that changed America. They actions emboldened the black educated classes and spearheaded a national movement that came to be called the Civil Rights Movement. It was natural then, that the revolution of the sixties would eventually settle the role of the university and access in education.

Two very decisive events motivated administrators at white colleges to open their doors more earnestly to the presence of black students: the assassination of Martin Luther King on April 4, 1968, and then three months later in June, the assassination of Robert F. Kennedy. As a consequence one finds in the late sixties through the mid-seventies an increased presence of students of color in predominantly white colleges and universities. When they arrived in larger numbers, however, the administration, faculty and student body did not always welcome them alike. In some cases, they were resented, feared, and avoided. It could be argued that they were misunderstood. In fact, it wasn't long after they arrived in larger numbers that the white administrators felt compelled to recruit black faculty and administrators from HBCUs to help them manage the presence of the black students on the white campuses. Of course, I could share with you many horror stories, but suffice it to say the situation today for students is much improved when compared to the late sixties and early seventies.

CHOOSING A PREDOMINANTLY WHITE SCHOOL

Of course, there are many circumstances where a predominantly white school may be a logical choice for your teen, when, for example, their major course of study is found there. This is perfectly fine if you have the academic foundation to do well at these schools, and if they are open to presences of students of color. Measuring that openness, however, can be difficult. Here are some questions to investigate when considering a predominantly white school:

- Are faculty of color represented across all academic disciplines or are they limited to those in the areas of ethnic studies?

- Are persons of color represented across all levels of the administration or are they relegated to lower-level administrative and staff positions?

- Are students of color generally happy there?

- Are students of color participating in all levels of the undergraduate experience?

- Does the university have a strong African-American and Hispanic American alumni association?

- Does the university address issues of race matters openly and fairly?

- Does the university discuss proactively issues of race, e.g. during freshmen orientation, or do they simply react to racial issues when they emerge?

- Does the university provide diversity training for faculty, staff, and students?

- What are the graduation rates of students of color in relationship to white students?

- Does the university offer any special incentives for students of color during the recruitment process?

- How do attrition and graduation rates compare between students of color and white students?

- Does the school offer raced-based scholarships? Are students of color generally pleased with their financial aid packages?

- What is the quality of life for students of color on campus?

- Is there an office to address issues of multi-cultural students? What is the staffing and funding allocation? Where are they physically positioned and how much influence do they have?

- How many tenured faculty of color does the university have?

- How are athletes of color treated in the academic setting? Do they feel respected? Are they assumed to be intellectually incompetent simply because they are athletes of color?

To answer these questions, your teen should speak to faculty, administrators, and students from all racial backgrounds, and when speaking to students, make sure your teen asks questions of both first-year and upper-class students.

THE ADVANTAGES AND DISADVANTAGES OF HBCUS

Advantages

- They provide another option just as women's colleges provide another option for females.

- They have a dedicated faculty who have the credentials to teach anywhere in the world, but they have elected to work at a college where they can make a difference in many black students' lives. While some work at Morehouse, Spelman, and Howard, to name a few of the most competitive black schools, others want to work at some of the lesser-known black schools that admit students who are faced with academic challenges and thus require more from this committed faculty once enrolled in higher education.

- Students can see themselves reflected throughout the institution. This can make them feel more comfortable and thus they will be more likely to take advantage of the opportunities available to them, making for a more complete undergraduate experience.

- They provide academically marginal students access into a higher educational opportunity.

- When recruiters are looking for students of color they tend to go to colleges where they exist in larger numbers, i.e. HBCUs.

- There tends to more diversity among the faculty, this is particularly the case at the larger schools, e.g. Howard University.

- They tend not to cost as much, and sometimes they do offer good financial aid packages.

- The social life on campus is informed by the cultural traditions of black culture and one does not have to compete with white organizations for visibility since it is an all-black school.

- Students are more likely to be exposed to mentors who come from a similar background and who have had the same experience since many faculty and administrators working at HBCUs themselves went to HBCUs.

Disadvantages

- They can be more conservative, particularly socially. For example, some black schools are not as open to gay and lesbian student organizations.

- Many of the dorms are still segregated across gender.

- Some black colleges still have curfews.

- They sometimes do not offer strong financial aid packages.

- The student body is more homogeneous, i.e. most of the students are all black or at the Hispanic-serving institutions, mostly Hispanic.

- They sometimes don't offer the elaborate facilities of many white colleges.

As your teen is thinking about whether a white, black, or Hispanic-serving institution is best for them, remember that our American higher education system offers a mosaic of opportunities ranging from black to white colleges, as well as women's to Jewish schools, and it is ok to attend a school that is all black or predominantly Hispanic. Students should not be forced to go to one or the other, but rather the one where they feel they will be most comfortable. Parents, respect your teen's decision and as a consumer advise them not be pigeonholed into attending a black school because someone in your family swears by them, or attending a white one because someone in the family has been ill informed about the quality of an education at a black school versus one at a white one. Unfortunately, still today black schools are informed by a historically legacy that they are all inferior and whenever one has a problem that problem is generalized to all of them unfairly. Like white schools, black colleges represent the same range of competence and incompetence as institutions at large and all have their value for the right student.

As an informed consumer, then, the student's goal is to know everything about the product that they will ultimately choose. I am sure your teen has had the experience of buying an electronic gadget like an Ipod, digital camera, or a Blackberry. They may have even read consumer magazines and talked to their friends about the experiences they had with the brands and the models they choose. Perhaps they even compared the warranties and service plans offered by different stores and surfed the Internet to get more detailed information. Essentially, choosing a college involves the same process, but this time the product is a four-year college education. Students and their families want to gather as much information as possible about schools so they can make informed decisions about where you apply.

When senior year rolls around, students will be inundated with college applications and other materials from the schools your teen has judged as possible matches. Hopefully as parents you will not have to exercise your veto power because the schools that are being considered are ones that you feel are also a good fit, knowing what you know about your teen.

Whether your teen is choosing a predominantly white school or a school where they are the majority, in the final analysis you must have clarity about what you expect to gain or lose from your college education. While parents have to be appropriately engaged, so too do counselors and teachers. Students should have their counselor and or teacher look over their applications and essays. Hopefully by this stage of the game your teen has visited campuses they are applying to, or at least talked with a representative of the school about campus life. Don't be afraid: millions of other students have gone through the process and have not only survived, but prospered. You can too.

● ● ● ●

As a minority college student who attends (and who has always attended) a predominately Caucasian institution, I would say that one of the most difficult things for me has been coping with the notion that the very system I yearn to place my faith in harbors some deeply rooted biases. It is not so much the blatant acts of racism, as it is the faint undercurrent of prejudice that seems to haunt this country's social structures and which is echoed by disparities across various demographics. I sometimes wonder if I am just imagining it. Most of the time I I can happily ignore racial differences between others and myself and immerse myself in my studies. But occasionally there are times when I am harshly reminded of them; one minor incident (which I do not consider overt racism) that comes to mind is when I was taking my seat before a math lecture and overheard a white student criticizing the university's initiatives to support minority involvement in the Engineering program (and did all I could to remain seated without turning around and firing up a debate with a complete stranger). And of course, every now and again one of my white friends describes to me the tasteless remarks blurted out by another white student under the mistaken assumption that openly racist remarks will not elicit scorn so long as no people of color are present to hear them.

The unfortunate truth is that even in a supposedly progressive environment such as a college campus, these things are certainly bound to happen and it would be naive to assume otherwise. Incidents such as these suggest to me that there remain some very large gaps in understanding between whites and minorities; namely, that different situations will be will often be interpreted very differently according to the race of the observer. The scary part about that is the possibility that these sorts of misunderstandings are irreconcilable. For example, judging from my own experience and understanding on how early social environment can have a significant influence on a person's success, I can appreciate the necessity for efforts to involve minorities in various academic fields in which they are underrepresented. But, by no means can I expect that those who lack my experience and perspective as a minority will share my understanding, particularly since we Americans are all raised to believe that we all single-handedly pave our own roads to success.

I as much as anyone would like to believe that each of us has a more or less equal shot, and I approach everything that I do with this conviction. However, when events such as those I described are more or less commonplace, and when it is ordinary for me to walk through the halls of the Physics building and not see more than one or two Black students on any given day of the week, I cannot help but wonder if, somehow, the cards are still stacked against us in ways that are not easily articulated.

—Patrick Jefferson

REFERENCES

Especially for Students of Color

The 2007-2009 African American Scholarship Guide for Students & Parents. Dante Lee. Jarmell Sims, ed.

African American Student's College Guide: Your One-Stop Resource for Choosing the Right College, Getting in, and Paying the Bill. Isaac Black. Wiley.

The Black Girl's Guide to College Success: What No One Really Tells You About College That You Must Know. Sheryl Walker. AuthorHouse.

The Black Student's Guide to Scholarships, Revised Edition. Barry Beckham. Madison Books.

Hispanic Scholarship Fund. http://www.hsf.net

THE FIRST-GENERATION COLLEGE-BOUND STUDENT

We all looked alike, but we were not all alike. More often, I was able to pretend to be something I wasn't. I was the invisible minority. Of course I was ashamed of this deception, but I wanted to affiliate with students from affluent backgrounds, and to the extent that I could, I did. I can recall one specific occasion when I was unable to join my friends on a visit to the Caribbean during spring break, where they would spend more money in a week than my father earned in three months. Frankly, I could not afford to go. I told them that my mother was ill and that I would be going home. This duplicity, denial, and shame lived with me throughout my years at college where because I was white, at a selective school, I was presumed to be at least middle class. The reality was, I was poor and ashamed of whom I was, and it was not until years after I graduated from college, that I was able to measure my success through my own eyes and not through the eyes of those friends who came from different places, places that positioned them as third- and fourth-generation college students.

—Anonymous

THIS IS THE VOICE OF an Italian-American female who went to a prestigious all-women's college and was the first in her family to attend college. Having graduated in 1989 at the top of her class from an urban high school in a working-class community, she was admitted to Wellesley College, a prestigious college in New England established historically for women who came from privileged backgrounds and whose families wanted them to receive a first-class education. In the late sixties and early seventies, like many of the selective institutions of its kind, Wellesley began in earnest to diversify its student body, thereby including not only more students of color, but also more students of economically disadvantaged communities.

Throughout my years in education I have had the opportunity and the honor of working with hundreds of students who were first in their families to attend and graduate from college. Their experience is at once similar and different from that of others. In fact, I was inspired to include this chapter as part of the book because of the similarities but mostly because of the differences.

First-generation college-bound students are likely to attend high schools that lack adequate resources. They also tend to come from families that are economically disadvantaged. These families rarely have individuals who can assist the student with the transition to, through, or beyond college. Moreover, these students tend to lack the resources in their communities to assist them as they enter graduate or professional school or the workplace. The world from home to the world of college and these other places is often quite different, but in these new places—college and beyond—all students are expected to adapt and excel. Learning how to negotiate these new environments presents significant and sometimes debilitating challenges, especially when there are no mentors or peers to guide them.

"First" students are not just different from those of a legacy of college graduates: their experiences are also different from other first-generation college-bound students. Some have difficulty negotiating class identity issues, while others have difficulty negotiating class and race identity. Others have problems when they return home and try to relate to members of their family and or community. Some may even face hostility and jealousy from members of their community who see the one they knew. Then there are those who choose, for sometimes the right and sometimes the wrong, not to be identified with their community even though they are welcomed at home. Finally, there are those who face additional challenges because English is their second language. These are just a few examples of the many obstacles facing the first-generation college bound. It is my hope that parents whose children will be first in the family to attend college, as well as others who work with these families, will be better advised on how to assist these young people through the process of preparing for, applying to, and getting through college. Clearly, the entire book aspires to achieve that goal, but for many families who are reading this book, and by extension this chapter, will not be first generation. They will come from backgrounds where they are empowered and thus can manage this process with more self-confidence. Too often, families who are first generation are managed by other peoples, policies, programs and goals, and what they will be able to do after reading this chapter, and hopefully whole book, is manage this process with greater confidence and determination.

A MESSAGE TO THE FIRST-GENERATION COLLEGE-BOUND STUDENT

You can do it. Do not let anyone tell you that you can't. This chapter is going to let your parents and guidance know how. As you probably already know, a college degree is a basic instrument on the road to career success and achievement. Obtaining that instrument has become increasingly competitive and expensive. You don't have to worry too much about cost, but you do have to concern yourself with academic performance in college-preparatory classes. If you perform well, you will be rewarded both financially and academically. Colleges will give you money if you qualify, and most first-generation college-bound students do.

There are many courses to think about, tests to take, applications to complete, and deadlines to meet before gaining admissions into those, what some call "hallowed halls of academe." The application process alone can be an overwhelming experience if you are "first," and that is why you have to plan.

How you have performed prior to high school will determine the courses you can take in high school and how you will perform in those courses. How you perform in high school will inform what colleges you will be able to attend, the money you will receive, and how you will excel once enrolled in college. If you have not performed as well as you might have, do not be discouraged, as you have the option of attending a community college for two years and then transferring to a four-year.

Another advantage of a college education is that it will impact the rest of your life. You will meet friends who will remain your friends for a lifetime. You may even meet your future partner. You may find your first job as a result of a recommendation from a professor or a referral from your college's career placement center. I hope I have convinced you of many of the challenges while also articulating some of the rewards. What follows in this section are some topic areas that families should address to make them more empowered throughout the process.

If you are a parent or guardian and have never been to college, I would you encourage to consider the following: planning, picking, packaging, presenting, paying, persisting, and profiting. These seven words are very important in planning for, applying to, and getting through college. That they have come up in different formats throughout the book is not by error. It has been deliberate, because of their importance, but here they take on special significance because first-generation college-bound youth and their parents do not have a history to rely on with this respect to this mission.

PLANNING

From the moment that your teen enters high school they should think of themselves as an asset and they should develop a plan to make that asset more desirable (See "College Applicant Profile," Appendix B). The way they do so is by taking advantage of all that the school has to offer. Do not worry if the school has limited resources and thus cannot offer much, but students must take advantage of what it does offer. When applying to college, students will not be held accountable for what a school does not offer, but they will be disadvantaged if they are perceived as a student who hasn't taken advantage of what is offered.

With respect to courses, think at least five academic classes times four years: four years of English, math, science, history, and foreign language. Those are the five solid academic areas in which colleges have an interest.

Colleges also like to see students challenge themselves, and if your teen is in a high school that offers honors and Advanced Placement classes, you should encourage them to take them. This will only strengthen their academic foundation and make them more marketable once they apply to college. Whether taking regular college preparatory or advanced ones if they are in the appropriate classes all for years and they do well, they will be viewed as an asset to any college and they will be rewarded in many ways.

As part of the plan your teen will be expected to sit for several test administrations: the PSAT, the practice test for the SAT, and the PLAN, which is the practice test for the ACT. Colleges do not require the PSAT or the PLAN. They do require that students submit either the SAT or the ACT.

Families that have the economic means will hire a private academic coach to help students prepare for these tests. Too often, first-generation college-bound students come from homes that do not have the resources for these services. Here is a case where families can contact the companies directly and ask about financial assistance. Parents can also speak to the school counselor to determine if they might know of some private funding. What is encouraging is that some schools do not require test scores, or they make them optional. Other schools will use them but will also rely on other areas of a student's application to determine if your teen would be successful at a college. Whether the scores are required or not, it is in the best interest of students to do well in those college-preparatory classes. The test show what your teen can accomplish in three and a half hours, while the grades are an indication of what they have done over four years. Scores alone are not a true marker of success in college but having a solid grade-point average (3.0+ over a 4.0 scale) alone can be a better indication of college success. Your teen should take control over that which he or she has more control. He or she has more control over the grade-point average than over the SAT or ACT score. This is not to say that students should not do what they can to prepare for and do well on the test. On the contrary, they should prepare for it and take it seriously. However, I do not want parents nor their teens to feel discouraged if they have challenges with the SAT and ACT. It does not mean that they cannot go to college. Nor does it mean if they score below average when compared to the scores at the college they attend, they will not excel. There simply may be other factors in their application that suggest they could excel, and most often those other factors have to do with the strength of their academic record.

SUPPORT FROM HOME FOR ACADEMICS

If you want your teen to be an asset, as a parent you have to lay the groundwork at home for that to happen. That can be done in several ways, but in general you have to provide your love and support constantly by being there for them. By setting a routine and a safe place to study at home, parents are encouraging academic engagement inside of the house. Students need a quiet place to study, and they should be expected to work on school-related assignments every night before a school day. If a student does not have homework, teens should be expected to read ahead and or review past assignments in preparation for future tests. This is called study. Too often teens do not know the difference between homework and study. Once the assignment has been completed, then the review of the material begins. Three hours a night, combining homework and study, is not unreasonable for teens today. Some teens who attend competitive high schools have five hours a night of academic work. If you expect your teen to excel academically, you have to monitor homework/study and you have to be engaged in the school on a regular basis. In that way you are not just telling them that education is important, you are showing them, while at the same time, helping them become an asset.

NON-ACADEMIC FACTORS

As you continue to think about how your teen can become an asset in high school and subsequently to a college, encourage them to become involved in extra-curricular activities, both in and out of school. You can support those interests, in some cases financially. It is important to note, however, your tax dollars pay for your child's public school education, and some of those funds provide resources for after-school activities. But, money aside, as parents you know that the real support does not come in the form of dollars, but rather in the form of emotional support. You can show that by simply showing up. If you are going to encourage your teen to play sports or participate in a school play, it is important for you to attend the sport events and/or the performances.

COMMUNITY-BASED ORGANIZATIONS

More and more today, community-based organizations are also providing college access programs to assist you and your families. These programs are not new, there are just more of them. In fact, Upward Bound Programs, which were spearheaded by the Lyndon B. Johnson administration in 1963, still exist today to prepare first-generation college-bound students from rural and urban areas gain access into higher education. Upward Bound and similar programs are a good resource for parents and students if they find that the resources at the high schools are limited. The quality of these programs vary so parents should do their homework by speaking with other parents whose students may currently or formerly have been in the program. A good litmus test would be the longevity of the program, its funding stream, and its placement rates of students in selective schools. Also, parents must make sure, when possible, that the counselors in the college access programs outside of the formal school setting are working in collaboration with your teen's guidance counselor. They both should be on the same page. Working at cross-purposes can put your teen at a disadvantage.

COUNT THE DOLLARS, NOT THE PENNIES

First-generation college-bound students tend to work not only in high school but also during their college years, and this sometimes puts them at yet another disadvantage. I recognize that some parents encourage their teens to work because they either need the financial help or at least if the teen works they will not need to depend on the parent as much to address the needs and wants of the teen. Working is good, for all the obvious reasons, but too much work can detract from a student's education, and from a planning perspective your teen should be focusing on their education so that they can save you and the family some in the long run. If a teen is working 20 hours a week or more and their GPA drops from a 3.5 to a 2.8 they are not going to be able to position themselves for a selective college that could offer them a full scholarship. Twenty hours a week at $7 an hour equals $560 a month before taxes. In a year they can earn $6,720 gross, and in four years they will have earned $26,880. Even if they saved all of the money, and of course they won't, they would still not have enough money to cover the average cost of a four-year college education at a public school $80,000 or a private college at $200,000. However, if you encouraged your teen to study more and work less, they could graduate with a GPA that could guarantee admissions to a selective school which would offer them a need- based financial aid package worth $200,000 and at some schools it could be all free money.

SUMMER ENRICHMENT

For students who are first in their families to go to college, attending a summer program, particularly on a college campus, can be rewarding in so many ways. A part from being away home alone, for the first time perhaps, and developing some independence before actually enrolling in college, it may be the first time that these students will face what is called academic rigor. Having these kinds of experiences prior to college enrollment is vital. It helps your teen academically when they return to their high school after the summer program. This assumes the program is offered earlier in high school, and it also increases the student's chances of doing well once in college. Parents can find out about these programs through school counselors, by calling colleges and universities, and speaking with an administrator who works for summer programs. Also, some of the boarding schools, high schools where students live throughout the school year, offer summer enrichment programs for high school kids.

EARLY FINANCIAL AID RESEARCH

As a parent you should not wait until the last minute to think about how your child's education will be paid for. In this case last minute is definitely too late. As a parent whose teen is first generation you probably don't have a great deal of disposable income, and if this is the case I would advise that you meet with your teen's counselor to determine what private scholarships are available early in high school. In that way not only will you know what is available, but you will also know what your teen has to achieve to compete for those scholarships once they are in senior year.

PICKING SCHOOLS

Picking, commonly known as the "college search" in the circles of guidance counselors and college advisors, is one of the most important assignments of your teen's young career, and as such it should not be taken lightly. Up until now you have helped your teen lay the foundation to apply to and get through college, now you have to assist him/her in choosing the right college for them among the thousands that exist.

In most cases, you can either depend on the school counselor or the college access provider outside of the school, and if you are fortunate you can use both as a resource. But let's assume that you are one of the rare parents who do not have access to either one. Then your best resource is to contact your local college directly. More and more colleges are reaching out into communities and helping families prepare their teens for college and also making the application process more transparent. In short, the college admissions officer would welcome your visit or come to your teen's school and answer any of your questions about the process. As a parent you have the right to this information so pick up the phone or go visit your local college.

Before calling or visiting a college or several colleges, you and your teen may want to sit down and focus your college search by asking two important questions. Your teen will have to answer: what do I bring to a college and what do I want in a college? He/she can answer the first question by reviewing their transcript, test scores, involvement in their in- and/or out-of-school activities, leadership, schools, and summer programs. The second question takes into consideration factors such as offered majors, if they have decided on one (they do not have to declare a major until the end of the second year of college), location, and size of school. Some students prefer urban over rural settings, while others have no preference. Religious-affiliated schools are a plus for some while a turn-off for others. As a parent, hopefully, you will not have to veto your teen's choice, though you may know them better than they know themselves. Ideally, you should let them make the choice of what type of schools they should apply to and ultimately where they decide to enroll.

PACKAGING AND PRESENTING

In the fall of the senior year your teen will be inundated with the college application and financial aid process. They will have to attend college fairs, complete applications, write essays, go for interviews, submit recommendations from teachers and sometimes counselors, prepare for and go for auditions (for performing art students), present portfolios (for visual art students), and register for the NCAA Clearing House (for athletes applying to DI, DIAA, or DII programs). Whether presenting a competed application, oneself in an interview or audition, presenting a portfolio, or an athletic tape, your teen has to be very deliberate about the way the contents are packaged and be mindful of their presentation. Also, they must be aware of how they present themselves not only in formal interviews, but also informal ones as well, for example, at college fairs when they are speaking with admissions officers, or at their schools when admissions representatives come to visit their high schools. Students should know that they are giving an impression in these situations, and they should package and present themselves in the best light. Certainly at a college fair they do not have to be in a suit and tie, but they should be dressed appropriately. Jeans and sneakers are ok at a fair, but a dress shirt and slacks and shoes are more appropriate for a formal interview.

PAYING: FINANCIAL AID

The financial aid process can be daunting for many parents, not just those who have teens who are first-generation college bound. But the key here is for parents to pay their taxes and to do so on time and use the resources available to them. Much of the information on your tax forms will be similar, and, in some cases, is the same as the information that is asked of you and your teen on the standard financial aid form that all schools require. This form is called the Free Application for Federal Student Aid (FAFSA). (See Chapter 7, "Financial Aid," for more details on the FAFSA.) It is important to keep in mind that financial aid is very time sensitive so students and their parents must complete the form on time and make sure it is completed correctly. Counselors at schools, college access providers, and college information centers in libraries in some of the urban centers in this country will be resources for families. You can also call the financial aid offices at one of the colleges to which your teen is applying and they can assist you with answering questions about the form.

Beyond the mechanics of completing the form and finding the right resource to help parents facilitate that goal, parents of first-generation college-bound students tend to have problems in three vital areas that hinder this process for their teen. Sometimes they are unaware of how to navigate the system. They do not know that they can and should negotiate the financial aid package if the college does not provide enough funds. They may also not know that they can reduce the cost of college if their teen becomes an asset to the college and can then obtain a Resident Advisors position (upper classmen live in one of the freshmen dorms and serve as advisors to first-year students and sometimes second-years too) which could provide them with a free room or board or both. Other schools offer stipends in lieu of free room and board while some offer all three. Knowing about these resources can help your teen reduce the cost of their education, but they have to know first that these resources exist and secondly how to navigate the system so they can access these services or at least be in a marketable position to be considered.

Some parents do not trust the system because they are being asked a lot of personal questions about their finances when the correct answers to these questions can only benefit their teen in the long run. Most parents who do not have a college education are not making a great deal of money, and thus they will qualify for need-based financial aid, but they have to trust that the system can and does work in their favor. In fact, if their teen is an asset and the family is poor, in this case the family could end up paying less than a thousand dollars a year for a college with a price tag of $50,000 a year.

A third concern is the problem with loans. These parents often are afraid to take out loans, and, by extension, their students do not want to take out loans. On the other hand, some of these families have no problem with taking out a loan for a new car. The cost of a four-year education is more important than the cost of a car, which in almost all cases will begin to depreciate as soon as one drives it off the lot. The investment in a college education can only appreciate in its value over a lifetime.

PERSISTING ONCE IN COLLEGE

You as parents know that getting into college for some teens is achieving a major milestone. They may have even been the first in their families to graduate from high school and now they are about to go off to college. While getting in is achieving one milestone, getting through is achieving another; this is particularly the case for the first-generation college bound since they have few if anyone to turn to assist them with this next important phase of their lives. The good news is that unlike some high schools, the resources on most college campuses abound. What parents and teens have to know is how to navigate so they can find them, how to communicate once they have found such, and how to self-advocate so they can get their needs met in an efficient and timely manner.

What many parents don't know is that some colleges have parent resources offices where parents can call to advocate on behalf of their teens. All colleges have student resources centers for a variety of issues, and some may even have offices that address the needs of first-generation college students specifically. Parents need to learn quickly what the resources are and how their teen can access them before a problem occurs; in other words, the accent should be on proactive and not reactive strategies. For example, if your teen has a roommate problem, and you don't have the resources to move her off campus, then what are the options on campus? Or your teen could be depressed around the holiday season or spring break because you do not have the money bring them home. Parents need to determine what college resources are available to assist students who may not be able to come home for all holidays throughout the year.

WORKING IN COLLEGE

It has already been noted that in high school first-generation college-bound students tend to have to or want to work. Unfortunately, the same phenomena exist at the college level. While your teen may be offered work-study as part of their financial aid package for the first year, I would advise that they not accept it. It is better to focus on their academics so they start out with a good GPA. As they become familiar with college life and have been successful in their transition year it may be more appropriate to consider a work-study job. On-campus work-study jobs may pay less than off-campus jobs, but on-campus ones are more accessible and more flexible since the employer respects the fact that your teen is a student first.

Paid internships are also recommended during the upper-class years of college since they could lead to a summer job and/or a full-time job in one's major after college, but keep in mind to advise your teen to be deliberate about time management and not to lose focus of the real reason why they are at college. Hopefully, your teen is one of those students who received a financial aid package that allows them the time and freedom to focus exclusively on their studies, but if they are not, urge them to work two jobs during the summer and save as much as they can so they won't have to depend on working so many hours when they return to college.

It is also important to note that these students sometimes can have a limited social life on campus because they are working so much. Thus, not only can the academic life of first-generation college students be affected, their social life can be impacted as well, thus rendering their entire undergraduate school years compromised because they are economically disadvantaged.

PROFITING

In the ideal world, I would want first-generation college students to have the same experience in college as their second-, third-, and fourth-generation college counterparts. However, we do not live in an ideal world, so my advice to parents has to be coached in reality. With the right long-term planning your teen will be advantaged and at least will not have to be preoccupied with money while in college. Does that mean that the playing field has been equalized? No, it does not, but it does make life easier when one does not have to worry about money and that would be the same for young people going through college.

If money is not an obstacle and one has the time to engage the undergraduate experiences more earnestly, then one should do so. It would be sinful to do otherwise since an opportunity denied is no different than one forgone, and we all know that there was a time in history that many poor families could not attend college.

You will find when you visit colleges that there are many students that persist. In other words, they finish college within a four- or five-year period and leave with a degree. However, many of these same students have failed to profit from more of what the undergraduate experience had to offer. They have not been involved in the college community, they have not participated in any educational or cultural programs in foreign countries, they have not established relationships with any professors, and thus they could not obtain a recommendation for a job or graduate or professional school if they needed one. While they have a degree, they have not developed a strong network of friends on campus so if they needed assistance from a friend's parent finding a job they would not have that option. Remember, education is not just what happens in the classroom. In fact, much of what a student learns in college will take place outside of the formal classroom setting from their peers. Your teen should be encouraged to profit from his/her college experiences in ways that will yield the greatest return on the investment that everyone has made including you as the parent. While you may not have provided most of the dollars for the education, you have provided other resources in the form of emotional support, time, and guidance, and you too deserve a return on your investment.

AFTER COLLEGE

First-generation college graduates return home with a mixed set of emotions, circumstances, challenges, and rewards. For some, social class and economic mobility can threaten an otherwise stable family if one or more members of the family are threatened by this new social standing of the college graduate. In other cases, the graduate may attach feelings of guilt do to his/her shift in values. In other cases their family members embrace them and their success, but they feel uncomfortable since they may question why they made it and a brother or cousin in the family did not. Still other graduates have parents who celebrate their success but they do not feel worthy of the celebration because they feel they are not as successful as their fellow classmates. They have continued feelings of being behind. They were behind when they arrived at college because of inferior schooling, they were behind once in college because of a poor educational foundation, or if their education was solid, they still had to navigate a foreign and sometimes foreboding social and cultural environment. And now that they are home, they cannot make the kind of money or obtain the kind of job that their fellow classmates have and on top of that some of them have loans to repay, hence they still feel left behind and not worthy of the celebration and pride felt by their parents and families. But of course all of this is in their own minds, and in most cases, unreasonable since they should not define success so narrowly and should not measure their success through the eyes of students who come from advantaged backgrounds.

SUBGROUP TRENDS ACROSS FIRST-GENERATION COLLEGE STUDENTS

There are a number of trends that I have witnessed over the years in working with different subgroups. As it is unwise to use a broad brush in defining patterns of behaviors for other identifiable groups, i.e. women, blacks, and Hispanic Americans, it is equally problematic do the same when discussing issues first-generation college students. Of course, there are some generalizations that are legitimate and much of those informed my earlier discussion about this important group of young people, and when there were differences particularly in the discussion of returning home, I did offer some variation. What follows is a brief overview of some of the specific characteristics associated with different subgroups. These observations are merely the ones I have observed and are not representative of a scientific study. They cannot thus be generalized across all students within each subgroup. Nonetheless, I think as parents you will find them interesting.

Freshmen and senior years can be equally problematic. In their first year they are told they are special but then they recognize the differences between economically advantaged and economically disadvantaged students that can make some feel insecure. These differences are more startling at the more selective schools, which tend to have a greater percentage of students from more affluent households. If they receive poor grades, this can make them feel more inadequate even though they have not had the same preparation as their peers and sometimes they have to work once in college, which takes them away from their studies.

As seniors if they don't receive the first job paying lots of money or they have not been admitted to a graduate or professional school they may feel inadequate if they judge their success narrowly or through some else's eyes.

White students who are first generation can mix in more since they do not have to reveal that they are economically disadvantaged. They are often described as the invisible minority as some light-skinned Hispanics are. Hispanics can also be invisible unless they have an accent; then their cover is revealed since the negative assumptions made by some about Hispanics in general can now be attributed to them.

Being invisible does not necessarily make it easier. It might be better to be obviously needy because in that way they can get some help from what the college has to offer students who are first generation.

Poor white students at rich white schools are marginalized. People don't want to talk about it because white folk don't like to admit that whites are poor too. Nevertheless, on these campuses class can raise its ugly head and first-generation college students who are white can feel it.

Hispanic parents have difficulty letting their daughters go away to college. This can also apply to the males but generally it is a female issue. On the other hand, black families in general encourage their teens to become independent and that means most do not have a problem with either gender leaving home.

Asians who are first in their families to go to college tend not to ask for help if they have a problem in class because they feel shameful since they are supposed to know. It is assumed that they are smart, and they realize that this is how they are stereotyped so they don't want to appear that they do not know.

African Americans and Hispanic Americans sometimes don't ask questions because it is assumed that they do not know and they don't want to appear to be unintelligent, so therefore they tend not to ask questions.

Some Asian students, particularly my Korean and Japanese, are more prone to depression if they receive poor grades because often shame is associated with not doing well academically. This self-loathing is not confined to first-generation students but is definitely a characteristic of those who are first.

White, Asian, and Hispanic Americans tend to work in study groups. Black students tend to think they have to do everything on their own. They assume that there is no one on whom they can rely. If they do not have a support system at home the problem is further aggravated. This puts them at a disadvantage and impacts their GPA negatively.

White students measure their success by the people they have come to know in college and in the white world. People of color measure their success through the eyes of their immediate family members. Blacks may not have someone in their family pushing them to and through college, but they may have someone in the church who acts as an advocate. People of color in general may feel compelled to help out their families while in college and thus they may be giving them some of the scholarship and financial aid money.

So as you can see, just through these few slices across these different groups, how daunting the experiences can be for students who are first in their families to attend college. But one can look at the glass half full and not half empty. It is indeed quite an honor to be the first in one's family to attend and graduate from college. It can also be a big responsibility but one that is not necessarily bad if the student comes home to a welcoming family.

When your teen comes home he will not be the same as he was when he left. This is particularly true of first-generation college graduates. In fact, if you are a wise parent, you will not expect him to be the same, and you will welcome and embrace his newfound wisdom. In fact, if families are clever they will leverage this new knowledge to help advance the family. On the other hand, when students come home they should not assume that they know it all. They owe a lot to their parents for the support that helped them manage the years in college. And while I recognize that not all college students have support from home, most do. That having been said, I believe that the values that informed the person that the first generation was able to become is in large part informed by the wisdom of the parents/guardians, and for that parents too should celebrate. I would hope that when a student returns home there be mutual respect on all sides. Parents may have something new to learn from their teen, and students will still have lots to learn from their parents. After all, that is what it should be all about– families helping each other move forward.

QUESTIONS TO ASK

Please take advantage of the following questions at the appropriate times. It will help increase your college knowledge and empower you as a parent as you are assisting your teen through the various processes of preparing for, applying to, and getting through college.

Planning in High School: Questions for School Counselor, Principal, Church Minister, College Access Provider in Your Community

- How do I prepare my teen for college?
- What courses should he/she be taking in high school?
- What is a standardized test?
- Does the school offer fee waivers for these exams?
- What is a college entrance exam?
- How does my teen prepare for them?
- What resources are in the library or in the community to assist my teen?

- What summer programs are available, and is there money available to defray their cost?

- Does your high school or community offer any tutoring programs for teens?

- How can I get involved in my teen's school one or two hours a week?

- How much homework can I expect my teen to have each night?

The College Application Process: School Counselors, College Access Providers, and College Admissions Officers

- Does your college offer application fee waivers?

- What is the fee waiver policy?

- Does the high school have college application fee waivers?

- Does the college offer fly-in programs for students and parents?

- Does the college offer an orientation program for parents?

- When are college applications generally due?

- When should a student expect to hear from a college?

- What is Early Decision and Early Action?

- What is Regular and Rolling Admissions?

- Does your college offer pre-college programs for first-generation college-bound students?

- What kind of programming is available for first-generation students once they are enrolled?

- Does your school have a resource center for students who have learning disabilities?

- Does your school have an organization serving the needs of students of color?

The Financial Aid Process-For School Counselors, College Access Providers, and Financial Aid Officers at College

- Where and when can I receive assistance completing the financial aid forms?

- What scholarship opportunities are available?

- How does the university allocate outside scholarship funds?
- If my teen receives outside monies can he use them to offset student loans and/or my parent contribution?
- Can the financial aid package be negotiated?
- Can a family expect to receive the same financial aid package all four years?
- How is the family contribution index calculated?
- When does a student have to notify the college that he is coming to your school?
- If a student sends a deposit to your school and changes his mind, is it refundable?

Getting Through College: Academic Deans and Counselors at College

- Who should my teen call if he is having a problem with his/her roommate?
- Who should my teen call if they are having a problem with a professor?
- Does your school offer any diversity training to address issues of race, gender, and social class?
- How is your academic advising program structured?
- How often can my teen meet with his/her academic advisor?
- At what point does my teen choose his/her major?
- What is the retention of students in general?
- What is the retention of first-generation college students?
- Is the faculty actively involved in the lives of students on your campus?
- How would you rate the social and the academic experiences of first-generation college students on your campus?
- Can my teen speak to a few first-generation students on your campus?
- Can I speak to some of the alumni who were first-generation college students on your campus?

● In your opinion, what challenges do first-generation college students face on your campus, and how is the faculty and administration addressing those needs?

These are a sampling of questions that will jump start any discussion you as a parent want to have at the various stages of your teen's education up to and through college, starting with the high school years. I hope this chapter has inspired you to motivate your teen to hold on to his dream. It can be realized with the right guidance, determination, and a bit of luck along the way. In closing this chapter, I offer you a second voice of a first-generation college graduate:

● ● ● ●

As a first-generation student you must believe in yourself because at times you may be the only one. "It is the pleasure of Howard University to inform you that you have been accepted for the fall semester 1992..." Wow, this was my second acceptance letter in as many days—I was ecstatic! But, there was no excitement or encouragement from my dad when I showed him the acceptance letters. And, later that spring, when I announced that I had won a scholarship from our church in the amount of $700.00 to assist with my college expenses, there was still no positive response. Being the first in my family to go to college was a source of great pride for my mother, who had always wanted more for her four daughters and two sons. On the other hand, my dad, having only attended grade school in rural South Carolina, seemed so far removed from the idea of a college education. Even, the colonel at my summer job in DC was not excited to hear that I had decided to attend Howard University in the fall and not accept the offer of a full-time position at the Department of Army. I thought to myself, "What is wrong with the male authority figures in my life—don't they want to see me succeed in college!" I was going to show them—not only will I earn a baccalaureate degree, but a master's degree and a doctorate degree, too! One day after classes in early December, my parents called me into their bedroom. My dad handed me an envelope and said, "This is from me and your mother for your college tuition." Inside the envelope were five $1000 bills. I was stunned and happy at the same time. He had dipped into his savings to ensure that I could return to college the next semester. Although he never said it, I knew he was proud of his oldest daughter. I felt a sense of pride as well, because I knew that I was setting the standard for my younger siblings and I would not let them down. Thank you, Daddy, for believing in me.

—Vera Faulkner

REFERENCES

First-Generation College Bound

Antonoff, Steven. *The College Finder: Choosing the School That's Right for You!* Westford, MA: Winter Green, Orchard House Press.

Gushman, Kathleen. *First in the Family: Advice from First-Generation Students, The High School Years.* Providence, RI: Next Generation Press.

---. *First in the Family: Advice about College from First-Generation Students, Your College Years.* Providence, RI: Next Generation Press.

FINANCIAL AID

During the college application process, I was informed that I would have to save some energy for applying for financial aid and that meant I had to complete the FAFSA and the CSS Profile. While most of my colleges only required the FAFSA some of them required both. Because my mother was unfamiliar with the process, I asked my guidance counselor for help. Before meeting with my guidance counselor, I talked to my mother about the information I would need prior to the meeting, and I also told her the kind of information I would share and the kind of information that would not be discussed. Since there are many parents in this country who are uncomfortable with sharing financial information, I made sure that I asked my mother for her permission before talking to my counselor about her finances. Luckily, my mother was not afraid to share her household income and expenses with my guidance counselor so when it came time to gather the information needed my mother gave me her W-2 forms and any other documents I needed to complete the forms with my guidance counselor.

Interpreting the financial aid packages was a challenge for my mother and me, so I asked my guidance counselor for assistance and she helped me interpret the various packages. What I believed to be a $20,000 scholarship from a university in the Northeast was in fact a $20,000 loan that I would have to take out yearly if I attended that school. Without my guidance counselor's help, I wouldn't have chosen the school I am going to now. In the end, I chose to attend the University of Virginia (UVA) because their financial aid package was the best out of all other colleges and I felt comfortable within UVA's environment both academically and socially.

—**Jasmine Drake**

WHAT IS THE FINANCIAL AID PROCESS?

The financial aid process is a systemic process designed to determine a student's eligibility, based on parents' and student's income, assets and financial resources, for federal and institutional need-based aid resources.

The process begins with viewing the required financial aid applications and gathering the necessary financial documents needed to complete the application. There are two financial aid applications, the Free Application for Federal Student Aid (FASFA) and the College Scholarship Service Profile (CSS Profile). It is highly recommended that your teen complete both applications online although the federal application has a paper version. Depending on the college, your teen will be required to complete one or both applications. The Financial Aid Offices at the colleges your teen is considering will be able to tell you which financial aid application to complete and submit.

Your teen's current federal tax and bank statements, social security number, and W-2s are several items they will need in order to complete the financial aid application. They may also need to collect documents related to your mortgage, business and farm records, untaxed income such as social security and welfare benefits, investments, and foreign tax returns.

THE PIN NUMBER

Your teen should register for a PIN number before they start filling out the financial aid application. PIN numbers are unique numbers assigned by the U.S. Department of Education to applicants and their parents. This number allows the applicant and one parent to sign the financial aid application electronically online. As a result, it keeps the applicant and parent from having to download a signature page to mail in to the application processing center. Having a PIN number will speed up your teen's application process.

To register for a PIN number, they must go to the following website: www.pin.ed.gov

THE FEDERAL AID APPLICATION (FAFSA)

The FAFSA (Free Application for Federal Student Aid) is the federal financial aid application used to produce an expected family contribution (EFC) from income, assets, and other financial resources information provided on the form by your teen. The processing of the application is free and will allow them to enter up to eight schools on a single application to receive the processed information.

The best time to complete the FAFSA is between January 1 and February 28 of each year. In most cases, this puts your teen within the early priority deadlines for financial aid consideration by most colleges. They should check with their college choices to find out their priority deadline dates.

The FAFSA is composed of seven steps or sections:

- **Step One:** Student personal and background information

- **Step Two:** Student income, assets, and financial resources information

- **Step Three:** Student dependency questions

- **Step Four:** Parents' income, assets, and financial resources information

- **Step Five:** Independent Student household size questions

- **Step Six:** School listing to send your information

- **Step Seven:** Signature section

The FAFSA application can be accessed at www.fafsa.ed.gov.

THE STUDENT AID REPORT

The Student Aid Report is received after the FAFSA application is processed. This report contains information relevant to your teen's eligibility for federal student aid. It also allows you and your teen to review the submitted processed data for any necessary corrections that might be needed for resubmission of the application. If corrections are needed, they can be done online with the PIN number or via a phone in most cases by providing the Data Release Number (DRN) number that will be located on the Student Aid Report. Lastly, the Student Aid Report will provide your teen with a calculated Expected Family Contribution. The calculated Expected Family Contribution, once determined, will be reported to each school listed on the FAFSA.

THE COLLEGE SCHOLARSHIP SERVICE APPLICATION (CSS PROFILE)

The CSS Profile financial aid application is designed to determine a family's eligibility for nonfederal student aid funds. In order to use the CSS Profile your teen must register online with a collegeboard.com account and debit card, credit card, or check. Students are encouraged to register at least two weeks before the priority application filing dates to meet the deadlines for scholarships and other aid programs.

Once your teen is registered, a personalized PROFILE application will be made available to complete. In order to complete the PROFILE, current year taxes for parents and student, along with information on other financial resources, will be needed.

Once completed and processed the PROFILE data will be sent to the schools listed on the application to determine eligibility for institutional financial aid, such as scholarship and institutional grants.

Your teen should check to find out if the CSS PROFILE is required by the Financial Aid Office of the schools they are considering.

The CSS PROFILE can be accessed at http://profileonline.collegeboard.com.

THE INSTITUTIONAL PROCESS

After the FAFSA and CSS PROFILE applications are processed and forwarded to the schools requested by the student, the different colleges will review the information received for financial aid eligibility. As part of the Financial Aid Office review process, each year the U.S. Department of Education randomly selects student financial aid applications for a process called "verification." Verification simply checks the information reported on the FAFSA against the tax documents used to complete the financial aid application. The Financial Aid Office will send your teen a letter asking for copies of tax forms and financial information for the current year to fulfill the "verification" requirement.

In addition to the tax information, your teen may be required to complete the following institutional documents utilized in the verification process:

- **Minimal Income Statement:** Used by Financial Aid Office to determine income and resources used by the family, if reported income is extremely low.

- **Dependent/Independent Verification Worksheet:** Used by the Financial Aid Office to verify untaxed income and household size.

- **Institutional Financial Aid Application:** Used by the Financial Aid Office to gather information on a student background and previous colleges attended.

The Financial Aid Office will send letters to students requesting the submission of all the necessary verification documents which normally can be downloaded from the college's website for completion and submission.

COST OF ATTENDANCE

The cost of attendance is created by the Financial Aid Office and may vary from school to school; however, they all will have the following major components:

- Tuition and fees
- Room and board

- Books and supplies

- Transportation

- Personal expenses

Schools may also include the fees associated with borrowing a student loan, a personal computer purchase, and other costs associated with a student with a disability.

When it comes to cost of attendance, the type of school your teen attends will have a significant impact on the amount they pay for a college education. Cost can vary tremendously among public colleges, private colleges, community colleges, vocational, technical, and trade schools. In most cases, financial need increases as the cost of attendance increases.

AWARD LETTER NOTIFICATIONS

The colleges that have accepted your teen for admission will begin sending out award letters normally in April. This will allow your teen to compare all the offers of financial aid from the different schools based on their cost of attendance. Some of these letters will list only direct cost where other letters may list all college costs. For example, an award letter may reflect the cost of tuition, fees, room, and board; however, these costs may vary depending on a variety of meal plans to select from and whether your teen lives on or off-campus. These are a few of the things to take into consideration when your teen is looking at the actual cost of the college. Don't forget about the cost of books and supplies because both can be expensive depending on the major and whether your teen chooses to buy new or used books.

There are two categories of financial aid that your teen's award notifications may have as offers to them. One category might be need-based which will consist of grants, scholarships, and work-study. These are funds, if offered, that your teen will not have to repay. The second category of awards might be non-need based loan funds. Loan funds, if offered, will have to be repaid.

Your teen should also know that they have the option in most cases to decide which financial aid funds, if offered, on the award letter they will accept or deny.

Lastly, they will need to be aware of the deadline to respond to the financial aid offer. If they fail to respond before the deadline, the offer will be rescinded and the funds redistributed to other waiting applicants.

If your teen has any questions they should contact the Financial Aid Office.

HELPING YOUR TEEN EVALUATE AND NEGOTIATE THE FINANCIAL AID AWARD OFFER

When it comes to evaluating the financial aid award offers, your teen will need to spread out the award letters so that they can compare the packages from the different colleges. This can be complicated because of the types and amount of financial aid that could be offered. An easy way for your teen to make the comparisons is to create a spreadsheet with the following headings and categories. List all the colleges by name, then make a list of the following items for each college: Cost of Attendance (tuition and fees, room and board, other expenses) = total cost of attendance; expected family contribution; Financial Aid Eligibility (scholarship and grants, student loans, work study job, other financial aid offers) = total aid offer.

Once your teen has the total cost and total aid they will have a sense of what will be required of them in order to fill the remaining difference in what the financial aid covers and the college costs. Have your teen look at the amount or percentage of the financial aid offer that is need-based compared to non-need-based financial aid.

Saying, "I want to negotiate the financial aid offer I received with the Financial Aid Office," can be viewed as very strong words. Your teen should keep in mind that the Financial Aid Office professionals are simply stewards of the institution's and federal government's funds and their job is to make sure that those funds are disbursed fairly and go to the neediest students. If your teen chooses to talk with the Financial Aid Office about the need for additional funds, a better approach would be to ask that their financial aid offer be given a review or reconsideration or they would like to appeal the offer due to specific reasons.

If their requested reason for an appeal of a financial aid offer is a good one, it does not hurt to make the request since they could receive more money. If the Financial Aid Office is unable to assist with your teen's present situation, they should stay in touch because they might be able to help them in the future.

THE FEDERAL FINANCIAL AID PROGRAMS

The Federal Pell Grant

The Federal Pell Grant program is a federal student aid program administered by the college for students who have not earned a bachelor's degree. The program is designed to offer assistance to students with the greatest need. Students can receive funding for enrollments of full time, three quarters time, half time and less than half time. Pell Grant funds are one of the few aid programs where the funds are portable, which means that funding can move with the student to different colleges and is not based on availability of funds at any one school. Eligibility for the Pell Grant is determined by the expected family contribution (EFC), calculated by the FAFSA and your teen's enrollment in college. The minimum and maximum under the program vary up to $5,550.

The Federal Supplemental Educational Opportunity Grant (FSEOG)

The Federal Supplemental Educational Opportunity Grant provides financial assistance to needy students who have not earned a bachelor's degree. If your teen qualifies for the Pell Grant, they will be given priority consideration for the FSEOG program; however, this program has limited funds so it's important to make the financial aid deadline. FSEOG award amounts vary from $100 to a maximum of $4,000 depending on the availability of school funds.

The Federal Perkins Loan Program

The Federal Perkins Loan Program is a low interest loan (5%). The loan is need-based and the interest is paid by the federal government while the student is enrolled in school at least half time. Students with exceptional need are required to be given priority by schools. Funding is based on the availability of the funds from funds being repaid by previous borrowers.

A student can borrow as much as $4,000 per year up to an aggregate of $20,000 as an undergraduate. Repayment begins nine months after graduation or after a student ceases to be enrolled at least half time. There is no penalty for repaying the full amount of the loan or part of the loan to avoid interest payments.

The Federal Work Study Program

The Federal Work Study Program is an employment program that allows students to work on-campus in administrative or academic offices and off-campus with community service organizations. The funds offered through the program are need-based and have no limit as the amount offered as long as it does not exceed the student's financial need. The hours per week vary from school to school, however, most will advise that a student work no more than twenty hours per week. The rates of pay will also vary depending on the type of work the student will be performing. Federal Work Study Program has limited funding so it is important that your teen apply for financial aid before the deadline.

The Federal Direct Student Loan Program (FDSLP)

The Federal Direct Student Loan Program is composed of three federally guaranteed loans. The Federal Direct Subsidized Stafford Loan and the Federal Direct Unsubsidized Loan are both low interest. Additionally, the Federal Direct Parent Loan for Undergraduate Students (PLUS) is a member of the federal guaranteed loans.

The Federal Direct Subsidized Loan is a need-based loan with interest that is paid by the federal government while the student is enrolled in school at least half time. Six months after graduation the student starts to repay the loan with interest. The amount borrowed may be limited by other financial aid offered to the student.

The Federal Direct Unsubsidized Loan is non-need based and the student is responsible for paying the interest while in school. The deferment of interest payments is available, but the interest will accrue if not paid while in school.

The student could receive either a Federal Subsidized or Unsubsidized Loan or a combination of both loans.

The maximum amounts a student can borrow are based on grade levels:

- $5,500 per year for first-year students; $3,500 of this may be subsidized.

- $6,500 per year for second-year students; $4,500 of this may be subsidized.

- $7,500 per year for third-year students and beyond; $5,500 of this may be subsidized.

The Direct Student Loan funds are made available through the federal government via U.S. Department of Education which eliminates having to use banks or other private lenders for these loans. The college's Financial Aid Office will normally have a simplified in-house application to apply for these loans. The interest rate is based on the 91-day T-Bill rate and the average one-year constant maturity Treasury yield (CMT). The rate is set July 1st of each year. For unsubidized loans the current rate is 6.8%. The College Cost Reduction and Access Act of 2007 temporarily reduced the fixed interest rate on newly originated subsidized loans for undergraduates to 4.5% (2010-2011) and 3.4% (2011-2012). In 2012-2013 the interest rate will return to 6.8%.

The Federal Direct Parent Loan for Undergraduate Students (PLUS)

The Federal Direct Parent Loan for Undergraduate Students (PLUS) is designed for the parents of an undergraduate student to borrow up to the cost of attendance of the student's educational cost, if necessary, minus any other financial aid the student receives. The credit history of the applicant is checked for any adverse activity. The repayment of the loan begins immediately after the last disbursement.

The PLUS Loan funds are made available through the federal government via the U.S. Department of Education and therefore no banks or other private lending institutions are needed to apply for the loan. The college Financial Aid Office will normally have a simplified in-house application to apply for the loan. The interest rate is presently fixed at 8.5%.

The Academic Competitive Grant (ACG)

This is a federal grant program for fulltime undergraduate students enrolled in an eligible program, who receive Pell Grant, and are U.S. citizens. The student must have completed a rigorous secondary school program of study. The student must also be enrolled in at least a two-year academic program with credits that will count towards a bachelor's degree or enrolled in a graduate degree program that includes three academic years of undergraduate education. Students must have completed high school after January 1, 2005, and have at least a 3.00 GPA for their first academic year in an eligible program.

The grant amounts are:

- Up to $750 for first-year students

- Up to $1,300 for second-year students

The National Science and Mathematics Access to Retain Talent Grant (SMART Grant)

This is a federal grant program for full-time undergraduate students who are in their third or fourth year of enrollment of an eligible program and who receive Pell Grants and are U.S. citizens. Students must be pursuing a degree in physical, life or computer sciences, engineering, technology, mathematics, or a critical-need foreign language and have at least a 3.00 cumulative GPA. The grant amounts are up to $4,000 for each of the third and fourth academic years.

SCHOLARSHIPS AND INSTITUTIONAL FINANCIAL AID PROGRAMS

Searching for scholarships can be a daunting task, but the Internet has made this process easier and it is far better than paying someone for something your teen can do for free. If your teen decides to use the Internet to find scholarships, they should use the free scholarship searches.

Here are some tips for your teen on finding scholarships:

- You should check with your employer about scholarships for children of employees.

- Consider scholarships through military and armed services.

- Look up professional associations and church membership awards.

- Check for scholarships on student and parental heritage.

- Research merit scholarships offered by state or national organizations.

- Join national competitions for scholarships.

- Talk with the high school counselor about local scholarships.

- Research schools that offer merit scholarships in your teen's area of interest.

Scholarships do not have to be repaid and are considered need-based financial aid.

NCAA ATHLETICS AND FINANCIAL AID

While Chapter 4 focused on the college athlete, I wish to stress again here the financial aid logistics and requirements for this special category of student. In order to be eligible to practice, play, and receive financial aid at a Division I school your teen must be able to present 14 core courses. To be eligible to practice, play, and receive financial aid at a Division II school, they must present 16 core courses.

- 4 years of English

- 3 years of mathematics (Algebra I or higher)

- 2 years of natural/physical science (one must be a lab science)

- 1 year of additional English, math or science

- 2 years of social studies

- 4 years of additional core courses (from any area listed above, or from foreign language, non-doctrinal religion, or philosophy)

NCAA athletes are required to take the SAT or ACT test. Both tests have a new writing component that is required by the SAT but is optional on the ACT. Presently the NCAA does not require the writing component. Additionally, information on test scores and how they are used by the NCAA can be obtained from your teen's high-school guidance counselor and at www.ncaa.org.

All student athletes are required to register with the NCAA Initial Eligibility Clearinghouse online.

Athletic scholarships are not plentiful and full-ride scholarships are rare and highly competitive. The key to receiving one is for your teen to start the process early and be an excellent athlete. They should contact their school, prepare to do well in the interview process, put together a good presentation of their talents and skills, be prepared to ask intelligent questions, and follow up with the coaches and school officials.

In the area of athletic scholarships, schools will offer two types. An institutional grant gives an athlete the flexibility to change his or her mind after signing with one college to change and sign with another college. The second type of scholarship is a conference grant, which will bind an athlete to a particular college once signed.

These scholarships could take the following forms:

- A full four-year ride covering all college expenses, room and board, tuition, and books.

- A scholarship for one year with a renewable contract. You and your teen should find out from the coach or recruiter the college's track record for renewing the scholarship, if the athlete meets all the academic, athletic, and other standards set by the school.

- A one-year trial grant with a verbal agreement between the athlete and the school that it will be renewed at the end of the year, based on academic and athletic performance on the team.

- A partial grant covering a portion of the college cost such as room and board or tuition and fees or books.

- The athlete could be offered a waiver of out-of-state fees that would allow the student to pay the same fees as an in-state student.

OTHER CONSIDERATIONS IN THE FINANCIAL AID PROCESS

Professional Judgment is a tool used in the Financial Aid Office to address special circumstances that may have occurred after the student files for financial aid. Some good examples of situations of this nature are divorce, loss of employment, death of a parent, hardship due to illness, and many other unusual things that could and do happen. If any of these events happen to the student during the application process they can only be addressed in the Financial Aid Office by requesting a professional judgment appeal.

If the Financial Aid Office reviews your teen's changed circumstances and approves their appeal, the student's financial aid file will be reprocessed with the adjustments made by the Financial Aid Office. This reprocessing could change your student's eligibility for financial aid.

SELECTIVE SERVICE

All males must register with the U.S. Selective Service Board when they reach the age of eighteen in order to be considered for federal financial aid. The selective service system is designed to create a database of eligible men to draft into the military, in case of war. Parents should be aware that a draft is not likely in the near future. See http://www.sss.gov/ for how to register online.

THE AMERICAN OPPORTUNITY TAX CREDIT

The American Opportunity Tax Credit (AOTC) replaces the Hope Tax Credit for 2009 tax filers. The credit is available for certain qualifying educational expenses that you pay for yourself, your spouse, or a dependent for which you claim an exemption on your tax return. The credit will cover qualifying expenses to the first four years of a teen's undergraduate education. Your teen can include student activity fees, expenses for course-related books, supplies, and equipment, only if the fees and expenses are paid to the college as a condition of their enrollment or attendance.

- The AOTC credit is worth up to $2,500 credit per eligible student.

- Available for first four years of postsecondary education.

- Student must be pursuing an undergraduate degree or other recognized educational credential.

- Student must be enrolled at least half time.

- Student cannot have any felony drug conviction on record.

THE LIFETIME LEARNING CREDIT

The Lifetime Learning Credit can be claimed for the qualified tuition and related expenses of the students in the taxpayer's family who are enrolled at in eligible educational institutions. Family can qualify for a credit amount equal to 20 percent of the taxpayer's first $10,000 of out-of-pocket qualified tuition and related expenses.

Some highlights of the Lifetime Learning Credit:

- A credit worth $2,000 per return.

- The credit is available for all year of postsecondary education and for courses to acquire or improve job skills.

- It is available for an unlimited number of years.

- In order to qualify for credit the student does not need to be pursuing a degree or other recognized education credential.

- Student can be enrolled for one or more courses and still receive the credit.

- The student can qualify for the credit even if the student has been convicted of felony drug conviction.

For more information on the tax credits view the IRS website: http://www.irs.gov/publications/p970/index.html.

HELPING YOUR TEEN REDUCE THE FOUR-YEAR COST OF COLLEGE

Freshman Year

- Leave the car at home.

- Live on campus.

- Decorate college dorm with furnishings from home.

- Don't buy all new clothes. Buy a few new basics and take the others from your high school senior year.

- Cancel the paid Internet service and use the free wireless service on-campus.

- Purchase a cell phone and disconnect the landline in the dorm room.

- Purchase used books online at www.bestbookbuys.com, www.half.com, www.thediag.com, and www.campusbookswap. com.

- Purchase a meal plan that will not waste money. If your teen doesn't like getting up for breakfast they should not buy a plan with breakfast as meals.

Sophomore Year

- Investigate ways to pay in-state tuition, if your teen is out-of-state.

- Prepare to take summer classes at the local community college and transfer them back to your teen's school.

- Register and pay bills on time to avoid late fees.

- Sell used textbooks.

- Get a job on or off campus.

- Reduce the number of trips home.

- Skip expensive spring break trips.

Junior Year

- Avoid unnecessary purchases with credit cards.

- Move off campus and share an apartment or room.

- Drop meal plan and cook food at home.

- Your teen should bring his or her car to school, but use public transportation or shuttle system provided by the college as much as possible.

- Get a paid summer internship.

Senior Year

- Save summer job earnings to purchase interview suit and cap and gown. Gowns usually are available as rentals.

- Tutor students for a fee.

The financial aid process may seem daunting, but getting an early start will cut down on frustration by allowing enough time for your teen to avoid the rush. Planning for college is challenging enough without having to spend a lot of time worrying about how and if your teen can afford the college of their choice.

● ● ● ●

Since this generation is so advanced in technology it does not come as a surprise that almost all of the financial aid applications are online. In this respect applying for financial aid is easier now than it has been in the past. Still, it is crucial to meet all the deadlines to ensure that you receive all of the aid that you can. If you have questions about the financial aid process and or applications, you do not have to rely solely on your guidance counselor. You can call the financial aid officer at one of the schools in which you have an interest.

Upon receiving the financial aid package, it should be read carefully as some of the aid may include loans. It is important that you are aware of the differences in aid and when in doubt, here again, do not always rely on your guidance counselor, call the financial aid counselor at the respective college. Now that you have been admitted, they will have even more of an investment in making sure that you come to their school.

Finally, if you are unhappy with the financial aid package, let the college know, you may be surprised when they inform you that they are willing to increase your scholarship allocation.

—Neferteneken Francis

GLOSSARY

American Opportunity Tax Credit (AOTC): This tax credit is worth up to $2,500 for tax filers and it is capped at $4,000. The credit is available only for expenses paid during the first four years of qualifying college education. For the 2010 tax year, the maximum credit remains $2,500 under the American Opportunity Tax Credit.

Award Letter: Is an official document issued by the Financial Aid Office of the college. It will reflect the financial aid awarded a student. The letter will be sent via electronic e-mail or the U.S. Postal mail.

Cost of Attendance: The total amount it will cost the student to attend a particular school. The cost of attendance includes room and board, tuition and fees, books and supplies, transportation, and personal expenses.

CSS Profile: A financial aid application with a processing fee used to determine eligibility for financial aid by some colleges. The application is usually a requirement of aid consideration by private colleges.

Dependent Student: An undergraduate student who is under the age of 24 and has no legal dependents, is not an orphan or ward of the court or veteran of the United States Armed Forces.

Deferment: An entitlement provided through student loans that allows your teen to temporarily postpone payments for several reasons, including employment, disability, returning to school, and personal hardship.

Eligibility: A term used when the calculated expected family contribution (EFC) is less than the cost of attendance (COA) of the educational institution.

Expected Family Contribution (EFC): The estimated amount, based on the processed FAFSA, the federal government says a family should be able to contribute to the cost of education, based on income, assets, and other contributions.

Federal Pell Grant: A federal grant aid program and as such the funds do not have to be repaid. Funds are awarded to students with exceptional need. Grant amounts depend on the expected family contribution (EFC).

Federal Perkins Loan: A federal loan for students managed by the college. Exceptional need is the first requirement, and interest is paid by the government while the student is enrolled at least half time.

Federal Supplemental Educational Opportunity Grant: A federal grant aid program. Funds received from the program do not have to be repaid. Funds are awarded based on need and availability by the college.

Federal Direct Subsidized Student Loan: A federal need-based loan that the government pays the interest on while the student is enrolled in school at least half time.

Federal Direct Unsubsidized Student Loan: A federal non-need based loan for which the student is responsible for paying the interest on the loan from the date of disbursement. Deferment options are available.

Federal Direct Parent Loan for Undergraduate Students (PLUS): A federally guaranteed loan utilized by parents of dependent students to cover college education costs. The loan repayment begins immediately after the full disbursement of the loan.

Federal Work Study: A need-based employment federal aid program that provides part-time employment opportunities to students on and off-campus to assist with educational costs.

Free Application for Federal Student Aid (FAFSA): The federal form used to apply for financial aid and determine eligibility for all federal aid programs.

Forbearance: An agreement with the lender, at its discretion, to postpone payments when your teen is having financial difficulty.

Grace Period: The amount of time allowed before principal repayment of loan must begin after the student graduates, leaves school, or drops below half time enrollment.

Lifetime Learning Tax Credit: A credit designed to aid students acquiring or improving job skills. The credit is equal to 20% of the first $10,000 of tuition-related expenses paid by a family. The maximum credit is usually $2,000 per year.

Merit-Based Aid: Financial assistance offered on the basis of personal achievement and individual characteristics without regard to financial need.

Need-Based Financial Aid: Financial aid resources awarded to students based on eligibility showing that the expected family contribution (EFC) is less than the college's cost of attendance (COA). The outcome of subtracting the EFC from the COA will yield a figure greater than zero which equates to need.

No Need: A term used when the calculated expected family contribution (EFC) is greater than the cost of attendance (COA) of the educational institution.

Promissory Note: A document that a borrower signs before receiving loan proceeds. The note includes information about the terms and conditions of the loan. It establishes that the borrower has promised to repay the loan.

Section 529 Plan: Plans established by states as college savings programs and pre-paid tuition plans that allow families to set aside money to grow federally tax-free, to cover college tuition, fees, supplies, books, and certain room and board costs.

Student Aid Report (SAR): A report sent to the student by the government to acknowledge that the FAFSA has been processed. The report allows the student to review the submitted information and make any necessary corrections needed for resubmission.

REFERENCES

Financial Aid

The Scholarship Book: The Complete Guide to Private Sector Scholarships, Grants, and Loans for Undergraduates. National Scholarship Research Service and Daniel J. Cassidy. Prentice Hall Trade.

The Ultimate Scholarship Book 2011. Gen and Kelly Tanabe. SuperCollege.

Winning Scholarships for College: An Insider's Guide. Marianne Ragins. Holt Paperbacks.

CHAPTER VIII

COLLEGE: GETTING IN AND GETTING THROUGH

Entering college for the right reasons is key to a successful college journey. People enter college for a variety of reasons, but if the reasons do not match the student's ambitions and goals, it will not be as fulfilling. Many students enter college with a vague career field or desired job title post graduation. Some let others directly or indirectly decide which path they should pursue, letting parents, friends, and faculty who influenced them along the way dictate their path out of a well-meaning sense of loyalty to their supporters. This in turn causes the student to lose him or herself and throughout their college tenure they function on automatic pilot just to finish. Therefore, enter college for the right reasons, and if you do not know the right reasons, do some serious soul searching; but come up with the final conclusion on your own and take ownership of your college destiny.

In retrospect, when I think of what helped me get through college two patterns come to mind. I needed to make sure I understood what the expectations were from each professor. I spoke with them often to gauge how I was doing in their class, and I also wanted to know how I could be more successful. I demanded feedback on papers and projects and always wanted to know how I could actively get a higher grade.

Which brings me to my second point—all of my close friends had a similar mindset. They checked in with their professors and were constantly striving to do better. I feel if one wants to be a productive student they have to make sure that they do not fall victim to negative outside pressure. Peer pressure can be both good and bad. Students need to surround themselves with those who share their goals, i.e. being around those of like minds increases the chances of being successful—in this case academic success.

—**Helena Edwards**

CONGRATULATIONS TO YOU AND YOUR family. Your teen has, with the support of family, friends, teachers and counselors, been admitted to college. They are in, but now they have to stay in and be productive while there. Ideally, they will enjoy their new home away from home, and if they do, they most likely will become engaged in the overall undergraduate experience.

Colleges too have an investment in your teen doing well. After all, a high rate of student attrition negatively affects their rankings. Consequently, they pay close attention to students, particularly freshmen, since that is the transitional year, and that is where most students face challenges. Institutions vary though as to the kind of and amount of attention they pay to transitioning new students to their campuses. Your teen will be integrating into a new community with a new set of rules and expectations. How well they will succeed in college will largely be determined on how well they can adapt to these new expectations.

Your teen will experience an orientation either during the summer preceding their first year of college or over a week in the fall preceding the start of classes. During that time they will meet several people representing various departments and programs. In general, the goal of this week is to orient the new students to the campus by identifying resources and key people associated with those resources. For example, they will meet employees from academic departments, student support services, residential life, and financial aid, to name a few.

Please do not let your teen be so consumed with high school graduation and getting ready to pack and go off to college and forget to read this section. Some, if not all, of this information will be covered at your teen's freshmen orientation, but I also know from experience that the quality of that information can vary and some topics may not be addressed. Succinctly, it is better to have the information and not need it rather than need it and not have it. What follows are some tips that will help your teen stay in and do well while they are in college.

When your teen thinks of a college or university there are many divisions, but generally everything can fall under two major areas, Academic Affairs and Student Affairs. Academic Affairs focuses on the academic areas of college, while Student Affairs addresses more of the social aspects. I would like to offer you some tips under Academic Affairs and then address Student Affairs separately. Please note I am not suggesting that once your teen is on campus these two departments should work separately. On the contrary, institutions that are successful do so through collaboration; therefore, you will see a joining of hands, so to speak, between the two. No longer is the student's well being seen as the province of those who work in Student Affairs. Today it is the responsibility of all administration, faculty, and staff to make sure that the community is a safe and nurturing one, so that all students can maximize their potential in being successful.

TIPS FOR YOUR TEEN: ACADEMIC AFFAIRS

Time Management: If you have not learned how to manage your time by now you will definitely face challenges. Think about who you are and how you learn. Recognize your limitations and seek support from an academic dean and/or a tutor or counselor to help you improve in this area. Set priorities and make a schedule. Make sure you stick to your schedule. Have a place for everything and keep everything in its place. You don't want to waste time spending one hour trying to find something that you should be able to put your hands on in one minute. But remember, there are resources on campus that will help you with time management and you only need to ask your resident advisor. If you can't find him/her go see your academic dean. Hopefully, you will know who the contact person is and may have even met that person at the Freshmen Orientation.

Academic Deans/Advisors: Before you arrive on campus you will most likely have already been assigned an academic dean, sometimes referred to as "academic advisor." An academic dean is to college what a guidance counselor is to high school. This is the person who will help you choose classes and a major and may advise you on summer opportunities, internships, and summer abroad programs. If you are entering college as an undeclared major you most likely will have two academic deans, one for your first two years, and one after you have declared a major for your last two years. The same way you established a relationship with your high school guidance counselor, you need to establish one with your academic dean. This is another resource should you be facing academic challenges. He/she may be able to advocate for you. Also, when it comes time to apply to graduate or professional schools this is the person that you will come to for guidance. You may also need to call on this individual to provide you with a character recommendation for a job, internship, fellowship, or graduate or professional school. Get to know them before you need to see them. And stay in touch with them after they have helped you out.

Choosing Classes: Unless you are in engineering, nursing, business, dance, or education, what are referred to as the professional majors, you will have some freedom over what classes you will choose and in some cases when you can choose to take them. This is particularly the case at the more selective colleges where students are granted a great deal of academic and social freedom. Be careful not to over-extend yourself. Just because you were at the top of your class in high school does not necessarily mean that you won't face challenges in college. In fact, if you do not choose your classes wisely, you most likely will face some challenges. Seek out the advice of your academic advisor and ask him or her to review your schedule. You should at least consider the advice you receive, although it may not always be sound. In these cases, you may want to consult your parents and use your own judgment.

Here an example might serve you well. If you are thinking about a pre-medicine major and you love science, do not take two science classes, Calculus, and Chinese the first semester of your freshmen year. You might be better served to take one math and one science, a writing class and something fun and light, like an Introduction to Film Studies freshman seminar. If you have never taken Chinese, you may want to audit the class at a local junior college after your freshmen year and enroll in Level I Chinese the first semester of your sophomore year.

Choosing a Major: If you are in the College of Arts and Sciences, sometimes called the College of Liberal Arts, you often do not have to declare your major until the end of sophomore year. Most students will fall into this category. If you think you have an idea of what you might want to major in, begin exploring those classes early. For example, if you have an interest in Psychology, you may want to take Introduction to Psychology in your freshmen year. If you decide it's not for you, you have not wasted your time since you can use that class to satisfy a distributional or elective requirement toward your graduation. You will have several people on campus who can help you explore major options: other students who are juniors or seniors who are majoring in a field in which you have an interest, your academic advisor, professors, and counselors in the Career Center. At some point you will want and need to know your career potential in a particular discipline. If you can, go with what will give you the greatest amount of pleasure. Choose a major that will give you the skill sets to engage a career that will be gratifying and rewarding. Hopefully, you will not choose one based solely on potential income.

Studying for Exams: Studying hard does not necessarily mean studying smart. People who study smart may study long hours but they also study in groups. Choosing your group and the dynamics of the group is very important or else you could end up doing most of the work. Don't wait until the last minute to study for an exam. Pace yourself. You know yourself and you should also know the group. Organize your reading schedule. If you have 22 books to read for one semester, determine how many pages you have to read over a four- or five-month period. In order to stay on top of your reading you may only need to read 75 pages a day.

That's better than waiting almost to the end of the semester where you may have to cram 7,000 pages in three weeks. Get help from a tutor and or the professor sooner rather than later.

Decoding Your Professor: Understanding who your professors are and what they want will help you do well in classes and also help you do well on the exams, papers, and projects. Professors are human too and they like to be valued. They also want to know you. If you are facing some personal challenges because of problems at home or on campus, you may want to share with your professors. When it comes to grading your performance, they could be more sympathetic and give you the benefit of the doubt, but you won't know that if you don't know them and they can't help you if they don't know you. Speak to other students who have studied under your professors and ask your fellow students if they can share past exams with you. At some schools previous exams are kept in the library and serve as guides for new students. If you feel uncomfortable with any material, go see your professors early in the semester rather than waiting to the last minute.

Writing Research Papers: No doubt by now you have already written several research papers. If you have, you have a competitive advantage over those students who have not. Independent of their major, most students will have to write, if not one, several research papers while in college. A research paper presents and argues a thesis. When you write a research paper, you use outside evidence to persuade the readers that your argument is valid or at least is worthy of serious consideration. Knowing how to write a good research paper is an essential skill for success in college. Make sure to ask your professors how they want you to give credit to those you may be quoting in your papers. You can be expelled from college for plagiarizing. Here are the basic steps you will need to complete as you write and research a paper:

- Select and narrow a topic
- Begin your research
- Evaluate your sources
- Take notes
- Outline
- Begin writing your first draft, including the thesis statement
- Document sources (speak to your professor about how this should be done as citation styles vary across study fields)

- Share with your professor

- Find more resources if necessary

- Revise first draft

- Share second draft with professor

- Re-write

- Proofread (may want to seek out staff from the Writing Lab)

- Write the final draft

TIPS FOR YOUR TEEN: STUDENT AFFAIRS

Time Management: Earlier tips about time management appeared under Academic Affairs, but students should also think about managing their time when thinking about the social aspects of college life. While typically the main reason students go to college is to earn a degree and by extension receive an education, we also recognize that much is learned outside of the classroom. Knowing how to balance your time so that your social life does not trump your academic responsibilities is key and ultimately will determine your success. You have to know yourself and know what your limitations are. You have an academic schedule already and now you need to include your social schedule, creating one schedule for the week. Remember, that your schedule is your own and not your friend's. You may need to study three hours for a math exam because your foundation in math is weaker and math was not your favorite subject. Or, you may not be able to go to the party on Thursday evening because you have an economics exam at 8 a.m. on Friday, while your roommate had his exam Thursday afternoon. Make sure you have fun and enjoy the social aspects of campus. Maintain a social schedule and leave room for some spontaneity, but don't forget the main reason for attending college—your education. Seek out a counselor on campus if you are having problems in this area.

Financial Management: Most students do not know how to manage money because they have never had to do so. If you have learned how to manage your funds, then you are one of the lucky ones. You have to develop a budget for yourself and just like you have to know yourself in terms of your academic and social limitations, you have to know your financial self. By creating a budget you will have a general sense of what you need and how much it will cost to take care of these needs over a specific period of time. If you have difficulty delaying gratification you might be better served by asking your parents to send you an allowance once a month or they can deposit the money in your bank account. If on the other hand you are not likely to spend your entire semester budget in one week, then you are in a safe position and won't run out of money. Whether or not you manage money well, all students would be best served to buy in bulk everything they need at the beginning of the school year. Here are some items you don't want to forget when you make a budget:

- **Personal essentials:** These include shampoo, toothpaste, mouth-wash, razors, and shaving cream.

- **Clothing:** Your budget does not need to include clothes since you will have purchased them before you leave for college. Remember that generally students bring too many clothes.

- **Books and supplies:** You cannot buy books for the year, but you might be able to buy supplies, e.g. pens, pencils, notebook paper, computer paper, ink cartridges for your printer, highlighters, etc.

- **Haircuts:** Research these services in your school community to find out cost and estimate how many times a school year you think you will need these services.

- **Laundry:** Most students wash their clothes in the dorm. So you can buy your detergent in bulk for the year, but you will have to budget your money over the academic year to pay for the washer and dryer fee. Inquire about this fee before your enroll in the college so that you include it in your budget prior to coming to school.

- **Entertainment:** Your room and board will be paid for but you may want to enjoy a dinner out once a semester or rather than rent a video, which you will have to include in your budget if you watch lots of them; you may want to go out to a movie from time to time. This too will have to be included in your budget as entertainment.

- **Transportation:** This will be based on how far you live and how often you plan to return home.

There is a lot to think about, but it does help to know yourself and what your needs are. Use your common sense when spending money. If you are at college with little or no money you will be stressed out and it will impact negatively on your academic performance.

Identity Formation: When you leave college you will not be the same person you were when you entered. You will experience new people, ideas, and situations that will challenge some of your values and beliefs in both positive and negative ways. Through your negotiations of these challenges you will incorporate new ways of thinking about old ideas and you will also invite in new ideas. You will also begin to look at your parents in different ways, in some ways more objectively. You will see qualities in you that you see in your parents that you may not like and you will see many qualities that you have inherited that you do like. You may identify with certain causes and certain groups that you parents may not approve of and you will face challenges, if and when you should reveal this new side of yourself. Coming to terms with who you are as you move from the transition from being neither fully dependent on your parents but not quite fully independent is both exciting and taxing but a phase that is necessary and in the final analysis is rewarding. I recommend strongly that, if you face challenges in this area, you seek out counseling. They can certainly help you process the issues that you may confront as you come to terms with your identity.

Diversity: Independent of who you are or where you go to school, everyone is going to experience something foreign and that is not necessarily a bad thing. After all, if you are going to go away for four years to college and come back the same way that you left, what would have been the point? Depending on where you go to school diversity will be defined quite broadly to include all kinds of differences or very narrowly to include only some. For example, in college you can be influenced by geographical, racial and cultural, religious, socio-economic as well as gender factors. You can also discuss diversity from the perspective of the student body and or the make up of the faculty and the administration. Diversity can also be seen from the perspective of the curriculum. If you have a chance to experience all of the above do so. The more you know about and are able to relate to and communicate with people who bring different perspectives, the more educated you will become. Moreover, you will be able to hold your own on the world stage and within and among a variety of social groups.

An important point for students to remember—particularly those of you who are first generation—you will bring a very important perspective to the college so do not underestimate your value, particularly to what it can bring to a diverse campus.

Finally, many colleges hold diversity training workshops for students and staff so that people are encouraged to embrace rather than be intimated by diversity. You are fortunate if you have chosen one of those schools.

Sexual Harassment: Colleges have very strict policies concerning sexual harassment and they do everything they can to protect you from being harassed or being violated. However, in the final analysis, you the student have the ultimate responsibility to govern your own behavior so that you will not be accused of sexual misconduct. Equally important, you have the responsibility to conduct yourself in a dignified manner or not to put yourself in a vulnerable position so that you will not fall prey to aggressive individuals. Using common sense can carry you a long way when you are at social functions or traveling to, from, and through campus, particularly if you are alone. In your orientation the Campus Police or Campus Security, which is what they are sometimes called, will provide you with the skill sets to be safe on and near campus. However, they cannot be everywhere so once again it is up to you to take care of yourself.

Drugs and Alcohol: Unfortunately one can find drugs and alcohol on all campuses. For students who are of legal age and who drink responsibly there is no problem. However, in too many cases, this is not the case. One can find upperclassmen drinking irresponsibly while also encouraging underage drinkers to do the same. Most colleges have very strict policies against drugs and underage drinking on campus. If you have a roommate who is engaged in illegal behavior, consult the Resident Advisor and/or the Dean of Students so that you will not be implicated because sometimes if drugs and alcohol are found in your room it can be difficult to determine to whom they belong. This situation can become particularly problematic if you live in a suite with several roommates and the alcohol is found in a common area. You could also contact the Dean of Housing and petition for a room change to avoid conflict, as well as avoid getting implicated in a situation over which you had no involvement and no control. The Dean of Housing and/or the Dean of Students may give you some advice on how to handle such situations. You can be assured they have had these types of complaints before and can offer assistance to you. Don't wait until the situation becomes a pattern and gets out of control before you act.

Roommates: When thinking about your roommate or roommates there are several recommendations. Be willing to negotiate: it's not always about you or them. Be considerate and don't pre-judge. Never claim a bed or a space until your roommate or roommates have arrived. Be respectful: don't play your music late in the evening if you know your roommate has an early class and needs to get to bed early. Communicate: maybe you can play the music late and loud, it may not be a concern for your roommate. Be responsible and be reasonable. Give the relationship time and give your roommate some space. Even under the best of circumstances, it is refreshing to come back to your room and have the space to yourself for three or four hours. Don't assume that your roommate is going to become your best friend. In this instance you are setting your expectations too high. All you can hope for is that you get along with your roommate and that there exists mutual respect. If you receive more, you are fortunate. Finally, try to avoid rooming with your best friend from high school. Usually it does not work out. You might want to find out what the roommate policy change is during freshmen orientation. At some schools, because of a housing shortage, it is sometimes difficult to change rooms. In any case, your Resident Advisor and eventually the Director of Housing are the point people who would advise you, should you have a conflict with your roommate.

Town-Gown Relationship: Know the community around you. After all, most students do not spend all of their time on campus, unless of course their campus is the town. Many colleges try to establish relationships with the surrounding community through employment opportunities and/or through service learning programs whereby students go into the community and provide tutorial services for young children or other support services for senior citizens. One can also find local school children visiting the campus for sponsored activities. You should be familiar with the community in which your college is located. If the college has established a positive relationship with the surrounding community, you can assume, for the most part, that students can move freely within and around that community without having to be pre-occupied with safety issues. Conversely, if the college has a contentious relationship with its neighbors, students may have problems in those neighborhoods.

In all cases, be alert, be aware, and be respectful.

Relationships: Relationships at college can be wonderful when they are working, but when they are not the situation can be quite overwhelming. If you have a class and/or live in the same dorm with your "ex," this can be quite emotionally unsettling. This problem is further exacerbated if you are attending a small college where you are running into your former partner and his or her friends several times a day. To help you work through this separation, seek comfort from your friends. Or if you need more help, seek counseling from the University Counseling Center and don't try to go it alone.

Returning Home: Remember when you return home you may have changed but your parents and other people in your circle will have not. You have to be patient and let them adjust to the new you. If you are lucky, they will be excited by what you have learned and how it has offered you some new perspectives. You might even become a change agent for them. On the other hand, if you come from a conservative family, you may have to suppress some of your new ideas so that the family can simply just get along. Most likely, you will know your family and know what they can and cannot absorb.

Your family will expect you to come back a changed person and will even welcome that change. That new wisdom and knowledge that you bring home cannot only become a change agent for your family, but for your community at large.

● ● ● ●

College is especially different from high school because unlike the typical high school teacher, college professors are not as likely to be as involved in assuring that each individual student is doing everything necessary to succeed in the class. More bluntly, college professors are not as likely to hold your hand as you complete the work required for the course. During college, the burden of being responsible for succeeding in the class rests more with the student—you must initiate contact with your professor when there is a question or concern. College professors tend to treat their students as adults and, as such, they expect students to be responsible for addressing with them any issue that needs to be addressed to succeed in the class.

—Justin Silvey
Brandeis University

GLOSSARY

Academic Dean: Sometimes called "academic advisor," the administrator at a college or university who advises students on class schedules, majors and various academic programs.

Alma Mater: The school, college, or university from which a person has graduated. The term is Latin for "dear mother."

Alumni : Graduates of a specific school or college.

Associate Degree: A degree that is granted by most two-year colleges and some four-year colleges at the end of two years of study.

Bursar's Office: Also called "Student's Accounts Office." The office that is responsible for billing and collection of colleges/universities charges.

Catalogue: A college or university publication that gives information about cost, courses, faculty, administration, admissions, and governance.

Class Load: The number of class units that a student takes within any given term or semester.

Commencement: Graduation ceremonies.

Community Colleges: Two-year regional colleges that offer an Associate Degree for part time or full time study.

Consortium: A voluntary association of colleges and universities that provides joint programs and services to enrolled students.

Convocation: An official ceremony commemorating the opening of the academic school year.

Core Courses: Classes that every student must take to qualify for graduation.

Credit Hour: A measure of completed college work. Usually colleges give one credit hour for each hour of class time during the week.

Default: Failure to repay a loan according to the terms agreed to when a student signed the promissory note. Defaulting on the student loan may affect credit rating for a long time.

Double Major: A course of study in which a student completes the requirements for two major degrees simultaneously.

Drop/Add: Revision of program of courses when a student wants to drop, change, or add a course.

Elective: Any course that is not required for a major field or general education requirement.

General Education Requirements: A group of basic courses for all students in a course of study at a college or university. Usually these courses cover broad subjects in the arts, social sciences, and natural sciences.

Greek Life: A system of fraternities and sororities consisting of a group of male students for the fraternities and female for the sororities organized in a club for social, professional, and academic reasons.

Honors Program: Special academic programs for exceptional students.

Independent Study: A course or course of study that allows a student to do all or part of the required course work on his/her own.

Intercollegiate: Activities between colleges and universities. Usually athletics, but can mean any activity.

Intramural Sports: Informal programs run by the athletic departments on a college campus. Competition is limited to students of that college or university.

REFERENCES

College: Getting In and Getting Though

Been There, Should've Done That: 995 Tips for Making the Most of College. Suzette Tyler. Front Porch Press.

The College Success Book: A Whole-Student Approach to Academic Excellence. James E. Groccia. Glenbridge Publishing.

Getting the Most Out of College. Arthur W. Chickering and Nancy K. Schlossberg. 2nd edition. Prentice Hall.

I'll Miss You Too: An Off-to-College Guide for Parents and Students. Margo E. Woodacre Bane and Steffany Bane. Sourcebooks.

You're on Your Own (But I'm Here If You Need Me): Mentoring Your Child During the College Years. Marjorie Savage. Fireside.

CONCLUSION

I INVITE YOUR TEEN TO enjoy the high school years. This guide aimed to present a comprehensive menu of how your teen should prepare for college, those considerations that influence how they choose an institution, along with those factors that need to be considered to influence their staying power. Whether in a public, private, parochial, charter, exam, independent day, or boarding school, I am hopeful that you and your teen will find this guide to be useful and informative.

Remember that educational planning is part of the college placement process and that the last minute is definitely too late. With that caveat, do not wait until your teen is in the middle of high school to look at this guide. Don't delay until he or she is a senior in high school to read Chapter Two on The College Application Process. The lessons I learned over the years are incorporated here for you and your teen's use, so take advantage of them to ensure that your teen is positioned to be a competitive high school student who will have multiple options available when they are ready to apply to college.

Your teen will also find it useful to take a moment away from the excitement of high school graduation, college admissions, and award letters to read Chapter Eight, which addresses what they need to know now that they are getting ready to attend college. It will admittedly be a challenge to sit down with your teen and take in even more information after they have graduated, but it will assuredly be worth your while. After all, this statement deserves repeating–*getting into college is achieving one milestone, but staying in and getting through is achieving another.* I know you have an investment in your teen getting through successfully, and I have the same investment. Good luck.

APPENDICES

STUDENT SELF-EVALUATION FOR COLLEGE EXPLORATION

YOU KNOW YOURSELF BETTER THAN anyone else, so your input is extremely important as we begin to explore colleges. Providing specific anecdotes where possible is particularly helpful in answering the below list of questions:

1. What are your greatest strengths and weaknesses? Your answer should include both academic and personal.

2. How would you rate your academic success? Does your transcript (do your evaluations) accurately reflect your abilities?

3. Have you been involved with any community service? If so, please describe the nature of the service and the extent to which you have been involved.

4. Outside of your academic classes, what other interests do you have? Examples might include sports, travel, religion, art, etc.

5. Are there academic or other qualities about you that make you particularly proud?

6. How do you spend your free time?

7. Are there any particular events that you see as turning points in your life? Please explain why you view them as such.

8. What is the best thing that has happened to you during your teen years (or high school years)?

9. What has been the most challenging or difficult thing about your teen years?

10. Do you have a job during the school year? How many hours per week do you work?

11. Describe your family. Comment on family background, language of household, important relationships, and educational background of your parents.

12. What words would you use to describe yourself?

13. Describe your ideal college.

14. Are there any particular colleges you would like to consider? Why?

15. Are there any special factors that will influence your decision about college, i.e. religion, distance from home, family pressure, work, etc.?

16. What aspect of the college application process concerns you most?

17. What aspect, if any, of getting through college concerns you most?

18. Is there anything else about you that will help you find the best college or university to match your skills and interests?

COLLEGE APPLICANT PROFILE

Name: _____

E-mail: _____

Date of Birth: _____ Social Security #: _____

Address: _____

_____

Phone #: _____

High School Name: _____

High School Phone #: _____

Profession: Mother _____

             Father _____

             Guardian _____

High School Course Information

	Course (Title, Honors/A.P.)	Grade/Mark
Math:	_____ (9)	_____
	_____ (10)	_____
	_____ (11)	_____
	_____ (12)	_____
English:	_____ (9)	_____
	_____ (10)	_____
	_____ (11)	_____
	_____ (12)	_____
Science:	_____ (9)	_____
	_____ (10)	_____
	_____ (11)	_____
	_____ (12)	_____
History:	_____ (9)	_____
	_____ (10)	_____
	_____ (11)	_____
	_____ (12)	_____

High School Course Information

Course (Title, Honors/A.P.)   *Grade/Mark*

Language:_____ (9) _____

_____ (10) _____

_____ (11) _____

_____ (12) _____

Electives:_____ (9) _____

_____ (10) _____

_____ (11) _____

_____ (12) _____

Class Rank: _____ of _____

Cumulative Grade-Point Average: _____

Standardized Test Scores

TEST	ATTEMPT	GRADE	DATE	MATH SCORE	CRITICAL READING SCORE	WRITING SCORE
PSAT:	(1st attempt)	_____	_____	_____	_____	_____
	(2nd attempt)	_____	_____	_____	_____	_____
SAT:	(1st attempt)	_____	_____	_____	_____	_____
	(2nd attempt)	_____	_____	_____	_____	_____

SAT Subject Test: TEST TITLE	GRADE	DATE	SCORE
_____	_____	_____	_____
_____	_____	_____	_____
_____	_____	_____	_____
_____	_____	_____	_____
_____	_____	_____	_____
_____	_____	_____	_____

TOEFL: TEST TITLE	GRADE	DATE	SCORE
_____	_____	_____	_____

AP: TEST TITLE	GRADE	DATE	SCORE
_____	_____	_____	_____
_____	_____	_____	_____
_____	_____	_____	_____
_____	_____	_____	_____
_____	_____	_____	_____
_____	_____	_____	_____

ACT:	GRADE	DATE	MATH	SCIENCE	ENG	READ	COMP

Activity	In and/or Out of School	No. of Years	Leadership

Summer Enrichment Programs

Freshman_____

Sophomore _____

Junior_____

Senior _____

Awards

Academic

_____
_____
_____
_____
_____
_____
_____
_____
_____
_____
_____
_____
_____
_____
_____
_____
_____
_____

Athletic

_____
_____
_____
_____
_____
_____
_____
_____
_____
_____
_____
_____
_____
_____
_____
_____
_____
_____

Community

_____
_____
_____
_____
_____
_____
_____
_____
_____
_____
_____
_____
_____
_____
_____
_____

Potential Schools

School Name	Applied	Accepted	Rejected	Wait-listed/ Application	Deferred Deadline

Do you fall into any one of the following categories?

❑ Athlete   ❑ Under-represented Groups   ❑ Special Talent
❑ Child of an Alumnus/a

Have you accomplished any of the following?

❑ Counselor Recommendation   ❑ Teacher Recommendation
❑ Essay   ❑ On-campus Interview   ❑ Alumni Interview

Have you or do you plan to apply to any schools through an early action/early decision program? _____
If so, what school? _____

Additional Notes _____

_____
_____
_____
_____
_____
_____
_____
_____
_____
_____
_____
_____
_____
_____
_____
_____
_____
_____
_____
_____
_____
_____

COLLEGE INFORMATION REQUEST LETTER

Malike Wilson
1334 ABC St. NW
Washington, DC 20011
malikewilson@abcmail.com

August 15, 2010

Mr. Sammie Robinson
Director of Admission
Williams College
Williamstown, MA 34566

Dear Mr. Robinson:

I am a senior at Wilson High School. I plan to enter college in the fall of 2012. I am interested in learning more about Williams College. I would appreciate if you would send me the following materials:

- an application form and a general bulletin explaining the entrance requirements, college costs, and course offerings;
- general financial aid information and any scholarship programs for students of color and/or first-generation college-bound students;
- special information related to your special interest groups, e.g. students of color, students with learning disabilities, and athletes;
- a video or CD-Rom, if available

Thank you very much for your consideration.

Sincerely,

Malike Wilson

SAMPLE THANK-YOU LETTER

Maria Reyes
4545 ABC Street, SE
Washington, DC 20011

October 1, 2010

Ms. Denise Walden
Associate Dean of Admissions
Colby College
Waterville, ME 40799

Dear Ms. Walden:

It was nice meeting you during your visit to Wilson High School. I also wanted to say thank you for taking the time to grant me a personal interview. I felt very comfortable during our conversation and you provided me with some helpful information about Colby College.

I will be completing my application by December and sending it to you before Christmas. I hope you had a safe trip back to Colby.

Sincerely,

Maria Reyes
Wilson High School
Class of 2012

COLLEGE APPLICATION PROCESS CHECKLIST

COLLEGE INFORMATION	College #1	College #2	College #3	College #4	College #5	College #6
Admissions contact person, phone, email address						
Information and application requested (date)						
Financial Aid forms requested (FAFSA)						
Scheduled campus visit						
APPLICATION DEADLINES						
TESTING DATES						
ACT completed (SCORE)						
SAT completed (SCORE)						
Number of SAT Subject Tests required						
Other tests taken (i.e. TOEFL)						
INTERVIEW						
On-campus: during visit to the school						
College representative high school visit (date)						
Thank-you notes						
APPLICATION						
Form completed and signed						
Essay completed						
Teacher recommendations requested						
Teacher recommendations mailed						
Other recommendations requested						
Other recommendations mailed						

COLLEGE INFORMATION	College #1	College #2	College #3	College #4	College #5	College #6
Transcript mailed						
Fee or fee waiver mailed						
Photograph (only if requested)						
Any other information requested by college						
Entire application copied for your records						
MID-YEAR						
7th-semester grades sent						
ADMISSION DECISIONS						
Accepted, wait listed, denied						
FINANCIAL AID OFFER						
Scholarships						
Grants						
Loans						
Work-Study						
FINAL DECISIONS						
Enrolling						
Deposits paid						
Not enrolling						
Courtesy notification completed (phone, postcard, email)						

TRANSCRIPT

Walker Jones High School
188 58th Street, New York, NY 10056

Kara L.
123 72nd Street
New York, NY 10043
212.888.8888

Expected Date of Graduation: June 2011
Class Rank: 32/547
Weighted GPA: 3.5/4.0
Un-Weighted GPA: 3.4/4.0
SAT Scores: Math-550 CR-510 Writing-600

Grade 9	2007–2008	
Courses	*Grade*	*Credit*
English 1	B+	1
Algebra 1	B	1
Biology	B	1
History W	B+	1
French 1	A	1
Art	A	1

Credits: 6
GPA: 3.3

Grade 10	2008–2009	
Courses	*Grade*	*Credit*
H-English 2	B+	1
Geometry	A-	1
Chemistry	A-	1
US History	B+	1
French 2	B+	1
Writing	A-	1

Credits: 6
Current GPA: 3.5
Cumulative GPA: 3.4

Grade 11	2009–2010	
Courses	*Grade*	*Credit*
AP English 3	A	1
Alg2/Trig.	B+	1
Physics	A	1
US Gov't.	B-	1
French 3	B+	1
Psychology	A	1

Credits: 6
Current GPA: 3.5
Cumulative GPA: 3.4

Grade 12	2010–2011	
Courses	*Grade**	*Credit*
AP English 4	B	
Pre-Calculus	B+	
AP Biology	B	
Thesis	C	
AP French	A	
Comp. Sci.	B	

Current GPA:
Cumulative GPA:
*First Quarter Senior Grades

Signature of Registrar _____ Date_____

SAMPLE RESUME

PENONE F.
341 ABC Street, NW.
Washington, DC 20001 202.888.1345
pfowler@abcmail.com

High School
Woodson Senior High School
3214 North ABC Street, NW
Washington, DC 20079

Academic Honors and Awards
2009–2010   National Honor Society
2009–2010   Spanish Honor Society
2006–2010   Honor Roll
2007–2010   Perfect Attendance
2009–2010   Eagle Scout

Athletics
2006–2007   Junior Varsity Basketball
2007–2010   Varsity Basketball
2008–2009   Captain-Basketball Team
2008–2009   Spring Track

Activities
2006–2007   Student Government-Class Representative
2009–2010   Treasurer of Junior and Senior Class
2009–2010   President, Business Club
2009–2011   Community Service-Davis Senior Citizens Home

Work Experience
2006–2007   Assistant to Accountant-Future Quest, Inc.
2009–2010   Cashier-Giant Foods

Summer
2008   The Lead Program. Kellogg School of Business
Northwestern University. Evanston, IL.

INTERNET SCHOLARSHIP RESOURCES

www.4scholarships4anything.com

www.freschinfo.com

www.scholarships.com

www.supercollege.com

www.collegequest.com

www.collegeboard.org/funfinder/html/ssrchtop.html

www.collegescholarships.com

www.smexpress.com

www.scholarship-page.com

www.collegenet.com

www.uncf.org

www.college-scholarships.com

www.collegefund.org

www.ajm.org

www.iefa.org

www.rhodesscholarship.com

www.gmsp.org

www.marine-scholar.org

www.jackierobinson.org

www.iie.org/cies

www.free-cash-grants-money-and-college-scholarship-loans.net

www.guaranteed-scholarship.com

www.scholarships.sjsu.edu/index.html

www.scholarships-education.com

www.scholarships.berkely.edu

www.scholarships-ar-us.org

www.udall.gov/p_scholarship.htm

www.act.org/goldwater

www.theihs.org/tabl/mfa.html

www.studentloan.citibank.com/slcsite/fr_schol.htm

www.nwc.cc.wy.us/campusserv.scholarship.htm

www.mason.gmu.edu/-his/mfa.html

www.lclark.edu/COLLEGE/FINAN/FINACAID/finameri/html

www.lemmermann.nexus.it/lemmermann/index.htm

www.aswa4.org/scholarship.htm

www.ag.ohio-state.edu/-natres/KWVEGC.html

www.cnet.navy.mil/nrotc/nschol.htm

www.gripvision.com/money.html

www.es.sunysb.edu/-webadm/external/asme/asmesch.html

ABOUT THE AUTHOR

DR. KPAKPUNDU EZEZE IS THE founder and President of Future Quest, Inc., a consulting firm that specializes in educational planning and college placement for high school students. Over the past thirty years Dr. Ezeze has developed a number of partnerships nationwide that have helped thousands of students to prepare for college. In the Washington, DC metropolitan area, these partnerships include Urban Alliance, College-Bound, The Ionia Whipper Home for Girls, the College Information Center at the Martin Luther King Memorial Library, Mentors, Inc., Jack & Jill, and Upward Bound Programs at Howard and Catholic Universities.

For over six years, Dr. Ezeze was the director of the Washington Tennis & Education Foundation's Center for Excellence (CFE), an educational planning and college placement enrichment program, which brings young tennis players together from under-resourced communities and introduces them to a range of competencies in public speaking, writing, interviewing skills, computer skills, and career opportunities.

Before coming to Washington, Dr. Ezeze served as a college consultant to students in Boston, Philadelphia, New York, Miami, and Princeton, New Jersey. Some of his clients included The Boys Choir of Harlem, New Jersey Nets Basketball Academic Camp, Salomon Brothers, Inc., Prudential Securities Adopt-a-School Programs, I Have a Dream Foundation, and The Ninety Second Street YMCA in New York.

His professional career includes experience as a guidance counselor in three school systems: Lexington, MA, Wellesley, MA and Arlington, VA. He has served as Assistant Dean in the College of Arts and Sciences at the University of Pennsylvania, Associate Program Director with the College Board Educational Testing Service, Academic Advisor at Wellesley College, Director for Upward Bound at Worcester College, and Admissions Associate for the Graduate School of Education at Harvard University.

Most recently, Dr. Ezeze has been involved with designing and implementing college advising programs for charter schools.